WHEN HOPE IS NOT ENOUGH
SECOND EDITION

A how-to guide for living with and loving someone with Borderline Personality Disorder

by Bon Dobbs

Second Edition

ISBN: 978-1-329-44409-6

ISBN: 978-1-329-44409-6

Table of Contents

Preface

What is this book about and for whom is it written?

This book is about living with, and loving, someone with Borderline Personality Disorder (abbreviated as BPD and also known as Emotional Regulation Disorder). The purpose of this book is to share effective tools and strategies to make your life easier in your relationship with this person.

Before you respond "my loved one doesn't have a personality disorder," read on, please. The most difficult relationships in our lives are with people that are disordered in one way or another. Your loved one may not qualify for the diagnosis of Borderline Personality Disorder, but if you continue reading, you may find many features of your loved one that reflect those of people with the disorder. I'm not saying that it is "right" to diagnose your loved one; I'm only saying that many, many people have these traits. I can help you navigate your relationship with someone with these traits, whether or not they actually have the disorder.

The intended audience of this book is the "Non-BPD," or the person who doesn't have the disorder, but cares for someone who does have the disorder (or a similar disorder). This "Non-BPD" could be a parent, partner, child or friend of the person with Borderline Personality Disorder.

Unlike many books on this subject, this book starts with the premise that you want to continue to have or to reestablish a relationship with this difficult person. If you are a spouse, I assume that you want to stay married. If you are a parent, I assume that you want to continue or to reestablish a relationship with your child (sometimes you may have no choice). If you are a child of a parent with the disorder, I assume you want to learn how to effectively interact with your parent. Finally, if you are a friend, I assume you want to continue to be friends with this person. I do not cover how to sever a relationship with someone with the disorder in this book.

If you actually have the disorder, I would suggest getting a different book. This book is not intended for a person with the disorder; however, it is unlikely that anything in this book would disturb you very much. There are some discussions of self-injury and other pain-management behavior –

so there is a possibility that portions of this book might be "triggering" of such behaviors if you are prone to them.

Also, unlike other books on this subject, I will tell you precisely how to deal with and talk to someone with the disorder. I found that, after reading some self-help books on this subject, I was left with little on the "how" side. I knew more about the disorder, but I didn't know what to do next. I hope that after reading this book, you will know exactly what to do next. I want you to have the "know-how."

So, if you fit the category of being a "Non-BPD" (or suspect you might) and you want to know what to do next... read on!

What's New in the Second Edition?

It's been seven years since I wrote and published *When Hope is Not Enough*, first edition. Since that time, this book has helped thousands of people in their relationships with a loved one with Borderline Personality Disorder. I've received hundreds of thank you emails and messages. For those, I am grateful that I was able to have a positive impact on my readers' lives.

I've found *When Hope is Not Enough* (sometimes called WHINE for brevity's sake) to be a valuable resource to the members of my Internet email support list. My internet support list has grown from thirty people in 2008 to a shade over one thousand in 2015.

What I also found was that several of the members of that list were commenting on helpful advice I provided on the list that was not referenced in the first edition of this book.

Originally, I chose to leave out the advanced tools in the first edition, but in creating a new edition, I felt it was better to include these advanced skills. People learn and accept different tools and strategies at different paces, and I found that certain more advanced members of my list were asking for more advanced tools to effectively deal with their loved ones with Borderline Personality Disorder.

Additionally, I modified my view of Borderline Personality Disorder and the "core" configuration of the disorder. I did this as a response to new research in the clinical field. At one time, few researchers were working in the borderline personality field. Now, there are many more all over the world.

Studies regarding genetics, neurotransmitters, neural activity and many others have appeared in the field of study since I wrote the first version of this book. I have modified certain areas of the book to reflect this more modern research. There has been a lot of research about Borderline Personality Disorder and about the biological causes of disorder in the past few years. Much of this research concerns brain function, genetic transmission and hormonal variations in those with the disorder.

I rewrote portions of the first edition to more accurately reflect what effectively works and to help you more easily implement these tools in your life. I found that my list members were able to more easily implement the tools if they used them in a certain order.

I have indicated in this edition of the book how to more simply put these tools into action in your life. I am so far removed from the mind-set that I had all those years ago, I had trouble remembering which order the tools would be most effectively applied. My list members were most generous in reminding me.

I added some exercises to certain tools that can help you pick up the tools and use them in your life. While the first edition had a description of most of the tools in this edition, some readers were left with a feeling of not knowing how to start practicing the tools, because there were few introductory exercises. I have tried to rectify that in this edition.

Finally, I added some additional "structure" to certain tools. This structure was thanks to one of my list members who took it upon herself to revise those tools. My thanks go out to her and to all of my list members who have contributed to a vital and effective community for support and advice. I love, trust and respect each one of you – you know who you are.

Bon

Introduction

Welcome! If you have found this book I can only assume that you are a loved one of someone with Borderline Personality Disorder (BPD) – either diagnosed or suspected. I know something about how you feel. I have been married to a woman with this disorder for two decades. We have children and one of my daughters also exhibits the signs of the disorder. I have been dealing with this frustrating emotional disorder for a long while now.

OK, first things first…

Before you read this book, you must know that I am not a mental health professional. I have no training in psychology or behavior modification, and no professional certifications of any kind (at least not in the mental health field).

I am a person who lives with and loves someone with BPD. I have taken it upon myself to learn as much as I can about this disorder and how to live more peacefully alongside someone with it. If you or your loved one is experiencing a mental health crisis, I urge you to contact a mental health professional immediately.

What I am (rather than what I'm not) is a loved one of someone with BPD. My wife has been diagnosed with the disorder and one of my daughters exhibits traits of the disorder. I have been trained in Dialectical Behavior Therapy Family Skills Training (DBT-FST) and in mentalization techniques. I have attended professional conferences regarding BPD. Since my daughter was a minor, I participated in my daughter's therapy. I have learned, practiced and honed my skills as a supporter of people with BPD.

Whether I can be considered an "authority" on the interpersonal struggles of a loved one of someone with BPD is arguable. Still, my previous books, Internet support list and blog have helped hundreds of people live a more peaceful and loving life with their BPD loved ones.

The guidelines and tools contained within this book are not intended to cure your loved one with BPD. I don't believe anyone has the ability to "cure" or to recover from BPD except the sufferer his/herself. Often, this recovery is only possible with the guidance of a knowledgeable mental health professional. Still, the only person who can take the steps necessary toward recovery is the person suffering the disorder.

The family members and loved ones can make the environment more suited to taking these steps, but the path toward recovery is one that only the sufferer can travel. That said, the skills in this book, once mastered, can help make taking this path much less arduous for the traveler and the traveling companions.

If you suspect that you have the disorder, I suggest that you turn to another text or to a mental health professional for guidance. This book was written specifically for those that do not have BPD, but are in a relationship with someone who does. At the same time, recommending this book to your family members and loved ones can help them understand the disorder (and you) more thoroughly and compassionately.

My story in brief

I knew that there was something wrong. I just didn't know what it was. We had been married for fifteen years before I figured it out. We had had four wonderful children together. But there was something wrong with my wife.

In a period of two years, she had been arrested for DUI twice; she had been investigated by Child Protective Services twice; she had become dependent on prescription drugs; and she had "run off" several times in the night.

She also had been very angry with me and the children on occasion, yelling at us and telling us that all of her problems were "our fault." I knew she had experienced deep depressions and that she was impulsive when taking the prescription medications. What I didn't know, I was soon to find out.

On a humid night in September 2005, I was putting my two year-old son to bed when my teenage daughter ran upstairs and into the room.

"Mom's hurt! You have to take her to the hospital!" she cried in a panic.

"What?" I responded, shaking myself awake and getting up from my son's bed where I had been sleeping next to him. "She's hurt?"

"Yes, hurry," my daughter urged me.

I went downstairs and found my wife in the kitchen. She was clearly under the influence of her prescription medication, and she had been drinking wine. She was standing next to the counter with a carving knife in one hand. Her arm was bleeding from ten or twelve scratch-like cuts.

I looked at her and knew immediately that she had inflicted these wounds on herself. The cuts were not very deep, but they were quite bloody.

"Please, don't take me to the hospital. They will put me in the psych ward," she said with tears in her eyes.

That's when I first discovered that my wife's illness was more than depression. It was something much more.

After that night, I began to research self-inflicted wounds. You see, this was one thing of which I had no understanding whatsoever. As I said, I knew my wife had experienced periods of depression, and I had also experienced periods of depression in my life – so I could relate to wanting to stay in bed for the day because you're depressed. I had also used alcohol on occasion to deal with the emotional pain in my life. (I never took prescription drugs, though).

But what about the self-inflicted injuries? I never had experienced any desire to hurt myself in that way. I knew that she wasn't attempting suicide; what, exactly, WAS she doing? Was she punishing herself? I was at a loss.

I began to research self-inflicted injury, self-harm and self-mutilation on the Internet. I found out the motivation for self-inflicted injury can be varied. One of those motivations, which I never considered on my own, was that the self-inflicted injury (whether it is "cutting" – like my wife did – or burning oneself or pulling out chunks of hair) serves to halt the pain that a person feels.

It seemed strange to me, but inflicting pain releases endorphins and serves to ease other pain. While self-punishment can be a motivation as well, I found out that it is more likely for a person to hurt him or herself to relieve pain than to specifically cause pain.

I also found out that the habit is something of a nervous one – in order to relieve the itching feeling of uneasiness, self-injury can serve to release that nervous energy. In addition, it can be a "shameful secret" in which the person who harms him or herself does so habitually and in secret. Generally, it is not a call for attention or for help. If it is hidden from the people who would answer that call, how could it be?

I also discovered something else when researching self-injury. That was, of course, Borderline Personality Disorder (BPD). A person doesn't have to have BPD in order to engage in self-harm. However, many of, but not all, people with BPD do engage in self-harming and parasuicidal (harming behaviors not meant to cause death) behaviors.

When I started following the links about BPD and about the behaviors involved in BPD, I realized I was reading a report on the mental state of my wife. It was quite disturbing for me because I had a pretty dim view of what BPD meant. I never understood the disorder completely.

The more I read, the more convinced I became that I was dealing with BPD in my wife. However, it wasn't good enough for me, a lay person, to diagnose my wife. What I decided to do was email our old therapist to see if he had some insights into a proper diagnosis or he could tell me whether I was barking up the wrong tree. After waiting a week or so, I received an email back confirming the borderline diagnosis (along with Major Depressive Disorder) for my wife. At that point, I officially became a "Non-BPD."

My journey did not stop there. I did several things to try to learn more about BPD. You see, I needed support. If you are anything like I was, you are confused, angry, frustrated, and sad. You are at your wit's end with your loved one's behavior.

The first thing I did was join an on-line email support list for Nons. The list is the largest community of Nons on the Internet. I also got a copy of a popular book for loved ones of people with the disorder and read it cover to cover.

At first, I thought that both of these resources were excellent, and I began to put into action the techniques I learned in the book and the advice I received on the Internet list. I soon found out that, at least with my wife, these techniques were not working consistently. I didn't know why the techniques were failing, but I decided to find out.

Desperate, I decided to attend a Dialectical Behavior Therapy Family Skills Training (DBT-FST) Workshop. Dialectical Behavior Therapy (or DBT) is a therapy designed by Dr. Marsha Linehan of the University of Washington to specifically help people with BPD. It was actually initially developed to help suicidal and parasuicidal women, but found to help BPD patients as well (although DBT therapists call the patients "clients").

The purpose of my family skills class was to expose Nons to some of the tools and techniques available within DBT and how to apply these skills to their day-to-day life.

After my attendance of the DBT-FST class, I started to believe that people with BPD had been given a very bad rap on the Internet. I understood much more about the disorder and realized that most Nons are not given the opportunity to learn the skills that can help improve their relationship with the person with BPD. I started a blog for the sole purpose of sharing the skills with other people.

Another Family Member Joins the Ranks

Right around the same time as my attendance in the DBT-FST class, my wife and I noticed that one of our daughters was having trouble in school. My wife and I decided to get an educational and psychosocial assessment done of our, then, eight year old daughter. The assessment was quite expensive and took months of interviews and neuropsychological testing.

When we received the report, what we found was very puzzling. It seemed that our daughter was inconsistent in the results of her educational testing. She scored extremely high on some measures and extremely low on other, related measures. It was odd. Even the tester/counselor was quite puzzled.

The solution to our daughter's performance on these tests was contained in the second half of the report, which was an analysis of her emotional and social development. It turns out that our daughter was unable to regulate her emotions. When she was calm and focused, she would score well on the tests. When she was anxious and afraid, she would score poorly.

The second half of the assessor's told the story of a girl who was easily triggered into emotional states and who was overwhelmed by these states. Our daughter told the assessor stories in which the main character's friends ran away from her forever. She was expecting doom to come to her. She was dreading the future.

Our daughter was naturally much more sensitive than her sisters. This emotional sensitivity translated into inconsistent test performance and poor learning strategies. She was easily triggered into emotionality, mostly negative (fear, anger or sadness), and the intensity of the emotions was such that she was unable to think clearly, learn effectively or be comfortable in social situations.

We were at an impasse as to how to proceed. She was a bright girl, doing very well in school when she was not fraught with powerful emotions. Of course, Borderline Personality Disorder is not diagnosed in children. It fit my daughter pretty thoroughly, although some of the adult behaviors associated with this condition had not yet emerged in her.

After much research, discussion and advisement from some of the experts in the field, who I had contacted out of desperation, I found a therapist near me who had adapted DBT for children. It was a wonderful discovery. I contacted the office of the therapist, and he agreed to accept my daughter as a patient.

Since my daughter was a minor, I was encouraged to participate in her therapy to some degree. I would take my daughter once a week to the therapy. For the first six months of the therapy, my daughter did not want to be there and distrusted the therapist. She was essentially silent for six months.

I would go into the therapist's office and the therapist and would talk about my daughter as she sat silently on the couch, her arms crossed and an angry look of "I don't want to be here" on her face.

After about six months, my daughter began to open up to the therapist. She accepted the therapy and threw herself into learning the skills. DBT is a skills-based form of Cognitive Behavior Therapy (CBT). The patient acquires the skills to deal with certain life situations.

It is close-ended – meaning, once the skills are acquired and mastered, the therapy ends. It took about eighteen months for that to happen with my daughter.

It also encourages the family members to acquire a certain set of skills that can aid in the patient's day-to-day interaction with people who are close. This includes parents, partners and siblings. I also participated in the therapy and learned the skills to effectively interact with my daughter. Since I'm the kind of person who does things fully, I decided to change my behavior and master the skills that were taught.

I practiced the skills in each interaction with my daughter and with other people with whom I came into contact. I did additional research and bounced ideas off of my friends in the Internet community. I adjusted the presentation of the skills as to more effectively communicate their efficacy with others.

I also noticed that the set of skills that I had acquired and that I had made second nature in my life were diametrically opposed to some of the skills that were being promoted by the self-help books I had originally read. These books were not only wrong; they were at some level harmful.

Here I was both a partner and a father of a person with Borderline Personality Disorder traits and the original resources to which I turned, to which hundreds of thousands of people have turned, were not only incorrect, they were potentially harmful?

For that reason, I decided to write this book.

About this Book

In this book, I will explain some characteristics of the disorder, but this is not intended to be a diagnostic guide. There are plenty of other books and resources that more fully describe the disorder and what behaviors come along with it.

When I wrote the first edition of this book the "Diagnostic Statistic Manual version four" (DSM-IV) was the diagnostic guide for use in the United States. At that time there were nine criteria for diagnosing BPD and if a person had five of these criteria, they were considered to have "met the criteria for BPD". Unfortunately, these criteria lead to many different combinations and permutations of the disorder.

Now, the DSM-V (Diagnostic Statistic Manual version five) has been released and the diagnostic criteria are almost completely different. I think the new criteria are much more reflective of people I've met (including my own family members) with BPD. Yet, I am not an expert in diagnosing anyone and I don't want to focus on those diagnostic criteria of the disorder.

Instead of focusing on those, I wanted to focus on the internal and behavioral "cornerstones" of BPD, at least in my experience. I have come into contact with hundreds of people with BPD and their loved ones, and the information about BPD in this book reflects those experiences.

A quick note about terminology: Throughout this book, I will use many terms which may be confusing to you. I will try to define these terms when they first appear. One of the most controversial terms that I will use, sparingly, is the term "Non" (or "Nons" or "Non-BPD"). This term originated in the support community some time ago, and it denotes a person who does not have the disorder but is in some sort of relationship with someone who does.

As a "Non" you can be a boyfriend or girlfriend, a husband or wife, a sibling, a parent, a child or a friend of someone with BPD. Personally, I don't like the term very much, because it creates an "us vs. them" dynamic. I believe that each person has a different capacity to regulate his or her emotions and that there is a wide spectrum of "Nons" and of people with BPD.

I also use the term "BPD" or "BPD's." This abbreviation indicates the person with BPD. While I'd prefer to use the term "a person with BPD" or "a loved one with borderline personality disorder" throughout, I use the abbreviation for the sake of brevity.

To be consistent throughout the book, I have decided to use the pronouns "her" or "she" when referring to someone with BPD, except when referencing a specific person with BPD that is identified as male. BPD is much more commonly diagnosed in women than in men. Men do get the disorder, but the breakdown in diagnosed persons is seventy-five percent female. Although I am using "she" and "her" throughout, the advice given applies to men with the disorder as well.

Recent studies have shown that this seventy-five percent female statistic to be inaccurate and that men and women get the disorder in equal numbers. The issue seems to be that women are more likely to seek treatment for BPD and the seventy-five percent figure comes from clinical studies (those in treatment), rather than from epidemiological ones (the general population). Recent epidemiological studies have shown that the actual occurrence of BPD is evenly split between men and women[1]. Women tend to seek treatment while men with the disorder tend to end up in jail as a consequence of some dysregulated behavior.

That being said, I still will refer to a person with BPD as "she" or "her" throughout this book. My apologies to the partners and parents of males with BPD.

There are many other examples of "jargon" used specifically in the support community. When I use one of these terms I will, as indicated above, try to define it to the best of my ability. Some of the terms are controversial and objectionable to me, and I will explain why I hold this opinion when I get to the term.

Some other terms in the book are used within the therapeutic community and are not well-understood in the support community. Unfortunately, I am forced to leave out some of these concepts because of copyright restrictions on the terms.

Finally, some of the terms I use are either my own or created by people on my email support list. Links to the list as well as other important resources can be found in the back of this book

I have heard many people say, especially on Internet sites, that the only thing to do with someone with BPD is to leave them. Sometimes, I have to agree that exiting the situation is more effective than continuing to live in confusion and pain.

At a conference on personality disorders, I heard Dr. John Gunderson, who is an expert in BPD and a talented clinician in treating BPD, say that he takes pride in his skills and gains satisfaction from his work because "if you can treat people with borderline personality disorder, you can treat anyone."[2]

[1] *Prevalence, Correlates, Disability, and Comorbidity of DSM-IV Borderline Personality Disorder: Results from the Wave 2 National Epidemiologic Survey on Alcohol and Related Conditions.* Bridget F. Grant, Ph.D.,et. al.; J Clin Psychiatry. 2008 Apr; 69(4): 533–545.

[2] *Psychodynamic Therapy of BPD: Developing Expertise*, John Gunderson, MD, International Society for the Study of Personality Disorders, 11th International Congress, The Mount Sinai School of Medicine, New York, NY, August 2009

People with BPD can be extraordinarily difficult people to interact with, let alone to live with and make a life with. Clinicians, therapists and psychologists spend at most a couple of hours a week with your loved one with BPD. As a loved one, you spend the rest of the time. It can be exhausting, frustrating and confusing.

I feel that skill acquisition is essential to making that time as enjoyable as it can be. Without a clear view of the dynamics of BPD and the role the disorder can play in interpersonal relationships, your life is likely to be hell on earth.

I have heard hundreds of stories from Non-BPD's about the crazy, out-of-control behavior that their loved one with BPD exhibits. If you don't understand the function of the behavior and the mental/emotional underpinnings, and if you are not told how to effectively react to such behavior, you are in for a ride (and perhaps you have already been on that ride for a while).

My approach has been to learn the skills necessary to make my life (and their lives) easier during those many hours spent together. Many partners ask, "Why bother?" This question is a valid one. Sometimes leaving the person is the only viable solution. Yet, I found that the "just leave" advice was not palatable to me. I love my wife and have chosen to stay with her.

For the parents of children with BPD, it isn't as easy as just leaving. Few mothers or fathers want to "dump" their child, even if he/she behaves in the way that is confusing, stressful and saddening to the parents. Still, most parents have deep and abiding love for their children despite the behavior, and the idea of leaving the child is just too painful.

For my own daughter, I could never think of a situation in which I would just cease to communicate with her. She is a young adult now. She's bright, generally out-going. She has many friends. I was very worried for her when she approached her teens. Normal teenage troubles can be enough to upset many teenagers, but my daughter was able to effectively navigate her teenage years.

She still has glimmers of BPD-like thinking and behavior. Yet, by applying the tools and skills from this book, I've been able to help her navigate her difficulties and overcome many of them. Of course, it's not all up to me. Her efforts in learning and applying the skills in her own life has empowered her and enabled her to do hard things.

I am often asked by parents whether there is any hope for their children with BPD or for the relationship between the parent and child. I believe that the answer to that question is "yes," but hope alone is not going to make it work effectively for both parent and child. In my opinion, any relationship between a loved one and a person with BPD requires skills.

It is almost as if we need to learn a new language, a language that the person with BPD has been speaking all along, and we heretofore haven't understood, before the relationship gets better, closer and more trusting.

Once the Non-BPD and the BPD begin speaking the same language, then the real healing can begin. Unfortunately, you (the Non-BPD) have to learn their language before they can start learning yours.

This book is an attempt to teach you fluency in the language of interpersonal relationships with someone with BPD. *When Hope is Not Enough*, first edition, was the basic version (even as difficult as many found it to learn and apply that language to their relationship), this is the "emersion" course that pushes you past where the first edition left you.

Some people are better at learning new languages than others, for various reasons. Some people are better at relating to someone with BPD than others as well.

The goal is to get you closer to a trusting, respectful and compassionate relationship with the person with BPD in your life. If that aligns with your goals for your relationship, then you've come the right place!

Chapter 1: What's up with that?

Since you are reading this book, you have probably asked yourself some form of the question above. You just can't understand why this person, who supposedly loves you, treats you with such disrespect and distain.

This is not the way life is supposed to be. Is it? You are confused, angry and in pain. Here are some questions that you can ask yourself to help to understand the source of the pain you feel:

- Do you fear coming home from work, or fear your loved one coming home from work, because you have no idea in which state of mind the person will be? Do you dread hearing the door open or entering the house, then immediately look for signs of your loved one's mood?
- Do you hold back your opinions about certain subjects for fear of being berated, criticized and judged?
- Do you not mention this person's erratic behavior for fear of being attacked or not believed by others outside the relationship?
- Do you feel lied to and/or manipulated? Does external evidence bear out the fact that your loved one has lied about his or her behavior?
- Do you feel that this person is constantly saying that everything is your fault and that you are to blame for all of his/her problems?
- Do you feel that this person won't listen to reason or that he/she specifically ignores the truth to support his/her erratic behavior? Do you feel he/she has an inability to take responsibility for his/her actions?
- Do you feel isolated from friends or from family members? Does he/she have a large fear of intimacy such that you feel disconnected from him or her most of the time as well?
- Does he/she rarely or never acknowledge your feelings? Does he/she never apologize for hurtful behavior?
- Does it feel that this person specifically sets up situations in which the intentions are to "destroy" you in some way (emotionally, financially, career-wise, etc.)?
- Is he/she like Dr. Jekyll and Mr. Hyde? Does it feel like these "switches" from friendliness to rage take place over short periods of time? Does he/she rage at you one minute and then, an hour later, act as if nothing happened?

- Does he/she look to you for answers and then attack you when you give them? Does he/she turn criticism of him or her into attacks on you and your behavior?

- Do you feel many times that the only way to have any peace in your life is to leave the presence of this person? Do your children or other family members feel the same way?

- Do you feel you carry around a secret about the embarrassing behavior that you "put up with" in your loved one? Do you protect him or her by not telling others, including friends and family members, about his/her behavior? Do you do this because you feel that others would either tell you to "just leave him/her" or they would judge you for being "weak" or "codependent"?

- Do you feel like the entire relationship is about him or her and how he/she feels? Do you feel that there is no room for your feelings? Have you asked yourself "what about me?"

If you answered "yes" to a large portion of the questions above, it is possible that you are in a relationship with someone who has BPD (and very probably that you are in a relationship with someone with BPD traits). Because you have been so isolated and secretive about your relationship, you also might feel that you are the only person in the world who feels this way and experiences this behavior.

You are not alone!

There are millions of people in the United States alone who suffer from BPD or a similar disorder. Estimates say that from one to six percent of the entire U.S. population experience this disorder.

That means that you have a fairly high chance of being involved with someone with BPD. If you are involved in a relationship with a person with BPD, whether you are a spouse, partner, parent, child or friend, you are considered a "Non-BPD" or "Non" for the purposes of this book.

The remainder of this book is focused on the Nons that are in a relationship with someone with BPD. When I use the term BPD in the rest of this book, I am referring to a "constellation" of conditions and disorders that present themselves in similar ways.

What I am describing here is a person who presents the traits of someone with BPD or behaves in a BPD-like fashion. Most of the tools will work with someone who has, say, a form of Post-Traumatic Stress Disorder

(PTSD) and behaves in a BPD-like way. It's not necessary to have a definite diagnosis.

Instead, I suggest you use the tools in this book to see if they are effective. If they are not, try them again. If they continue to be ineffective, then you're going to have to look elsewhere. Even if you determine that your loved one does not have BPD or a similar disorder, the tools in this book can still help you in your relationship with a difficult person.

What is important about BPD-like conditions and disorders is that they have a core component in common, which is called **emotional dysregulation**. A disturbance to one's emotional regulation system can exhibit itself in a number of ways, but the behavior of the BPD and the feelings of the Non are generally consistent and reflected in the questions above.

I put the words **emotional dysregulation** in bold because that concept is vital for you to understand what BPD is all about. What upsets the Nons most about the disorder is the behaviors associated with BPD – raging, lying, substance abuse, unfaithfulness, dangerous risk-taking and others. While emotional dysregulation is not the cause of BPD, it is one of the most vital features of the disorder.

The Nons feel put-upon and under siege, yet what motivates the behaviors of the person with BPD is that she is awash with negative emotional states. She has a reduced capacity to regulate her emotions.

Dr. Marsha Linehan, the developer of Dialectical Behavior Therapy (DBT), states it this way:

The components of emotion vulnerability are sensitivity to emotional stimuli, emotional intensity, and slow return to emotional baseline. "High sensitivity" refers to the tendency to pick up emotional cues, especially negative cues, react quickly, and have a low threshold for emotional reaction. In other words, it does not take much to provoke an emotional reaction. "Emotional intensity" refers to extreme reactions to emotional stimuli, which frequently disrupt cognitive processing and the ability to self soothe. "Slow return to baseline" refers to reactions being long lasting, which in turn leads to narrowing of attention towards mood-congruent aspects of the environment, biased memory, and biased interpretations, all of which contribute to maintaining the original mood state and a heightened state of arousal. [3]

Essentially, what you're dealing with is someone who reacts strongly and emotionally to the slightest provocation, who will dwell on those intense emotional reactions for periods longer than you might. A person with BPD-like traits heats up quickly and cools down slowly.

I'm sure that if you have been dealing with such a person for an extended period of time, you will have noticed that she seems to fly off the handle at the slightest comment or action, no matter how unintended the "offense."

Someone with BPD will be more sensitive to emotional cues and triggers from the environment, will react more intensely to these cues, and will take longer to "return to baseline," or will be under the effects of strong emotions for longer than other, less emotional people.

Many times, because of the low tolerance of emotional cues or triggers, the person with BPD will react with alarm even though their emotional reaction does not match the reality of the environment. Dr. Paul Ekman calls the period in which emotions influence your decision-making the "refractory period (or state)":

For a while we are in a refractory state, during which time our thinking cannot incorporate information that does not fit, maintain or justify the emotion that we are feeling. This refractory state may be of more benefit than harm if it is brief, lasting only for a second or two. In that short window, it focuses our attention on the problem at hand, using the most relevant knowledge that can guide our initial actions, as well as preparations for further actions. Difficulties can arise or inappropriate emotional behavior may occur when the refractory period lasts much longer, for minute or perhaps even hours. A too-long refractory period biases the way we see the world and ourselves. [4]

Ekman is not specifically talking about BPD or people with BPD. His book applies to emotions in all people. However, the last two lines of the quote help illustrate what is actually going on with someone with BPD. A person with BPD gets into powerful emotional states more easily than other people, and her refractory period lasts longer than with other

---

[3] Linehan, Marsha "Dialectical Behavior Therapy (DBT) for Borderline Personality Disorder" From *The Journal*, March 1, 1997, Vol. 8/Iss. 1

[4] Ekman, Paul, *Emotions Revealed*, Holt Paperbacks; 2nd edition, March 20, 2007, Pages 39-40

people. A person with BPD is like a cork floating on a stormy sea of negative emotions.

What a Non can find useful about this view of BPD is that it is basically a sub-class of other mood disorders. Medications like mood-stabilizers and anti-depressants do help people with BPD, but they might not offer complete relief. These medications will not halt impulsive and dangerous behaviors. BPD is a severe mental illness with emotional and behavioral components. There is no magic pill that will cure the disorder. However, some medications do help those with the disorder.

While it seems almost completely intractable, there is hope. The tools that I am offering you in this book can help to calm the waters and to point the direction toward healing. I have seen it with my own eyes in both my wife and daughter.

For now, you should reflect on that fact that BPD is chiefly an emotional disorder with behavioral aspects that arise from strong negative emotional states.

In the next chapter I will briefly explain emotions and their role in the life of a person with BPD. The purpose of this explanation is for you to understand a little more about how it may feel to have the disorder and how and why emotion-based tools actually work. If you do not accept the idea that BPD is primarily an emotional disorder, the tools are not going to be effective for you.

It is important that you understand what is going on with your loved one. Only by understanding what is going on can you learn how you can do anything about it.

I am going to focus on four of the symptoms which, in my opinion, are the foundation for all the others and for the behaviors. These four symptoms are:

1. **Emotional dysregulation** (which I have just explained and is the "cornerstone" of the foundation);
2. **Impulsivity** (which combined with emotional dysregulation forms the motivation behind many of the "nonsensical" behaviors)
3. **Shame** (which motivates many of the mistrust, sensitivity to judgment and black-and-white thinking aspects of the disorder).

4. **Preoccupation with Interpersonal Relationships** (Or attachment relationships, which causes an "obsession" with others, their feelings toward the BPD and the fear of abandonment).

In the Frequently Asked Questions portion of this book, I address other symptoms and behaviors.

Now, you might be saying to yourself, "Hey! What about me? Why are you talking so much about how THEY feel? I don't care how they feel! I just want to get on with my life! I just want to figure out how to deal with them when I have to without getting raged at!"

Believe me, I'm getting to that. Be patient and let me explain some features of the disorder so that you know why the skills work.

Emotional Dysregulation

I previously explained what emotional dysregulation (the opposite of regulation) is and how a BPD reacts to emotional situations. I will delve into it more deeply because, as I have said, emotional dysregulation is a cornerstone of BPD.

People with BPD are highly emotionally reactive to external stimuli and easily upset by events that they perceive as threatening to them. Often, the "actual" events are not really threatening at all. However, the person will perceive the events as threatening and typically will react with a high state of agitation, sadness, anger or fear.

Having wildly-swinging out-of-control emotions is no fun at all. It fact it hurts a great deal. Emotional pain is almost constant in BPD and, since emotions affect both the body and the mind, it hurts through and through. Any disease that upsets the emotional system is going to be extremely painful for the sufferer.

Recent studies have indicated that this pain is an outgrowth of a debt of u-opioids in the sufferer's brain. While there seems to be too few of these pain-killing neurochemicals, the receptors for u-opioids are overactive. This combination of too little u-opioids and overactive receptors results in a state of constant pain, emptiness and lack of well-being. If correct, this brain chemistry combination explains the "dead inside" feeling of BPD as well as the opiate abuse and self-injury common in BPD.[5]

That is why I called my Internet group, "Anything to Stop the Pain" (ATSTP). I wanted to remind the members that their loved ones are in a lot of emotional pain and that those people would do anything (even the extreme, irrational behavior that they were actually doing) to stop it.

I like to compare it to someone actually being on fire. She will do anything to put out the flames, including running right over you if you're standing in her way on the way to the lake.

The quelling of emotional pain is one of the main motivations for substance abuse and impulsive behaviors (like dangerous driving, unprotected sex and binge spending). Each of these behaviors either makes the person with BPD feel better (and more deserving) or temporarily deadens the emotional pain.

Because the person with BPD has such extreme emotional pain, she can at times take that pain out on you. Like the "person on fire" example, YOU can get burned if she runs up to you and transmits the fire to you. YOU can be hurt as she bowls you over on the way to the lake that she believes will squelch her fire.   It hurts, regardless of whether you're bowled over… or burned.

Impulsivity

Based on emotional reactions, people with BPD are likely to be impulsive. It is not a "do it if it feels good" kind of thing. Impulsiveness when someone is emotionally dysregulated is geared to halt the emotional pain.

What happens is that the person with BPD gets "under the influence" of their strong negative emotional states, and, because emotions are immediate and strong, if a person makes a decision based on that emotion, the decision is likely to be impulsive. If the emotion is a negative one, like deep sadness to the point of pain, the impulsivity is likely to be in the area of pain relief or pain avoidance.

This reason is why people with BPD might go on shopping sprees or overeat or drink-and-drive. She isn't driving under the influence. She is

[5] *An Opioid Deficit in Borderline Personality Disorder: Self-Cutting, Substance Abuse, and Social Dysfunction,* The American Journal of Psychiatry, Antonia S. New, M.D., Barbara Stanley, Ph.D., Volume 167 Issue 8, August 2010, pp. 882-885

getting under the influence (in this case of negative emotional states) and then driving. If the emotional state is fear, a person with BPD is likely to run away, even if it is not "practical" at the time.

On two occasions, my wife has been emotionally dysregulated (angry with me) and dropped everything gone to the airport and flown to a foreign country. Now, that's impulsive. Unfortunately for her, while she was "getting back at me" by giving herself something she felt she deserved at the time, once the emotions passed (like half way over the ocean on her way to Europe), the shame of what she was doing impulsively was huge.

This increased level of impulsivity will likely get more pronounced if the person with BPD uses alcohol or drugs (even prescription drugs) to ease their pain, as such mind-altering substances reduce the barriers to impulsive action.

It may manifest itself in self-destructive impulses, like unprotected sex, dangerous driving or shopping that one cannot afford. Sometimes even suicidal behavior might occur in reaction to other symptoms (shame, ruminating, etc.) with the idea that death will halt the emotional pain forever. At times, the suicidal behavior is "accidental" as in the case of an overdose, which was done impulsively and for the purpose of pain relief. Keep in mind; we are dealing with some serious business here.

Shame

One of the most marked features of BPD is a sense of pervasive shame experienced by the sufferer. Dr. Richard Moskowitz says this on his website about the role of shame in BPD:

Shame is fundamental to the experience of anyone with BPD and is the most crucial emotion that must be addressed if recovery is to occur. Shame is often confused with guilt, but these emotions have very different meanings. Shame is about who we are, while guilt is about what we do. Shame therefore reflects more lasting beliefs about the self than guilt. When we feel guilt, we expect retribution for what we've done. When we feel shame, we expect contempt from others and feel contempt for ourselves. [6]

As you can see, shame is different from guilt. When someone feels guilt they are embarrassed or judgmental about something that they did. That

[6] Moskowitz, Richard, From the URL: http://www.soulselfhelp.on.ca/drm10shame.html

is, you feel guilty when you do something bad or wrong. When someone feels shame they are embarrassed or judgmental about who they are.

Guilt says I've made a mistake; shame says I am a mistake. [7]

The person with BPD is likely to feel deep shame about who she is and will likely consider herself, deep inside, to be a bad person. The natural reaction to shame is to cover it up and to hide it from others. It may be that your loved one has never exhibited shame to you. If she has not revealed this sense of shame, she is behaving in a completely natural manner. It is not a matter of trusting you or not trusting you. The natural reaction to shame is to hide.

Letting another person know that you carry around a feeling of shame involves much vulnerability. That vulnerability can feel threatening to the person with BPD. In the second section of this book, I will talk about how to deal with shame in your loved one. For now, it is important that you know that it is there, even if it is not readily visible to you.

Shame is why people with BPD are NOT psychopaths. I often get comments on my blog indicating that people with BPD are psychopaths. I like to point out that while there is a vernacular usage of the term psychopath, there is also a clinical one. A clinical psychopath (someone with psychopathy) will have no shame and will behave in a "callous and unemotional" fashion towards others. People with dysregulated emotional states and who are filled with shame are not psychopathic.

This sense of shame is one of the core features of BPD. People with toxic and core shame often exhibit "push-pull" behavior in which you, as a partner or parent, are loved and cherished one day and hated and reviled the next.

She may run from a relationship if you get too close. She wants to be able the control the inevitable ending of the relationship. In her mind, which has a sense of "background shame," she expects that one day you will see through her and discover that she is a bad person, judge her as unworthy of love and leave. This dynamic gives rise to the fear of abandonment and sensitivity to judgment.

---

[7] Bradshaw, John, From the URL: www.eqi.com

The interplay between shame and the other symptoms of BPD cannot be understated. Understanding shame is the key to understanding the motivations and behaviors of someone with BPD.

Dr. John Bradshaw talks extensively about toxic shame in his book *Healing the Shame that Binds You*. He calls this internal shame "binding shame" and notes:

The shame binding of feelings, needs and natural instinctual drives, is a key factor in changing healthy shame into toxic shame. To be shame-bound means that whenever you feel any feeling, and need or any drive, you immediately feel ashamed. The dynamic core of your human life is grounded in your feelings, your needs and your drives. When these are bound by shame, you are shamed to the core.[8]

It is also important to know that this shame prevents many people with BPD from going into therapy. The person with BPD will experience two distinct shame reactions when considering therapy. One is the fear that the therapist will be able to "see right through her" and judge her as a bad or broken person. The other is that, because the shame backs up the idea within her that she is bad or broken, that the therapy will fail to heal her.

This feeling is particularly unpleasant because then her shame would be confirmed professionally and, therefore, in her belief system, she is beyond help. Often, someone with BPD who is in therapy will drop out when the therapist approaches this sense of shame.

She would be exposed. Think about that word – exposed. Imagine you're exposed. You're naked for the entire world to see. It's an unpleasant, sickening feeling: one that a person with BPD lives with all day, every day.

The other two core features of BPD also contribute to the shame. First, a person with BPD will become emotional dysregulated because of her interpretation of an event. That may cause impulsivity and irrational behavior. Then, after the emotional dysregulation is gone, the BP may feel embarrassed and shameful about the behavior. My wife's impulsive travels are excellent examples of this shame-inducing behavior.

---

[8] Bradshaw, John, *Healing the Shame that Binds You*, from website.

She may not express this shame and may defend her behavior to you, because to be seen as shameful again marks her as "different." (Dr. Marsha Linehan calls BPD the "I don't fit in" disorder.[9])

Since the origin of the behavior was her feelings and being emotionally sensitive is "just how she is," if the behavior is judged as "bad" or "wrong" then a connection is made between that judgment and feelings. She feels this way and it is wrong to feel this way, but she can't help feeling this way.

In the next chapter I will explain the nature of emotions and how they can be an issue with BPD. Hang in there, we will get to the tools that can help you from getting burned or run over.

Preoccupation with Interpersonal Relationships

This feature is a new one that I have added to my "model" of BPD. I added it because I attended the International Society for the Study of Personality Disorders (ISSPD) and listened to Dr. John Gunderson present a detailed model of his experience with BPD. The purpose of the presentation was to present a "real world" clinical model of BPD from the viewpoint of someone with many years of experience treating the disorder. One of the features that Dr. Gunderson provided was this "preoccupation with attachments."[10]

I believe this feature is born of an unstable sense of self. A person with BPD has difficulty "locating herself in the world." While two of the other "core" features of BPD are "systems related" (meaning, those features are based on subsystems of the mind – the emotional regulation system, the impulse control system), shame and the preoccupation with interpersonal relationships are based more on a person with BPD's view of herself. While it might seem that interpersonal relationships are outside of self, a more complex picture arises as we look more deeply into the mental configuration of BPD.

[9] Quote from "Back From the Edge" - Borderline Personality Disorder Documentary, New York Presbyterian Hospital, Feb 2, 2012

[10] Psychodynamic Therapy of BPD: Developing Expertise, John Gunderson, MD, International Society for the Study of Personality Disorders, 11th International Congress, The Mount Sinai School of Medicine, New York, NY, AUGUST 2009

A recent study showed that the number one trigger of systems dysregulation (like wildly swinging emotions and impulsive behavior) is interpersonal distress. This interpersonal distress is more important as a trigger of dysregulated behavior than sweeping/major life changes – in fact major life changes, such as changing jobs, getting married, having a child, were ranked last of nine factors that trigger BPD distress.[11]

The interpersonal, moment-to-moment perception of the state of an important relationship is the most important trigger. That can be bad news for someone in a close relationship with someone with BPD. The person with BPD will be continuously scanning the interpersonal landscape for threats. Since shame is involved, people with BPD are likely to use others to regulate their internal systems and their self-view. In other words, a person with BPD uses others as a mirror to view their self.

Why is this so? I believe that a person with BPD's lack of internal regulation causes her to internalize other people and use others to self-regulate. This is why a person with BPD will both try to control the behavior of others (usually only those to whom they are attached) and feel controlled at the same time. Also, the loss of an external emotional regulator feels like core abandonment and triggers panic.

When someone has an inability to locate herself in the world, which very possibly arises from the emotional instability as a child, she seeks to have others locate her for her. She needs others to verify and validate that she's "ok". Unfortunately, because few of us are taught the language of emotional regulation, a person with BPD will likely learn that the interpersonal landscape is not safe; it is full of threats to their very self.

It's not an easy situation in which to live. If a person requires external validation and regulation, there develops a sense of a lack of control. Others are unpredictable, don't understand how it feels and can damage the very core of her being. This leads to a semi-paranoid state about others. There is an assumption that other people's intentions are malevolent toward the person with BPD.

People with BPD have described this internal feeling of emptiness and lack of internal controls as feeling "dead inside," which is, in itself, tragic.

---

[11] Elements of affective instability associated with suicidal behaviour in patients with borderline personality disorder. Links PS, Eynan R, Heisel MJ, Nisenbaum R., Can J Psychiatry. 2008 Feb;53(2):112-6.

Extending this feeling to others through this preoccupation with close interpersonal relationships leaves a person with BPD with the feeling that others contribute to this unpleasant internal feeling. In other words, "it's your fault that I feel this way." It's a very "effect and cause" way of thinking. I feel bad – something or someone must be making me feel this way.

Many Non-BPDs ask me why their loved ones with BPD don't seem to trust them. To me, this aspect of BPD is a significant factor, along with other biological factors which I will explain later in this book.

All of that being said, interpersonal relationships play a huge role in BPD. Social connections and attachments, including parent/child attachments, are the focal point of a person with BPD's sense of well-being. When these trigger dysregulation and/or ineffective modes of thinking and behavior, a person with BPD is lost in the world, floating free in a threatening sea of feelings, thoughts and behaviors.

Other Symptoms

What about manipulation? What about lying and blaming and raging? What about verbal and physical abuse? These are excellent questions. As a loved one of someone with BPD, you are subjected to many irrational and abusive situations.

Those situations and your loved one's behaviors are difficult to understand or withstand. I have personally been lied to, blamed and raged at on numerous occasions. However, by applying the tools that I will explain later in this book, I have been able to reduce the rage and emotion-driven behaviors in both my wife and my daughter. I have heard from my coaching clients and my list members that the first thing that goes away when they applied the skills in this book was the raging.

Remember though: these skills are not a cure-all. In fact, they are not a "cure" at all.

The purpose of the tools is to get through the moment and more quickly insure that the BP returns to baseline or exits the refractory period. That will help calm the waters. Real healing can only occur when the BPD is out of the emotional dysregulation. Getting the BPD out of emotional dysregulation is the first step.

I believe that behaviors can be explained by their root causes, which are the symptoms I have previously explained: emotional dysregulation, impulsiveness, shame and a preoccupation with interpersonal relationships.

Go Slowly

You must understand that in order for the tools in this book to work properly, they need to be understood and applied in a step-wise fashion. I have often said to my list members that "you can't boil the ocean" which means that you can't do everything all at once. You can't jump to the end before you walk the path.

Instead, you have to take one small step at a time in a longer journey. The goal of all of these tools, attitudes, skills and approaches is (in my mind) a compassionate, trusting, respectful and two-way relationship in which both parties feel known, heard, understood and worthy.

Achieving that goal is hitting a grand slam so to speak. Yet, I feel that you must be given the fundamentals and practice those fundamentals before you can hit one out of the park. To that end, I will start with emotions which are the first layer to peel back from the onion that is BPD.

Chapter 2: What are emotions and why do we have them?

Emotions are built-in mechanisms for keeping us safe. The "base" of emotions in our brain is in the limbic system, deep within the core and just above the brain stem. I like to refer to emotions as the "land-bridge" between the mind and the body.

When you experience emotions both your body and mind react. If you feel fearful, your body reacts by speeding up your heart-rate, contracting capillaries in your extremities (that is why you can "go pale"), and releasing adrenaline into your bloodstream. Your emotion, fear in this case, is preparing your body to run away fast, which is the natural reaction to fear.

Emotions are, in some ways, a "mind reflex" that protects you and your body's survival. Emotions are basic survival mechanisms. Even animals have some form of emotion – fear, for example – that prey can use to escape predators. While some might argue that emotions are a left-over vestige of a distant past, an "animal" version of higher thought, I would disagree. We still need emotions to inform us about the environment. In any event, everyone has emotions and everyone can learn to deal with them effectively. That being said, people with BPD are in a position of requiring additional help to effectively regulate with their emotions.

Emotions are almost immediate. They arise quickly and dissipate quickly. They are not "moods." Emotions last a short period of time – minutes, hours – but are unlikely to last more than a day or two. Moods last a longer time, sometimes weeks or months. Your "temperament" is of an even longer duration and with you most of their life. Because emotional reactions are immediate and short-acting, a person can be angry one minute and joyful the next. The bad news is that such reactions are unpredictable. The good news is that they will pass quickly in most people.

Dr. Paul Ekman has demonstrated that there are seven basic, universal emotions: anger, fear, sadness, joy, disgust, contempt and surprise. [12]

---

[12] Ekman, Paul, *Emotions Revealed.*, Page 11.

Ekman has researched emotions over several decades and found that, for these seven emotions, while cultural cues that stimulate them may differ, every person in every culture displays these emotions. They also display them in the same manner on their faces. Ekman created the Facial Action Coding System (FACS) to categorize each expression and how each expression relates to each basic emotion.

For the purposes of this book, I will focus on the basic emotions: anger, sadness, joy, fear, contempt and disgust. Each one can be felt in combination with another, meaning you can feel sad and angry at the same time, depending on the cue and your "belief" about the cue. When I say "belief" I refer to the meaning of the cue to you.

As stated, Ekman found that there were cultural differences in the meaning of the cues. In some cultures, the people eat cats or dogs — a practice that an American would mostly likely find disgusting. There are certainly things in American culture that others around the world might think is unholy or disgusting. The cue for the emotion is different in different cultures.

The natural reactions to the particular emotions, however, are universal. All people, regardless of culture, will display the same facial expression and feel the same physiological effects of a particular emotion. All people will also feel compelled to react in a similar fashion to a particular emotion. While the actual behavior may differ, the impulse to act on each emotion — to laugh when happy, to cry when sad and to fight when angry — is the same in each and every person.[13]

We need our emotions for protection. When a car swerves in front of yours on the highway, your mind takes that cue as dangerous, triggers fear and almost automatically reacts to swerve out of the way. Even after the fear has dissipated, you may still feel the fear in your body.

I remember once when I was on the highway (and talking on the cell phone), and I saw a car seem to fly into the air two lanes over from me and a few cars in front. It was as if everything was happening in slow motion, because a postal truck, one of those with a van-like cab and a boxy truck-like back, turned directly into my lane to avoid the flying car. My fear immediately rose. I knew there was a threat. I dropped the phone, slammed on the brakes (with all of the junk in my car hurtling towards

---

[13] Ekman, Paul, *Emotions Revealed*, General Concept.

me), and turned the wheel. I guided my car into the emergency lane between the highway and the divider and missed the postal truck by inches. I was safe and unharmed, but it still took my body about half an hour to recover from the physiological effects of fear. I was shaky and drained and had to pull off the road to recover. I later learned that two people were killed in the car that vaulted into the air.

Now you might be saying, "I can understand why we need emotions in a situation like that, but what about regular decision-making? Shouldn't we decide things based on the facts and our rational assessment of the facts?"

Actually, the answer is "no." Even in the modern world we need our emotions to help us make wise decisions.

Emotions function in three important ways. These are:

- Emotions can help to communicate with and to influence other people.
- Emotions can organize and contribute to the motivation of actions and behaviors.
- Emotions can provide information about our environment.

If you lack the ability to make meaning out of emotions, you have a diminished capability to do one or all of the above.

Consider the strange case of Phineas Gage, which is retold and analyzed in neurologist Antonio R. Damasio's *Descartes' Error: Emotion, Reason, and the Human Brain*. Gage was a railroad foreman who, because of an unexpected explosion, had a rail spike penetrate his head. The two-foot steel spike entered his brain below the right cheek and exited through the top of his head, effectively severing his pre-frontal cortex from the rest of his brain. He essentially received an unexpected pre-frontal lobotomy.

While the "base" of emotions is deep within the brain, the ability to make "sense" of the emotions is within the pre-frontal cortex. The pre-frontal cortex helps "synthesize" emotional information and find meaning in it. The effect on Gage was dramatic. Dr. J. M. Harlow was quoted at the time saying:

Gage was fitful, irreverent, indulging at times in the grossest profanity (which was not previously his custom), manifesting but little deference for his fellows, impatient of restraint or advice when it conflicts with his desires, at times pertinaciously obstinate, yet capricious and vacillating, devising many plans of future operations, which are no sooner arranged than they are abandoned in turn for others appearing more feasible. [14]

While the language is certainly nineteenth century, neurologist Damasio notes in his text that he met a modern-day Gage in the form of a patient named Elliot. This patient began experiencing problems after a tumor placed pressure on the pre-frontal cortex. The text says that Elliot had trouble experiencing any emotion, including positive ones:

This was astounding. Try to imagine it. Try to imagine not feeling pleasure when you contemplate a painting you love or hear a favorite piece of music. Try to imagine yourself forever robbed of that possibility and yet aware of the intellectual contents of the visual or musical stimulus, and also aware that once it did give you pleasure. [15]

Damasio goes on to say that in addition to being unable to experience positive or negative affect, Elliot could not make sound decisions. Elliot's life spiraled out of control. Before his condition worsened, he was married, had children and a promising career. After his pre-frontal cortex was damaged by the tumor, Elliot lost his job, amassed large gambling debts and went through a protracted divorce.

Emotions play a huge role in our lives and in our decision-making. Many people believe that a person can't make sound decisions if they are "too emotional." Most people place value in being rational (as opposed to rash). However, studies have shown that every decision – from buying ice cream to hiring an employee – has an emotional component. We just don't notice the emotional component often because it is so built-in that it just seems natural, unless the emotions are expressed for everyone to see.

We usually only notice the emotions of people that "wear their heart on their sleeve." Yet, everyone has emotions. When something just doesn't "feel right," that is your emotional system contributing to a decision. We need both our emotions and our rational mind to make sound, wise decisions. If one of the two faculties is out-of-kilter, the decision-making process suffers.

---

[14] Harlow, J.M. (1868). "Recovery from a Passage of an Iron Bar through the Head". *Publications of the Massachusetts Medical Society* 2: 327-347

[15] Damasio, Antonio R, *Descartes' Error Emotion, Reason, and the Human Brain*, 1994, page 45

Typically, people do the natural thing when responding to their emotions.

The natural thing for each of the "basic" emotions is as follows:

Emotion - Reflex

- Fear - Flee
- Anger - Attack
- Joy - Rejoice, smile, laugh
- Disgust - Turn away
- Contempt - Judge others
- Surprise - Jump back
- Sadness - Cry, withdrawal

Typically, any person will feel compelled to do the natural thing as a result of these emotions. These emotions are "reflexive" emotions and can save a person's life. Your body and mind react to these emotions reflexively. If the reflexive emotion is not aligned with reality, it can cause problems.

It is possible to turn reflexive emotions into "reflective" emotions. Reflective emotions can encourage wise choices because they are combined in our mind with rationality. In fact, these two types of emotions are configured differently in our brains.[16]

With BPD, the emotional system is out-of-kilter and that affects the decision- making process. They are naturally more reflexive as a result of emotions than a less emotionally sensitive person. Additionally, a person with BPD has poor impulse control so that misguided decisions often lead directly to inappropriate behavior. Clearly, the problem is in her brain and with her emotional regulation capacities.

A person with BPD's brain is working against them by upsetting the emotional regulation system. It is impossible for a person with BPD not to feel those emotions.

---

[16] *Neural Correlates of Borderline Personality Disorder and What They Might Teach Us*, Harold W. Koenigsberg, MD, International Society for the Study of Personality Disorders, 11th International Congress, The Mount Sinai School of Medicine, New York, NY, AUGUST 2009

The emotions are not right or wrong, they just are. These emotions do not arise out of nowhere. In fact, they are triggered by the internalized "sensors" (which are thoughts, beliefs and other mental states). There are two basic things that one can change emotionally: behavior and thoughts. This book will start with behavior – which seems more difficult to change, but is actually easier – and then move on to changing thoughts.

Emotions and BPD

A person with BPD is characterized by having a diminished ability to regulate her emotions during interactions with other people. This means that someone with BPD will likely react much more emotionally to a given situation than someone without BPD. A person with BPD is likely to get angry and, at times, fly into a rage at seemingly trivial events and interactions. She also will have a tendency to personalize external events.

In other words, the person suffering from BPD will believe that other people's behavior and comments are "about her," sometimes interpreting veiled criticism or judgment of her behavior when the evidence shows that there is none. The person with BPD is also likely to be seemingly obsessed with blame and fault-finding. You will likely hear a person with BPD say, "It's not my fault!" or "I did nothing wrong!" These comments and fault-avoidant behaviors are a consequence of sensitivity to judgment and rejection.

Everyone has both an in-born and learned capacity to regulate his or her emotions. I will discuss what factors contribute to these capacities and how you, as a loved one of someone with BPD, can cope with the problem. As stated earlier, reflexive emotions play a vital role in our ability to survive in a sometimes threatening environment. They are "mind reflexes" that protect and inform the mind of the state of the body and the body's assessment of the immediate surroundings. Unfortunately, as with BPD, the messages that are sent are sometimes not in tune with the actual environment - there may indeed be no basis in reality for her reactions.

An ancient Hindu text characterizes this "misperception" of reality in the following manner: "A rope may be momentarily perceived as a snake before ignorance is lifted."[17] The importance of this "ignorance" is that

[17] Sankaras Aparoksanubhuti, verse 44

during the time the rope is perceived as a snake, your emotions react almost automatically. (I say "almost" because if you have been taught to love snakes and not to fear them, you will not have a fear reaction even if you misperceive the rope as a snake).

You feel fear, it is real, and you jump away. Your body reacts as well. When I say "feel fear," I really mean it. Your heart rate increases, the capillaries in your extremities contract to save blood for vital organs, adrenaline is released to your blood stream. Your fear is real and felt directly. However, it is based on a misperception of reality. When you see that it is actually a rope, you might feel foolish or you might, if you had BPD, still try to convince everyone else that it is really a snake even though others can see it is a rope.

The reason for this behavior is that the feelings are so immediate and seem so "true" that you have to make "reality" match your feelings, rather than the other way around. When an emotional reaction conflicts with the state of the environment for whatever reason, it is said to be a "misaligned" emotional reaction.

What I realized about this story after I published the first edition of this book was that humans get more utility from a "false positive" (thinking a rope is a snake) than a "false negative" (thinking a snake is a rope). It allows us to better survive in a threatening world. Considering the "false alarms" (positives) that a person with BPD experiences, this threat-awareness, for whatever reason, seems to be on a hair trigger for someone with BPD. All of these false positives serve to keep the person with BPD in a constant state of crisis and fear.

Emotional Profiles and BPD

Each person has a unique emotional profile, despite the fact that all of us experience the same basic emotions. This profile is based on five independent factors. When I say "independent" here, I am saying factors that can each be unique in each individual and are not dependent on each other. The emotional profile factors are:

1. **Tolerance (When).** This is the sensitivity a person has to triggering events. Those with a high sense of threat awareness (like people with BPD) are likely to have this factor set at "hair trigger."

2. **Onset (How Fast).** This is how quickly the emotion gets to full intensity.

3. **Intensity (How High).** This is how intense the emotion affects a particular person.

4. **Duration (How Long).** How long the emotion lasts and continues to affect the person's thinking.

5. **Recovery duration (When Over).** How long it takes a person to "get over" the emotional reaction.

A person with BPD will likely have an emotional profile in which all five aspects are poorly regulated. That is, the tolerance will be low and they will react at the slightest provocation. The onset will be fast and they will react quickly to the trigger. The intensity will be high, and their experience and expression of the emotion is likely to be strong. The duration will be long and it will last a longer time at top intensity. Their "return to baseline" will take longer and they will be emotionally upset longer than others might. In other words, people with BPD are likely to be an emotional volcano, ready to erupt at any minute.

For this reason, a person will BPD can be difficult to deal with and to understand how they get upset at the most "trivial" of things. Poor emotional regulation can cause other symptoms to arise as the person with BPD becomes emotionally dysregulated. This term emotionally dysregulated (or just dysregulated) is used to denote the state in which a person with BPD is overcome with powerful and, at many times, misaligned emotional reactions.

Remember that emotions don't arise on their own; they are based on cues or triggers from the environment and compared by our "emotional immune system" to the meaning of the cue. For a person with BPD, the meaning can be misjudged or, as is often the case, the sensitivity to emotional cues is greatly heightened.

An example is a heat-sensing system that helps to detect and suppress fires. Sometimes companies will install heat-sensing equipment in addition to smoke detectors so that they can protect assets that need a certain temperature to operate (e.g. computer equipment which might cease working at a high temperature). The setting at which an alarm goes off might be 80 degrees Fahrenheit.

In the case of someone with BPD, the setting (or "tolerance" as it is called in the control community) is naturally set much lower, at 50 degrees Fahrenheit. That means that the alarm will be raised much more often and lead to a reaction to the alarm. In other words, people with BPD will experience many, many (what you would consider) false alarms. These false alarms seem completely real to them, because their tolerance for emotional triggers is set very low. They are constantly running a fire drill. Unfortunately for you, the BP may drag you along unwillingly and unwittingly for the drill.

Chapter 3: What causes BPD?

Another theme of my online list is a detailed discussion of the causes of BPD. There are people in various "camps" as to the causes, and especially lively is the debate on "nature vs. nurture."

My take on the situation is that there appears to be both "nature" causes and "nurture" causes and that either can have varying degrees of influence on the severity of the illness.

My other take on this discussion is that I'd like for it to be brief because, in my opinion, WHY this person in your life has BPD is not as important to me as WHAT do you do to make your life easier. No matter what causes it, the facts remain:

- A person you love or with which you have some relationship has a serious problem.
- A person you love is very difficult to live with at times.
- A person you love is causing you pain and suffering and is in pain herself.

Many people find themselves compelled to find out the "whys" of BPD and to understand what caused the disorder in their loved one. Searching for a "why" can be disheartening, because the causes of the disorder can often not be attributed to a single factor, either biological or environmental. Some researchers believe it is completely biological, some that it is completely environmental. Some believe that it is a form of Post-Traumatic Stress Disorder. Others believe it is akin to a rapid-cycling form of Bipolar Disorder.

In the first edition of this book I used the equifinality model, created by Joseph Santoro, Michael Tisbe, and Michael Katsarakes, to explain the causes of BPD.[18] Since there has been much additional research as to the causes of BPD, I found it necessary for me to rewrite this section for the second edition.

---

[18] Santoro Ph.D., Joseph, Michael Tisbe, M.D., Michael Katsarakes, "An Equifinality Model of Borderline Personality Disorder" from American Academy of Experts in Traumatic Stress website.

Regardless of how the disorder is caused, the skills explained in this book are likely to be effective at reducing the chaos in your relationship with this person. That is where the "how" comes into play. You can be effective whether or not you know exactly why the person has BPD.

I will discuss the two causes – biological and environmental – because there are several important points that you will need to understand before you can apply the tools effectively.

In the first chapter of this book, I spoke about the core components of BPD. It is important for you to understand that these components do not cause BPD, they are features of BPD.

Biological Causes

Clearly, there is some evidence of biological (and possibly genetic) causes of BPD. Some people naturally have less of an ability to regulate their emotions than others. In psychology, this "tendency to experience unpleasant emotions easily, such as anger, anxiety, depression, or vulnerability; sometimes called emotional instability" is labeled "Neuroticism" and is considered one of the "Big Five" personality traits.[19] Although this factor also has environmental influences, some of the "initial setting" of emotional instability seems to be biological and likely inheritable.

Thus, the tendency of a particular person to develop (or not to develop) BPD seems to be, at least partially, in-born. Others who have less of a propensity toward BPD can be said to have a natural immunity against developing it. Neuroticism has environmental factors and other biological factors such as brain injury.

Just being born with (or without) neuroticism does not insure that a person will (or will not) develop BPD. However, some people seem to have a pre-disposition that makes it more likely that they will develop BPD.

Certain areas of the brain are also more active and other areas less active in those that have BPD. The amgydala, which is an almond-sized organ

---

[19] Mount, M. K. & Barrick, M. R. (1998). "Five reasons why the 'Big Five article has been frequently cited," *Personnel Psychology*, 51, Pages 849-857

within the limbic system, is more active in people with BPD. The pre-frontal cortex where logical, rational thinking and emotional input is integrated shows less activity when the person is emotional. Undoubtedly, there are neural foundations for the emotional dysregulation that is common for someone with BPD.

More recently, studies have been looking into the brain chemistry of people with BPD. There have been studies about opioid disturbance in the brain. They propose that the feeling of inner deadness, the inability to tolerate aloneness, the vast abuse of pain killers and the frequency of self-injury, all can be explained in the disordered opioid system.[20]

Other studies have investigated the levels of oxytocin in the blood streams of people with BPD. Oxytocin is known as the "love chemical" and is probably a key ingredient in attachment. Low level of oxytocin can lead to mistrust and even paranoia.

Additionally, vasopressin has been considered as a contributing factor to heightened aggression. In mammals, vasopressin levels contribute to a number of social behaviors including selective aggression toward peers. It has been suggested that people with BPD have a surplus of vasopressin and that this may contribute to increased levels of social aggression.[21]

If any of the above situations are true and can be shown to have a causative effect on borderline personality disorder, I feel we need to completely rethink the way consider the sufferers. If the disorder is completely caused by biological factors beyond your control, how can the disorder be considered a "personality" disorder at all?

Instead, borderline personality disorder should be renamed and treated like bipolar I. In the first paper about the opioid debt, it was suggested that buprenorphine might be used to effectively treat BPD.

[20] *Borderline personality disorder: a dysregulation of the endogenous opioid system?*, Bandelow B, Schmahl C, Falkai P, Wedekind D.,Psychol Rev. 2010 Apr;117(2):623-36. doi: 10.1037/a0018095.

[21] The interpersonal dimension of borderline personality disorder: toward a neuropeptide model, Stanley B, Siever LJ., Am J Psychiatry. 2010 Jan;167(1):24-39. doi: 10.1176/appi.ajp.2009.09050744. Epub 2009 Dec 1.

Buprenorphine is an opioid receptor antagonist/opioid-like combination used to treat opioid addiction (like heroin abuse). It comes in a number of varieties with the most well-known being Suboxone. I am not currently aware of studies about this or other similar medications. I am also not a doctor and can't recommend any medication.

My wife once reported to me that she only felt "normal" when she had about 20 milligrams of Vicodin inside her body. She no longer uses pain killers, but at that time (about 10 years ago), she was using them frequently. I could see firsthand how the idea of opioid dysfunction could be a cause of BPD.

Environmental Causes

Much has been said of the role of the environment and emotional disorders. Often, doctors blame the parents of someone with BPD for causing the disorder. While the environment plays a key role in BPD, I hesitate to point fingers at someone's parents. Many people with BPD have experienced parental abuse and/or neglect, but not all of the people with BPD have. A more important factor in developing BPD seems to be what Marsha Linehan calls the "Invalidating Environment."

The Invalidating Environment is one in which emotional responses, particularly negative emotional responses, are met with derision, dismissal or scorn. This reaction does not have to be abuse. When someone who is biologically vulnerable to strong emotional responses has their emotional reactions met with invalidation, the person can start to develop BPD. The following internal situation begins to develop:

[The] effect of an invalidating environment, especially when basic emotions such as fear, anger, and sadness are invalidated, is that a person in such an environment does not learn when to trust her own emotional responses as valid reflections of individual and situational events. Thus, she is unable to validate and trust herself… If communication of negative emotions is punished, as it often is in invalidating environment, then a response of shame follows experiencing the intense emotion in the first place and expressing it publicly in the second. [22]

If the parents or peers of someone who is biologically vulnerable to experiencing powerful emotions do not accept as valid the expression of

[22] Linehan, Marsha, *Cognitive-Behavioral Treatment of Borderline Personality Disorder*, pg 72

those emotions, the person lives in an invalidating environment. Since emotions are natural expressions of how one's mind measures the surrounding environment, the invalidation is of something natural and something that cannot be "controlled."

While one's behavior as a reaction to negative emotions can be controlled (and I will talk about this in more detail later), the arising of the negative emotions are, for the most part, beyond the conscious control of the person. Therefore, when the expression of this subconscious reaction is met with dismissal, the person begins to feel broken and defective and develops a low self-image. She begins to have a "response of shame."

Invalidation of this sort is embodied in several forms. The most common form of emotional invalidation comes from telling the person that their emotional expressions are "wrong" or "bad" and from punishing the individual for being upset in some way. Additionally, the punishment of emotional responses, particular corporal punishment, can have a lasting effect on the person. She learns that feeling angry or sad gets her punished and she will try to suppress these feelings.

Unfortunately, emotions cannot be completely suppressed and, when the emotions arise as a natural reaction to external (like a threat) or internal states (like being tired or run-down), the cycle of invalidation begins all over again.

Emotions can be self-feeding and, if the person experiencing the emotion tries to push them away, the emotions can come back stronger than before. Emotions can also generate other emotions – that is, you can be angry that you are sad – which can generate more emotional dysregulation.

A person with BPD can also be affected by the emotional states and reactions of others, especially those who are important figures in her life. As stated, emotions can build on themselves. This is true whether the emotions are internal (within the person with BPD) or external (within and expressed by the person with whom the person with BPD has a close relationship). As the negative emotions build within a particular encounter, the person with BPD is likely to become more emotionally dysregulated if the other person expresses disapproval of the expressed emotions or if the other person expresses strong negative emotions of his own.

More recent studies have considered PTSD and BPD to be distinct, although the disorders can be comorbid. In essence, BPD is not a form of PTSD, but the severity of BPD can be accelerated with comorbid PTSD. [23] Thus, it's not a traumatic childhood that causes BPD; although a traumatic childhood can make the symptoms and dysfunction of BPD much more severe.

Attachment and BPD

This section is new to the second addition of this book. Since I wrote the first edition, I started learning about mentalization techniques (which I will talk about later in this edition). Mentalization-based treatment (MBT) was pioneered by Drs. Peter Fonagy and Anthony Bateman, beginning in the early 2000's. It is a form of psychodynamic psychotherapy and is not skills-based like Dialectical Behavior Therapy.

The pioneers of MBT have cited attachment (using attachment theory) as a critical dysfunction in borderline personality disorder. When a primary attachment figure fails to properly mirror the mind states of an infant, a disturbance in attachment can take place.

I will be unable to do this rather complex and detailed theory justice in these pages. It is not a "blame it on the mother" situation though. Although proper mirroring of the infant's mental states can help reduce attachment anxiety, improper mirroring is not the sole factor in attachment disorder. When attachment anxiety develops, the person can end up being highly avoidant in either a dismissive or fearful fashion.

If the view of self developed in the attachment process contains much anxiety, a highly preoccupied view of others develops. In this way, the "preoccupation with attachment relationships" can be explained in BPD.

Whether or not attachment is a root cause of BPD or whether or not mirroring is a cause of attachment disorder/anxiety, attachment theory is still useful to understand the disorder. The poor attachment developed in childhood would likely exacerbate issues in the interpersonal domain.

---

[23] *Comorbidity of borderline personality disorder and posttraumatic stress disorder in the U.S. population.*,Pagura J, Stein MB, Bolton JM, Cox BJ, Grant B, Sareen J. ,J Psychiatr Res. 2010 Dec;44(16):1190-8. doi: 10.1016/j.jpsychires.2010.04.016. Epub 2010 May 26.

A common theme of crisis in BPD is interpersonal disturbances – romantic relationship issues, conflict with friends or family – and this theme is reflective of attachment stressors, rather than everyday stressors, like lost keys and work deadlines.

In 2008, Dr. Paul Links published a study that ranked the interpersonal "triggers" of emotional dysregulation in people with BPD.[24] In descending order of importance the triggers are:

1. Interpersonal Issues
2. Daily Life
3. Internal Psychological States
4. Physical States
5. Media Stimuli
6. Therapy
7. Memories
8. Impulsivity
9. Major Life Change/Stress

Since interpersonal issues are the number one trigger for emotional dysregulation and affect instability, this study would suggest that attachment is important in the functioning of emotional dysregulation.

I certainly have noticed and noted on my blog that the intensity of the emotional dysregulation is influenced and heightened if the attachment figure is of more importance (i.e. a parent or partner). In other words, the importance of the attachment seems to explain to severity of the emotional dysregulation.

This might resolve the strange conundrum: Why can my loved one with BPD behave normally at work, but is a raging "demon" with me? How can she control it in certain situations, but not within the family? In reality, there's just less at stake outside of the house, because the attachment relationship is not as strong or important.

When the attachment system is over-stimulated, much puzzling behavior can occur. Some examples of this are: rapid intimacy, self-harm, blaming, raging, idealization and others.

[24] *Elements of affective instability associated with suicidal behaviour in patients with borderline personality disorder.* Links PS, Eynan R, Heisel MJ, Nisenbaum R., Can J Psychiatry. 2008 Feb;53(2):112-6.

Bateman goes on to say that disordered attachment results in a poor representation of one's self inside one's self, which is called "the alien self". The child is unable to locate himself as an intentional being and internalizes the characteristics of the other person into the self. This creates an unstable self and a feeling of not really knowing who you are. [25]

This is a painful state, one of confusion, and one that results, according to the attachment theorists, in BPD.

Whatever the cause of BPD, it is important to note that it has to be approached in an effective manner. Your loved one is suffering. You are suffering. The remainder of this book is intended to teach you how to reduce (even eliminate) that suffering.

[25] Bateman, Anthony, via website, https://www.ucl.ac.uk/psychoanalysis/people/bateman

Chapter 4: The BPD Dynamic

While emotional dysregulation is an internal state – one that can build upon itself – the effects of emotional dysregulation are most often expressed in relation to other people. This is where you come in.

Having a relationship with someone who has BPD can be exhausting, both emotionally and physically. The main cause of this exhaustion is the BPD Dynamic, which is the typical direction of the interaction between someone with BPD and another person.

The Event

Some event happens in the world that triggers an emotional reaction within the person with BPD. This emotional reaction could be the result of someone else's statement that the person with BPD views as either judgmental or invalidating or both. Since the person with BPD self-judges and self-invalidates, she expects judgment and invalidation from the world around her. Often, the "event" is misaligned externally and internally. What this means is that it is only she that has associated certain events with certain emotions.

When someone with BPD gets "hot" she heats up quickly and stays hot longer than someone without BPD. She also has a lower emotional tolerance to external or internal triggers. Therefore, what someone without BPD might consider nothing, a person with BPD will consider threatening and react quickly and strongly.

One of the most interesting findings of a study in which scientists used functional magnetic resonance imagining (fMRI) to measure the emotional reaction (limbic system activation) of patients with BPD is that these people react to neutral faces in the same manner they react to angry faces. In essence, when shown a picture of a person with a neutral expression, people with BPD showed amygdala activation as if the picture was one of a person with an angry expression.[26] These people expect

[26] Donegan NH, Sanislow CA, Blumberg HP, Fulbright RK, Lacadie C, Skudlarski P, Gore JC, Olson IR, McGlashan TH, Wexler BE, "Amygdala hyperreactivity in borderline personality disorder: implications for emotional dysregulation", Biological Psychiatry, 2003 Dec 1, 54(11), Pages 1284-93

judgment and anger in others towards them and react physically and mentally to neutral situations as if they are threatening. They are likely to find "meaning" that is judgmental or threatening in an event which others would see as meaningless.

A member of my list compared this reactivity to neutral faces to neutral feedback on eBay. As a buyer on eBay, you don't give neutral feedback to a seller when everything about the sale is perfect. You give neutral feedback when something is wrong. A person with BPD will interpret a neutral face as "something wrong."

Still, this false interpretation doesn't mean that the feeling of being threatened or judged is not "real" to the person with BPD. It is felt and experienced as valid as any other event that triggers an emotion. In therapeutic circles, the event is often referred to as the "precipitating event."

The Interpretation

The event doesn't actually trigger the emotion directly. In fact, it is the interpretation of a particular event that triggers the emotion within someone. Different people can interpret the same event in different ways. As stated above about neutral faces, a person with BPD is more likely to be triggered by a negative interpretation of an event. For example, let's say that your wife has BPD and you are working outside the home. Let's further say that you come home an hour later than usual because you have a large project at work. Coming home an hour later is the event. Since you wife has BPD, she is more likely to interpret this event in a negative way.

Because of the symptoms of rejection sensitivity, shame and personalization (see FAQ), she is also more likely to interpret the event in a way that directly affects her in a negative, even catastrophic manner. She interprets it as "you're having an affair" and that is why you are late. What emotion is triggered when a wife thinks her husband is having an affair? Shame? Sadness? Fear? Anger? In this case, I would suspect that a mix of all of those emotions might be triggered in the following way:

Shame

"I am not a good enough wife. I don't have sex with him enough, so he has to go find a new woman." Now shame is not a base emotion. It is really a world-view in which the person that feels shame is a "bad person" or "inadequate person." It is closely related to guilt and embarrassment (which are emotions), but stronger and more primal than each. As I have previously mentioned, shame is one of the core aspects of BPD and can be triggered easily.

Shame is a painful feeling (arguably the most painful) and a person with BPD will quickly move on to other feelings to reduce the pain that comes along with feeling shame. Those other feelings are triggered more easily in a person with BPD because of the emotional dysregulation feature.

Sadness

"This relationship is over. It was the focus of my entire life and now it is over."

Fear

"He's going to divorce me and I will never be able to make it alone."

Anger

"How DARE he have an affair! I'll show him! The bastard!"

Now that the interpretation is in place, the emotions are triggered and the dysregulation begins. Anger is a very powerful emotion and, in most cases, anger will trump the others. So, even though your wife may experience each of these emotions quickly as the interpretation of the event arises, the reaction will most likely be one of anger.

Emotional and Physical Feelings

Emotions involve both the body and the mind. When your wife experiences these emotions, her body will automatically react to each one. Each emotion has a physical configuration. If she experiences these emotions, consider this quotation from Peter Steinke's Healthy Congregations:

When stress and anxiety are high, the R (reptilian) system is exaggerated. In other words, people become more thoughtless, more instinctive, and more automatic. The same is true concerning the feeling brain. Once fueled by limbic-derived feelings, we have less access to the thinking brain. Both brains have ensured the survival of the individual and the species. Necessary to survival, feelings have an insistent quality and are hardwired into the nervous system. With strong arousal, the limbic brain can be driven to continue. The reactive force can go on for hours. Highly excited emotional states are like poison ivy - we become all itch.[27]

What we see is that, once the emotional system becomes engaged, the body reacts automatically and reacts in a way that is "hard-wired" in our brains and bodies. We may feel a knot in the stomach, sweaty palms, and a loss of blood to the extremities, a rise in blood pressure or other automatic physical reactions. We also will, if even for a microsecond, display the emotion on our face. It is impossible to stop, although it can be suppressed quickly.

Dr. Paul Ekman, who was mentioned in the emotions section of this book, found that this display of emotion was (for many emotions) universal and cross-cultural. He found the same displays to the same emotions on the faces of tribes-people deep in New Guinea that he found in modern societies. [28] The body reactions and facial expressions are the same each time a particular emotion is experienced.

Action Impulses

Now that the emotion has been felt by your wife, she will have an impulse to act in a certain fashion – her behaviors are based on the emotions experienced. The natural way to react to each emotion is indicated below:

Shame, embarrassment or guilt. The natural reaction is to hide or remove oneself from the situation.

Sadness. The natural reaction is to cry or to behave in a depressed manner – to mourn or have the desire to stay in bed and disengage from the world.

Fear. The natural reaction is to run away to escape a threat.

Anger. The natural reaction is to attack, scream or display some other behavior that will cause fear in the object of the anger.

[27] Steinke, Peter, *Healthy Congregations: A Systems Approach*, 1996, pg. 36

[28] Ekman, Paul, *Emotions Revealed*, General Concept.

60

The reaction to the emotion is usually the natural one. What is in misalignment is the interpretation of the event. In this situation let's suppose that you are not having an affair, and your wife's interpretation of the fact that you came home an hour late is completely misaligned with reality.

Even if this is the case, she will still have action impulses as stated above. Why? Because the action impulses are not based on the event itself, but based on the emotion that she feels which is in turn based on her misaligned interpretation of the event. Since her emotional tolerance is low and her other symptoms are present, the interpretation kicks off the emotions.

We will discuss realigning her interpretations with reality later in this book. Suffice it to say that, at this point in the interaction, the problem is not the misalignment, but the emotional reaction to the misaligned interpretation. The problem is the emotion, not the event or the interpretation.

Unfortunately, as I mentioned in the symptoms section, one of the symptoms of BPD is impulsivity. Since these are action impulses, they are subject to the poor impulse control that is common in BPD. Therefore, it is likely that a person with react to the felt emotions in a way that is natural. Unfortunately for you, the natural reaction to anger is attacking behavior or rage.

Expression and Behavior

Since the emotions are dysregulated and overwhelming, your wife will now express her emotions and behave in a certain manner. She may say, "You are having an affair, you bastard! I can tell!" and throw a vegetable peeler at you (if one is handy). She will in some way try to communicate her emotions to you. This expression is sort of like "emotional vomit." The bad emotions build up inside of her and they must come out. Vomiting them up helps relieve the tension.

By yelling and attacking, she is trying to communicate her anger. This can lead to a misunderstanding because you are shocked that you just got hit in the head with a vegetable peeler. You can't understand why she would react this way. Now, this is an important point and you should read it carefully and try to understand it closely.

Remember the problem is not the event (you coming home an hour late) it is that your wife is angry. She is doing what most anyone would do when they are angry – she is expressing her anger and trying to communicate that she is angry.

The natural reaction to anger is to attack or to display the anger to hurt, scare or intimidate the other person (or animal). This is why cats puff themselves up and try to appear bigger when they encounter another threatening cat. Even though your wife's reaction seems completely crazy and out of touch with reality, she is expressing, behaving and reacting to her anger in a natural way. Once the anger is gone, the problem will be gone. Without anger there is no need to rage at you.

This step is the one at which most books about emotional disorders stop, but since this is a book for the people that are in a relationship with a person with BPD, I will go beyond just explanation of the cause, to actual steps you can take to help your loved one with BPD through these moments.

Your (Emotional) Reaction

OK, now here is the place where you have a choice of what to do. Just as your wife will naturally feel angry based on her interpretation of the event, you also go through the same process. If you have been yelled at and had a vegetable peeler thrown at your head, I suspect that you are likely to interpret that event as threatening. You have been attacked and the natural reaction to an attack is either fear or anger.

It depends on how threatening the display or anger (and attack) are to you. If you interpret your wife's reaction as extremely threatening – that is, threatening to life or limb, like she is going to go into the other room and get a shotgun out next – you will likely feel fear and get out of the house as soon as possible.

If you feel that the display is not quite that threatening, you will likely feel anger too. In addition to either emotion, you are also likely to feel bewilderment about how she can possibly think that you're having an affair. But here is where I have to remind you that it is not the belief of your "affair" that caused the peeler-throwing, it is the anger in her.

Let's say you don't immediately react as if she's going to try to kill you next. Let's say you are angry that she threw something at you and screamed at you – that she is essentially in a rage about something that never happened. What is your reaction then? You will go through the same process as she did and arrive at a similar state. You might not be as "hot" as she is or take as long to "cool down" as she does, but you will still experience the emotion and have "action impulses" yourself. We all do in the face of strong emotions.

Her emotional dysregulation will most often cause you to be dysregulated as well and, after time, you will start to integrate interpretations that become misaligned with reality and kick off negative emotions as well. You might say, as a reaction to your anger, "You crazy bitch! You're completely nuts! I'm not having an affair, but I wish I was to get away from this crap!" So, basically, you attack back, and do so with judgment (she's crazy) and with threats. But your reaction, like hers, is the natural reaction to your anger.

And around and around it goes

This process of event, interpretation, emotional/physical feeling, action impulses, expression and behavior, and reaction will continue until one of the parties leaves the confrontation for one reason or another. It is the same way with expressions of anger in nature – at some point someone will have to back down, unless it escalates to violence and the authorities become involved.

The point here is that emotions and emotional behavior will feed off themselves and continue the cycle of dysregulation. As it continues, the emotions become stronger and you become dysregulated just as she does.

On top of that, the behavior based on those emotions, while natural, becomes conditioned. What this means is that every time you do something and link a feeling with a particular behavior, the more likely you are to exhibit that same behavior based on that same feeling. The linkage between the feeling (anger) and the behavior (yell back) becomes stronger – it becomes a conditioned behavior.

Conditioning between feelings and behavior is extremely difficult to break. The brain pathways get less resistant. It's like you're sledding. As you go down the hill through the snow in the same route, over and over, the route gets more slippery, the snow more packed. Eventually, the route is frozen solid and the sled can speed down the one route, but not any others.

At some point the resistance to action impulses gets lower and lower and you become impulsive and reactive to the action impulses as well. Your emotional tolerance starts to drop and your behaviors become more and more repetitive. You and your wife are stuck in a cycle of interacting that seems to go on forever and that you feel that you will never be able to break.

Conditioned Behavior

Although I just outlined the BPD Dynamic, you must understand that ingraining this behavior doesn't happen in just one encounter. It happens over a period of time as you become "trained" to respond in a certain way to emotional dysregulation in your loved one. What happens is that you begin to develop conditioned behavior, as I stated above.

Conditioning takes time and reinforcement. It occurs as you and your loved one repeat certain behaviors again and again. You might ask yourself: how can it be that anyone would do something over and over when it was not healthy for them? Basically, the behavior that you and your loved one practice is an adaptation to the emotional dysregulation. It is an attempt to make sense of the "craziness."

Many adaptations can be unhealthy. If you consider smoking cigarettes as an adaptation to either shame for not being "cool," a way to manage stress and pain, or some way to lose weight (depending on your reason for starting the first place), the repeated behavior becomes "conditioned" and becomes a maladaptive, unhealthy way of dealing with the original issue. While cigarette smoking clearly has a biological and addictive quality, I am suggesting that behavioral adaptations to emotional situations also have a biological and addictive quality.

The release of endorphins within the brain when the painful feelings are assuaged does provide some relief and can be "conditioned." We gradually teach ourselves, through reinforcement, that a certain behavior brings relief, even if that behavior is unhealthy or maladaptive. Eventually, this behavior will repeat itself almost automatically when the same (or similar) situations and emotions arise.

Conditioned behavior is a significant problem in BPD. Behavior that was once adaptive can become, over time, maladaptive. If your loved one is the child of an alcoholic, for example, constant vigilance to look for potential threats or safety concerns (i.e. mom's drunk and passed out and

I need to get away from her or dad's drunk and he might hit me) is adaptive in that situation.

The emotions involved in that situation, particularly fear or anger, cause the vigilance and lead to other behaviors. In time, these behaviors become both conditioned (easier to repeat) and linked with the particular emotion. Therefore, when your wife accuses you of cheating, even though it is not true, she could be repeating the same sort of "threat awareness" that was required in her childhood.

In other words, she has been "conditioned" to look for threats, perceives them when they don't exist and tries to attack them head-on to rid herself of the painful emotions that come with those threats. She has adapted in a way that was effective in her childhood, but is ineffective and harmful to her current situation.

On top of the conditioning, she may also have a natural in-born diminished capacity to regulate her emotions, so those emotions arise more easily, even when they are not warranted. Additionally, she may have an in-born tendency to act impulsively, which further brings down the barriers when she gets "action impulses." Basically, she is just doing what she has learned and doing it in a way that is natural to her.

Depending on how you react to a person with BPD's behaviors, you can begin the road toward acting and reacting in maladaptive ways yourself. In the second section of this book, I will discuss, at length, the ways to protect yourself from maladaptive conditioned behavior and ways to help your loved one loosen the bonds that conditioned behavior and emotional dysregulation have over them. But if you are also conditioned to interact in a certain way, you might have to loosen those bonds on yourself first, before you help the other person with theirs. You will definitely have to examine your conditioning, and you will quite possibly have to re-train yourself in some areas.

Learned Helplessness and PTSD

Another concept that is new to this edition is the idea of learned helplessness and PTSD as Non-BP's. Personally, I think this concept applies to both people with BPD and those who loved them. Not so long ago I was reading a "Non-BPD Staying" book, written by a very popular author who I have spoken with a few times. This book mentioned the idea of "Stockholm Syndrome" sometimes occurs within the Non-BPD's mind.

Stockholm Syndrome is a condition in which a person who is abducted begins to feel sympathy for and identify with his or her abductor(s). It was coined following a six-day hostage crisis in 1973 in Stockholm, Sweden in which the captors began to feel emotionally attached to their abductors.

This other Non-BPD book likens the state of the mind of a BPD to those captors; that is, the abused person (the Non-BPD) begins to develop an emotional attachment to the person with BPD because of this dynamic. Stockholm Syndrome has also been used in the context of a weaker abused person (such as a child) bonding to a more powerful abuser.

While it is not a professionally recognized diagnosis, several high-profile abduction and abuse cases have mentioned the syndrome in the popular press, including the high-profile case of Patty Hearst.

I believe that application of Stockholm Syndrome to a BPD/Non-BPD relationship is inaccurate in almost every case. While there may be certain cases in which this dynamic exists, of all of the individuals that I have met in person and online, I have yet to see any that could be properly described as Stockholm Syndrome.

One problem in my mind with the application of this label is that it creates a defined abuser/abused polar relationship and discounts the real affection one may have for the (supposed) love one in your life. Mistreatment certainly goes both way in any relationship and in the case of a BPD/Non-BPD relationship, that mistreatment can arise to the level of abuse. I don't, however, think it can arise to the level of abductor, captor or terrorist on either part.

It may feel that way at times, but relationships go through many changes during the course of months and years and to say that the overriding factor contributing to the relationship is only and solely one of abuse and mistreatment, that would indicate (to me at least) that the relationship is not based on love and one which might likely be better off terminated.

Still, if you are this person's parent or child, it may not be possible to terminate such as relationship. Instead, you have to find ways to break the cycle of abuse. It is difficult, no doubt. Stockholm Syndrome is, in my mind, an extreme form of co-dependency.

A more useful concept is that of learned helplessness. One of the major differences between Stockholm Syndrome and learned helplessness is that the former is psychodynamic or psychoanalytic (through attachment and/or object relationship explanations) and the latter is behavioral.

Before I began to research BPD and the "plight" of the Non-BP, I was never much of a behaviorist. Once I started to understand what actually worked with BPD, I have warmed up to the idea of behavioral therapies in general and to DBT specifically (because it is something of a hybrid approach to acceptance and change, whereas CBT is typical places more emphasis on change).

There are several differences between the idea of learned helplessness and Stockholm Syndrome. First, I need to define learned helplessness such that you understand the concept and why it may apply to you (or your BP loved one).

Learned helplessness is a state in which a person (or an animal, which is a major difference because it operates at a lower brain level than does the psychoanalytic-derived object relations model that explains Stockholm Syndrome) discovers that no behavior can counteract the pain and suffering that that person is feeling.

Learned helplessness is a psychological condition in which a human being or an animal has learned to act or behave helpless in a particular situation, even when it has the power to change its unpleasant or even harmful circumstance. Learned helplessness theory is the view that clinical depression and related mental illnesses result from a perceived absence of control over the outcome of a situation. [29]

The idea of learned helplessness is derived from a behavioral experiment by Seligman and Maier in 1967. These researchers took dogs and placed them in experimental conditions in which one group of dogs could stop shocks coming from a grid beneath their feet by pressing a lever. In other words, pressing the lever was the behavior that allowed them to escape pain.

These dogs learned to press the level repeatedly to escape the suffering induced by the electric shocks. Another group of dogs also had the grid and the lever, but in their case pressing the lever did nothing to alleviate

[29] Seligman, M. E. P. (1972). "Learned helplessness". Annual Review of Medicine 23 (1): 407–412. doi:10.1146/annurev.me.23.020172.002203.

the painful shocks. The shocks did not increase or decrease by behaving in any particular fashion. The lever did nothing to stop the pain they were feeling. These dogs learned that they were completely helpless to lessen their pain.

Eventually, these dogs merely "laid down on the grid" and accepted the shocks without attempting a behavior which might remove the shocks. This reaction is the essence of learned helplessness. If a person learns that, no matter what they try, nothing works to alleviate their pain, they eventually give up on trying and "lay down on the grid."

I believe this idea better describes the dynamic between any other person (including the BP/Non-BPD relationship) than does Stockholm Syndrome. I say this because unlike Stockholm Syndrome in which one party is deemed the abuser and the other the abused, learned helplessness is about pain avoidance – either on the BP or Non-BPD side.

If what you try, over and over, doesn't work to alleviate pain, then you eventually learn that the pain is unavoidable and you "lie down on the grid" and accept the pain as unavoidable – or you go nuclear and terminate the relationship or commit suicide. If everything you do, even if you try the diametrically opposed action to the previous action and that doesn't work, results in suffering and equal pain, eventually you are going to learn that you are helpless to the pain – this is what learned helplessness is all about.

I don't think this concept is only about the Non-BPD (which the idea of Stockholm Syndrome assumes – that is, there is one abuser and one abused, which in a loving relationship seem ridiculous to me. I mean, after all, we are talking about "loved ones" and families are we not?). No, the idea of learned helplessness cuts both ways because both parties are using ineffective methods to remove pain and both parties end up banging their head up against to wall of ineffectiveness. If nothing works, despair rules and the only solution is to accept your fate and "lay down on the grid."

The way out of learned helplessness is a reconditioning of one's behavior in which the pain can be removed. That is another difference in the idea of Stockholm Syndrome and learned helplessness. The mechanics of Stockholm Syndrome are impossible to counteract (I suppose it's years of psychoanalytic therapy or other ideas that this "Non-BP" book purports), while the mechanics of learned helplessness are difficult, yet possible, to counteract. What one has to do to counteract the condition of learned helplessness is find a behavior or technique that is not helpless. One has to find a technique or behavior that one can practice and be effective to alleviate the suffering of the condition in which one is currently helpless.

While I have yet to talk about the tools to counteract this and other relationship issues that can arise from an ineffective BPD/Non-BPD relationship, I just wrote about conditioned behavior and I am about to write about emotional memory.

Conditioned behavior and learned helplessness can happen in both humans and in animals. These two concepts are interrelated. I'm not sure about emotional memory and if it applies to animals. If whatever you try to reduce your pain doesn't work, you eventually learn that nothing works – that is the state of learned helplessness.

Within the framework of the BPD dynamic, if you find that your reactions and behaviors are ineffectual, these reactions and behaviors are ineffective at reducing your suffering and at fostering a calmer relationship. Learned helplessness is related to conditioned behavior and learned helplessness can grow out of the BPD dynamic if you continue to perpetuate ineffective behavior.

Unlike Stockholm Syndrome, learned helplessness is born out of trust. Stockholm Syndrome is born out of abuse and/or hostage-taking. Your loved one is not (however it may feel at times) a kidnapper, terrorist or, intentionally, an abuser. They (and you) are trying to get needs met.

The relationship generally is born out of trust and presumed love, whether romantic, familiar or friendly (or a combination of each). The basic premise of the nature of the relationship is a significant difference between Stockholm Syndrome and learned helplessness.

It is not just the nature of the concepts academically (one is psychodynamic, the other behavioral), it is the foundation for the relationship that is divergent.

The dogs in the learned helplessness experiments essentially trusted and relied upon their "owners" – they needed food and shelter provided by the experimenters (which in a way makes their case more tragic). In the case of Stockholm Syndrome, the initial state between subject and object is adversarial. The abusers or abductors are part of the initial part in the equation, as are the abused and the abducted. There is a clear perpetuator and a clear victim, but in my mind, no such clear lines between these categories exist in a BPD/Non-BPD relationship. Certainly, Non-BP's do feel embattled and, at times, overwhelmed, but, upon reflection, so do people with BPD. Both groups are behaving in ways that are ineffective and ineffectual for reducing pain, for increasing understanding and for maintaining calm in the relationship.

One of the keys to understanding learned helplessness is to understand that no effective behavior can be found to escape pain. While people with BPD might resort to "extreme" behavior to reduce their pain (such as cutting, risk-taking behavior, drug taking and others) Non-BPD's may be less likely to do so. I say "may be" less likely because I suspect that alcoholism and other such behavioral adaptations might be more prevalent in Non-BPD's than in the general population because these are behavioral adaptations that act on the pain directly, yet these adaptations are ineffective and may create other interpersonal and personal consequences.

It is possible that (as in the dogs) there is no behavioral adaptation that has any effective impact on the suffering. You feel stuck and there's no way out. You've tried everything and nothing works. That, in effect, requires that you "lie down on the grid" and accept your punishment. The trust and presumed love you felt in the beginning of the relationship is exposed as ineffective, and you feel trapped in pain. I think this is a mild form of PTSD.

The point is, if you can't do anything to get you out of pain, you're stuck, helpless and hopeless. I called this book *When Hope is Not Enough* for a reason, and here's where my intentions become clear: you can't hope for a better and more effective solution when everything you have tried thus far doesn't relieve the suffering and pain you feel. You stop pressing any lever because nothing relieves the pain; thus, you're stuck in pain and suffering.

Unlike Stockholm Syndrome, I can offer you a way out of learned helplessness. The way out is through the application of tools that you can apply to the BPD dynamic that can break you out of hopelessness. And unlike psychodynamic explanations, which can take years, this escape can take much less time. All you have to do is dedicate yourself and practice.

This form of PTSD/learned helplessness hurts and feels as if you are trapped in a cage of conditioned behavior. Yet, if you learn and apply the tools in this book, you can change the BPD dynamic and take your life back.

I'm introducing you to a new dynamic that can open the escape window. I have seen in this work in my life and, possibly more importantly, in the lives of the people on my list. There's hope, but real hope only comes through the application of the skills that dismiss learned helplessness and PTSD forever.

Emotional Memory

Emotional memory functions in a way that is far different than regular, time-based memory. While any memory can be colored by emotions, some memories are particularly emotional. My wife, for example, can remember her shaming at the hands of middle school bullies more vividly than what she had for breakfast yesterday. Consider this quotation from Wikipedia's entry on "Emotion and Memory":

Emotion can have a powerful impact on memory. Numerous studies have shown that the most vivid autobiographical memories tend to be of emotional events, which are likely to be recalled more often and with more clarity and detail than neutral events. The activity of emotionally enhanced memory retention can be linked to human evolution; during early development, responsive behavior to environmental events would have progressed as a process of trial and error. Survival depended on behavioral patterns that were repeated or reinforced through life and death situations. Through evolution, this process of learning became genetically embedded in humans and all animal species in what is known as "fight or flight" instinct. [30]

The "most vivid autobiographical memories tend to be of emotional events" is the most compelling statement in this paragraph and it is the one to which I'd like to reply. Based on experience with people with BPD, I have come to notice that these emotional memories become linked within one's mind and outside of time.

In other words, a distance of many years does not diminish the linkage between an emotional-laden memory and an event currently taking place. A person with BPD will link long ago negative emotional experiences with current events because it "feels the same." In that way, the person with BPD will act on these emotional memories in a way that is

[30] http://en.wikipedia.org/wiki/Emotional_memory

inappropriate for the current situation. The sense of time is lost completely when it comes to emotional memory.

As a response to this quality, one of my list members (who wishes to remain anonymous) crafted a brilliant "Top 20" list of the internal beliefs of someone with BPD. I will reproduce them here, slightly edited. I think this member did an excellent job of summarizing the feelings of BPD, especially with respect to emotional memory.

THE TOP 20 RULES FOR BPD

(An experimental outlook)

1. All time is in the present. If something makes me feel bad now, it is linked directly to the greatest pain I ever experienced -- and that pain is happening now, too. Time can't heal any wounds because time never really passes. Everything -- past, present, and future -- is NOW.
2. If I do something I feel is wrong, I am unworthy of living. Therefore, admitting I am wrong -- or that I did something to hurt someone -- feels just like committing suicide. I don't want to die, so I can't acknowledge that I am wrong. Even to the judges inside me.
3. I am wrong means I AM wrong. It's not about what I did; it's about who I am as a person. This is also true of other people. If they do/did something wrong, they are unfixable. If I do/did something wrong, I am broken.
4. I am constantly being judged by people who don't understand my situation. Including myself. And the penalty for being judged as being wrong is death. (see #2)
5. Memories are the files in my mental "cabinet." Because I am always being judged, I need to use those files like a lawyer. Therefore, only the memories that suit my current feeling will be called up. Those that present evidence that contradicts that feeling will not be considered admissible... or will be doctored to preserve my innocence. Again, it's a matter of my life or my death.
6. I am like a ship with a thin, fragile hull -- any hole will sink me. Therefore, anything that approaches near enough is a danger, and must be kept away. At all costs.
7. Everyone is just an extension of me -- so if I can't control them, it means I can't control myself. Likewise, when someone steps outside my control, I -- by definition -- lose control.

8. I cannot bear pain -- therefore I must find someone else to bear it for me. If they don't take the weight of my pain, I will be crushed. Literally.

9. If I take responsibility for making something happen, I will have to deal with disappointment. At some point, it won't work, and that means I will have been wrong, which will feel like death. I cannot risk death, so I can't risk taking responsibility.

10. Relationships are attractive, but will end in disappointment. They are like cigarettes and drugs -- soothing at first, but they'll kill you. However, they are addictive. This makes them toxic.

11. I was abused and need shelter. But whatever shelter I run to, they will eventually abuse me. So I must be constantly on guard, to prevent being violated. If I let down my guard, I will be abused again. There is only one thing that leads to abuse: trust.

12. Asking me to be calm in the face of what I believe is a danger is like asking the Scarecrow not to be afraid when the Wicked Witch holds up the burning broom.

13. Thought is reality. If I think of something, it is already done. If someone else mentions something, they have already made it happen.

14. Anyone who wants something wants it right now. Including me. All needs must be satisfied instantly, or something is wrong. And wrong means death.

15. I would never hurt me or anyone else. Therefore, if that occurs, it means someone other than me did it.

16. The way the world operates is "effect and cause." If I feel a certain way, I will find a cause for it that does not involve me, because otherwise I will be judged as wrong. And I cannot be judged as wrong.

17. Other people created the shame I carry. Therefore, only other people can remove it. I was rendered powerless to do anything about it the moment it happened. I was powerless then, therefore I am powerless now.

18. The world is how I feel. Anything that does not reflect/support my feeling must be annihilated. When it comes to feelings and ideas other than what I experience, I am like the Taliban. Those alien forces threaten who I am, and so must be removed from my midst.

19. If you agree with me, you agree with my feelings, which ARE me. If you disagree with me, you disagree with my feelings. But, because my feelings are me -- if you disagree with me, you kill me.

20. There is no greater weakness than vulnerability. Open yourself up, and all you will be is exposed. And if you are exposed, you can only rely on trust -- trust is the cause of abuse.

As you can see, these beliefs are rooted in emotional memory (all time is the present), emotional reasoning (my feelings are me), shame (if I am wrong, I AM wrong) and lack of trust (trust = abuse).

While a person with BPD's autobiographical history doesn't actually have to include abuse, the emotional invalidation that they have experienced throughout their lives feels like actual abuse, because it is a denial and invalidation of their feelings and, therefore, their very nature and being.

Actual abuse, especially sexual abuse, is the ultimate form of invalidation since the person functions as a "toy" or "whipping post" for the abuser, rather than an actual person.

Chapter 5: What now?

Now that I have explained the symptoms, causes, dynamic and basic beliefs of someone with BPD, it is time to turn to the "tools" section of this book. In this section, I will teach you how to immunize yourself from BPD and how to help someone who has BPD.

Like any tools that you use in life, you have to learn how to use them, learn which tool is appropriate for which job and practice using the tool until you build mastery over that particular tool. Some of the tools are basic "common sense," while others are counterintuitive and difficult to master. Some of these tools you have probably heard of before, especially if you have done any research into BPD, PTSD or ERD. Some of these tools have probably never been explained to you before.

I will start by talking about what doesn't work with someone with BPD and explain why. Some of these strategies are mentioned on the Internet and in other books as effective strategies. Despite this, they are not ultimately effective. How do I know? I have tried each of these things repeatedly and know these things do NOT work.

After explaining what doesn't work, I will explain the "mindset" that one must have to be effective in relation to someone with BPD. Unfortunately, one can't approach the tools that do work with a regular, run-of-the-mill mindset. At least for me, I had to change the way I looked at interpersonal relationships in order for the tools to be effective. This change is neither bad nor good – it is just different than I originally viewed the world.

What doesn't work

Like I said, if you do any research on BPD, you will find a plethora of advice from all types of people. There are Internet support groups, self-help books and personal stories that tell you what to do as a Non. Some of this advice is good and works effectively with someone with BPD. Some of this advice is not good and is ineffective with someone with BPD. Some of this advice is misperceived by the Non and applied in a way that is not intended by the advice giver. The most misunderstood tool is boundaries.

Boundaries

Interestingly, I am including boundaries in both the "what doesn't work" and "what works" sections. The reason is that boundaries can be effective if they are properly understood. Most people who try to create and apply boundaries to their BP relationship do so improperly and with misunderstanding. This misunderstanding is amplified across the Internet and in publications about dealing with a highly emotional person. The misunderstanding arises in two forms: One is the meaning of a boundary, and the second is to whom the boundary applies.

A member of my Internet list summarized the correct view of boundaries, and I'd like to use his summary as a tool for understanding boundaries and dismissing the misperceptions.

"In essence, boundaries are what you do with YOURSELF — AFTER the line's been crossed. And eventually, they become what you do to put yourself in a position so the line CAN'T be crossed. They really have nothing to do with the "perpetrator.""

If that's confusing, think of it this way:

1. The law says: Don't go over 55 mph. (That's a rule, not a boundary.)
2. A speeder goes 85 mph. (That's breaking a rule, not breaking a boundary.)
3. You're a passenger in a car while the speeder is driving. (You're in a dangerous situation. Boundaries still aren't a factor.)
4. You tell the driver they should slow down. (That's a plea, not a boundary.)
5. They don't, so you yell at them that they should. (That's still a plea.)
6. You tell them if they don't slow down, that they'll get a ticket. (That's a threat of consequences, not enforcing a boundary.)
7. Next time they ask you to ride with them, you don't. (THAT'S a boundary.)

See, the thing is — Boundaries can't be enforced, because they're not rules. You either do them, or you don't.

The idea even works in the traffic parallel. What's a boundary on a road? A concrete divider. Cars CAN'T go over that. On the other hand, yellow lines are just rules that say "Don't drive over this." So they have to be enforced.

So, how can you tell a rule from a boundary? If you have to enforce it, it's not a boundary."

- an ATSTP member on boundaries

Many people believe that a "boundary" is equivalent to a rule and that they have to enforce their personal boundaries with a person who has BPD. This is not the case. A personal boundary is not a rule that needs to be enforced. Instead, a personal boundary is a limit that one puts on one's own behavior.

In the above example, the personal boundary is that you refuse to get into the car with someone who makes you feel unsafe. That is a choice that you make about your own behavior and a limit on the behavior you're willing to engage in.

This leads me to the second, more common misconception about boundaries. Boundaries are not about the other person's behavior at all. They are about your behavior. Often the idea of boundaries is mentioned with respect to children. Many people will advise you to "enforce boundaries" for children so that they will understand the limits of behavior. In actuality, these are not boundaries at all. They are rules. Since boundaries are about your behavior, not another person's, boundaries can only be respected based on your own behavior.

When someone with BPD "crosses your personal boundary" what they are really doing is breaking an agreed-upon rule set up between you and the other person. Only you can "cross your personal boundary." If you, as a result of the person with BPD's behavior, decide to cross your personal boundaries, you have made that decision yourself. You cannot control other people's behavior with a boundary – especially when that behavior is based on emotions. I will talk about behavior modification and "controlling" behavior later in this book, but, for now, let's assume that the only person's behavior you can control is your own.

When you "set a boundary" for someone with BPD, what you are actually doing is "laying down the law" (i.e. setting up a rule) to them. You are telling them that they can't do a particular something which you find unacceptable. This is not a boundary at all. It is a rule.

Often, when people are faced with inappropriate behavior (or behavior they find inappropriate) the suggestion is to create a personal boundary. What is really being suggested is that you create a rule for the other person, not a boundary. Remember boundaries can only be crossed by you. Some "rules" are unspoken and commonly understood. Some are governed by the law. Rules are rules and they have to be enforced. Boundaries do not have to be enforced. It is important for you to understand the difference between rules and boundaries so that you can effectively use boundaries with your loved one.

Now that I have explained the definition of a boundary, I will explain why, when applied improperly, they are ineffective. If what you are really creating for someone with BPD is a rule, then we should no longer call it a boundary. That is where we need to dismiss the idea of a boundary as applying to anyone else besides yourself.

People with BPD may have trouble applying and sticking to their own personal boundaries, but there is nothing you can do about that. You can't control another person's behavior with a boundary. Additionally, you can't control another person's behavior with a rule either. You can try, but more often than not, the rule will be broken by the person with BPD. Why? Because they are acting on their feelings which fuel the action impulses. They don't feel like sticking to the rule - I say that not to be flippant - because emotions are a powerful motivating factor for behavior.

A good example of rule-breaking by an emotionally dysregulated person is a preschooler. Let's say that you have a four year old boy. Kids that young have the tendency to get emotionally dysregulated, especially when they are over-tired or have some other physical issue (like a cold). They just haven't learned to apply emotional regulation skills yet. Three and four year olds can be all emotion at times. Let's say in turn you have created a rule for your son that he must go to bed by eight PM. When eight approaches, he is tired and grouchy from a long day. Because of his tiredness, he feels extremely emotional and, when you tell him it is bedtime, he pitches a fit, screaming and yelling not to go to bed. Let me be clear, this is not a case of crossing a boundary, because you have to enforce the rule of eight PM bedtime.

Sometimes you will hear parenting experts (of which I am not one, just a parent myself) informing you that your son is "pushing boundaries" with this behavior. This is not the case. What is usually happening is that your child is suffering from a brief period of emotional dysregulation caused by biological factors (he's tired) and environmental factors (you told him it's bedtime). I'm not going to supply a solution to this particular problem at this point. While there are several solutions that you can try, some are more effective than others. The point here is that your son does not respect the rule that you have created because he is emotional and out-of-sorts. The same logic applies to someone with BPD when they are emotionally dysregulated.

Ultimatums

An ultimatum is actually another form of a rule, one that borders on black-mail. The basic equation in an ultimatum is: if you do this, I will do that. And the "that" is typically a severe punishment. Ultimatums are like the "nuclear option" in war. If one country attacks another, the attacked country will obliterate the attacking one. One famous ultimatum was sent from Austria-Hungary to Serbia and triggered World War One. It was an ultimatum that came after the assassination of Arch Duke Ferdinand and one with which the Serbian government couldn't comply.

Ultimatums almost always have a destructive outcome. They don't work with people with BPD for the same reasons rules don't. You can't control another person's behavior with threats, no matter how severe the consequences. You can use consequences to help control another person's behavior, but these consequences have to apply directly to the other person's behavior and have to be analyzed. More on consequences later.

Ultimatums will not work. While the person with BPD is likely to understand the idea of an ultimatum (and maybe even issue a few themselves), because it is a form of black-and-white thinking, they are unlikely to comply with the ultimatum's request. The only option left for you is the "nuclear" one.

Behavior Contracts

Some therapists recommend developing behavior contracts with patients who have BPD. I do not believe that behavior contracts will be effective for someone with BPD. For the same reason that ultimatums and rules will not work, behavior contracts will not work. The idea of vowing to another person to act a certain way and to, furthermore, formalize that vow in a contract is ridiculous.

A person with BPD acts as their emotions inform them to act. When the person gets dysregulated, for whatever the reason, the behavior contract will be forgotten. On top of that, the contract sets up a dynamic of certain failure for the person with BPD. This failure merely fuels additional shame and feeds the illness.

If boundaries (in the sense that they are understood by the general public), ultimatums and behavior contracts do not work, what does?

Before I answer that question, I want to note that the approach that I present in this book may differ greatly from approaches that you have encountered in the past. You may have heard that the above approaches – those involving boundaries, ultimatums and behavior contracts or, collectively, "tough love" is the proper approach when it comes to BPD. You may have even heard this from therapists or from recognizable and respected self-help books on the subject. I have learned from experience that these approaches are ineffective with BPD. Believe me, I have tried all of these approaches and found that, after a period of time, each of them fails. What may work at first does not work in the long run. The success from each of these approaches is intermittent at best.

I am here to teach you what does work. Each of the tools I propose has been used and tested by me and by people in my Internet group. My purpose for collecting these tools into one source is to try to provide a compendium that you can refer to and become successful with.

While others, including "experts" on Non-BPD's, may recommend some tools that are diametrically opposed to what I offer, I assure you that what I am advising I have done with my wife and daughter and gained significant positive results. While some of the tools may be difficult to implement in your life and some may seem counterintuitive, these tools are effective in managing a Non-BPD/BPD relationship.

Depending on your background, biological make-up and sensibilities about the world, you may have an easier or more difficult time understanding and implementing these tools in your life. I have seen the evolution of many Non-BPD's on my Internet list and some take more time than others to get their minds around the tools and practice them in their lives.

I do want to note that when the Non-BPD begins to utilize these tools, most experience a vast improvement in their relationship with their loved one with BPD. Again, some of the attitudes and tools I present might go against your natural inclinations and even your value system. Even if this is the case, I would implore you to try each one out and see the results in your relationship.

What holds us back before we start

I often see on my support list "newbies" who are not teachable. They arrive at the list seemingly willing to listen to the experienced members, yet in reality they subconsciously feel they have it all figured out. The experience of the "old timers" is extraordinarily valuable. In fact, that experience is the greatest asset available on the list. It is why I decided to revise this book to reflect the teaching from the sharing of that experience. Many newcomers to the list are unwilling to listen to guidance from the experienced members. When someone is unable or unwilling to listen to wise advice, this person usually has one of the next few approaches as a hindrance to progress.

Willfulness

Willfulness is the opposite of willingness. If you have an open mind, you have the willingness. You're teachable. Yet, if your mind is closed and unwilling to listen to suggestions, things will not change. I've heard it said that insanity is doing the same thing over and over and expecting different results. To me, that's a willful, close-minded approach to the Non/BPD relationship.

The skills I offer in this book are counterintuitive. They go against many of the things that we have been taught to believe about relationships. If a concept is alien to your current way of thinking, if you don't believe that it will work, only willingness will provide the key to open the closed mind. Without a willingness to listen, to reflect and to experiment with concepts that you may think will never work, nothing will change.

I've also heard it said: nothing changes if nothing changes. Nothing changes without willingness and an open mind.

I have a mother on my email support list who told me that it was in a single interaction when her mind opened and her willingness began to flower. She had made a statement about the meaning of a particular behavior of her daughter with BPD. I responded to her interpretation of the behavior with the words: "That may or may not be the case." I suggested another interpretation of the motivation behind the behavior.

These words immediately opened the mind of the mother. She never before considered that her interpretation of her daughter's motivations and behaviors was inaccurate. She was approaching the interaction with her daughter knowing (actually assuming that she knew) the answer before the question was even posed. She was unwilling to hear another interpretation of the behavior. She was closed-minded and willful. Once I suggested another possible interpretation of the motivation of the behavior, her mind immediately opened (even if just a crack) to the possibility of an alternative meaning. Willingness is a key that opens the closed mind.

Shoulds

Many of us have a picture in our minds of what life should be like – what is "normal" in a relationship. These shoulds are expectations of how our partner or child ought to behave. They are based on our up-bringing, our values and our expectations of what's "normal" or expected/deserved in a given time. For example, when you've been married for five years, you should own a home or you should have a child. Or when your child is eighteen years old, she should graduate from high school and go to college.

Unfortunately, these shoulds lead to a great deal of suffering for both you and the other person in the relationship. Steven Stosny, a psychologist and blogger for *Psychology Today*, has a blog called "anger in the age of entitlement." In my mind, that title encapsulates the "shoulds."

We feel as though we deserve to be treated a particular way. We feel we deserve certain things in life. Things should be different. Our partner should cook dinner more. Our adult child should have a better job (or a job at all). Things shouldn't be like they are!

In many ways, we are still being willful when we concentrate on shoulds. We want to remake the world in our image – the image of what we believe is normal. I'll talk more about how to get out of the shoulds in the next few chapters. I wanted to mention the shoulds here because they are one of the biggest stumbling blocks to achieving effectiveness with our loved ones.

Control

When I attended the dialectical behavior therapy family skills training ten years ago, the leader of the group said to me: "You're very controlling." I was taken aback. I thought: "The nerve of this woman! To say I'm controlling! I'm here because I love my wife! I don't want to control her!"

Upon reflection, I have to admit, the group leader was right. I was very controlling. What was more embarrassing about that quality of my nature was that I was completely blind to the fact. I was controlling without even realizing it. I thought I was actually helping my wife with her behavior, because I knew better.

Clearly, what she was doing at the time – doctor shopping, drunk driving, spending sprees – was not the best behavior in the world. I was so afraid of the consequences (some of which actually came to pass) that I thought I could save her from herself. It wasn't until the group leader told me I was controlling that I could see that she was right.

I was controlling because I was afraid. I was afraid that my wife would get arrested (she did) or that she would accidentally kill herself (she didn't). What I didn't realize was that I couldn't live her life for her. I couldn't save her from herself.

My problem was that I was trying to control her behavior, rather than focusing on my own. I see people approaching their relationship with a loved one with BPD doing this just about every day. This area is where the misapplication of boundaries looms large. If you don't understand where what you can control (you and your behavior) ends and what you can't control (your loved one and her behavior) begins, you are the person who has a problem with boundaries, not your loved one.

My approach to this issue is: you can only control yourself, your approach, and your behavior. You can only control you.

Victimhood

I speak with many loved ones of people with BPD who are very put upon. The world has not treated them right. Their loved one has emotionally abused them most horribly.

While it is true that many of these people have been treated rather poorly by their loved one with BPD, the idea that there's nothing that can be done about it, that it is their lot in life, is just inaccurate. If you're destined to be a victim for the rest of your life, that it is BPD's fault that you're suffering, why bother to read this (or any other) book?

The reality is that if you believe you're the victim and have no role or efficacy when it comes to your relationship, you're going to end up suffering much more than you're suffering now. That's because you're experiencing the learned helplessness that I spoke about earlier in the last chapter.

I've heard it said that if it's someone else's problem, you have no solution. Meaning, if the fault lies outside of yourself, there's no way for you to work on the problem. I believe that in each interaction with our loved ones, we contribute to either effectiveness or ineffectiveness. When we contribute to ineffectiveness, everyone suffers.

While I don't believe in walking on eggshells around our loved ones with BPD, I do believe that an effective approach that takes into consideration the facts about the real world (not the way we wished the world to be) opens the trap of victimhood. Yet, you have to take responsibility for your own words and actions – you have to recognize how you might be pouring gasoline onto a raging fire, rather than water to extinguish it.

If you're burned, you might feel like a victim; I will teach you in the next few chapters how to recognize your contribution to the interactions and how to make this contribution as effective as possible. You just have to be willing to accept your role and change your approach and stop playing the victim.

The skills in the next few chapters will empower you out of the victim role. I will teach you what you can control and what you can't. I will teach you how to get out of the shoulds.

I will teach you what to do and how to do it.

Chapter 6: Getting Ready to Get Ready

In the first edition of this book, I didn't have this chapter. What I found through my list members and "newbie" Non-BPD's was that many of them were not yet ready to get ready.

When new members "wash up on the shores" of the Anything to Stop the Pain list, they are confused, angry, helpless and exhausted. One thing I also noticed is that new members are emotionally entangled with their loved ones with BPD.

Sometimes when people speak of boundaries, they use the phrase "where you end and I begin." The word boundary has many meanings, and I will explain what I believe is an effective boundary a little later. Yet, this idea of "where you stop and I begin" is very important when you're entangled in another person's emotions.

I decided to write this chapter to help you learn to heal, to unpack your emotional baggage, to give you skills to help yourself emotionally. Through this you can detangle the morass of emotional issues that may be keeping you in confusion and pain. Many of the tools that I describe later in this book can be applied to yourself. Here I'd like to spell out a simple process of emotional healing that can make you feel better and more capable with your loved one with BPD.

Sorting out what's yours and what's theirs

When I meet with Non-BPD's on "coaching" or "consultation" calls, I find that many times the emotional issues of the Non-BPD's are intertwined with those of the person with BPD. This is a big problem when it comes to solving emotional issues and sorting out what is what in a relationship.

One thing that I usually recommend to Non-BPD's is to ask themselves if the issue at hand is actually an issue to the person with BPD. Let me give an example… I met with a mother of a son with BPD. The son is about 20 years old. He is smart and living on his own, but all of his expenses are being paid by his parents.

The mother wants him to get a job. The son is perfectly fine not having a job. His expenses are completely paid for. Why would he bother getting a job?

The issue of his unemployment is the mother's issue. She feels bad asking her new husband to contribute to her son's life and livelihood. It hurts her and makes her sad that her son has no career prospects. She had aspirations and a vision of what it would be like to have an adult son, what it would be like when her son grew up.

His being unemployed does not meet her expectations and goals for her son. She's living in the shoulds. It makes her sad and worried about her son's future. While it is perfectly natural to be afraid, sad and worried about your child's future, **those are her emotions and not his**.

It is not his issue or his goal to get a job. Certainly, if the mother decides to cut his expenses to the point where it will be impossible for him to live without working, it will likely cause pain, anger and possibly rage within the son. Yet, the issue of the job is his mother's. While he might have a better future and more prospects if he began working, it is not his goal to work. His goal is (like most people with BPD) to feel better.

Perhaps he shies away from getting a job because he would feel "on stage" and judged at work, but we need to reserve the discussion on how to deal with that for later in this book.

The first thing you must do is to understand what is yours and what is theirs. You may be surprised that even things that you have thought is all their problem is really a problem that you are harboring.

On this list I often "hear" (read email really) people say something like:

- "I'm scared that she might…"
- "I get angry when he…"
- "It makes me sad when I think about…"

If a person starts a sentence with "I [verb like am/feel] [emotion] toward the person with BPD" it clues me into the idea that the person is attributing personal emotions to the person with BPD.

No one can MAKE you feel anything. Owning how you feel and understanding that it is your feeling can help you draw the line between your feelings and theirs. Know that your feelings are what make you feel good or bad, and these feelings really only affect you. Understanding your own feelings and what triggers those feelings is very important to getting free of ineffective patterns and emotional entanglement.

I would encourage you to be open and brave about what's about you and what's not about you. I will go into much more detail about that issue (whether it is about you or not) later. For now, let's consider that each person is the center of their own emotional universe. If you feel it, you must own it, even if your loved one with BPD is unable to do the same.

Once these problems and issues are sorted out into what is yours and what is theirs, it is also important to reduce the problem to basic emotions. The problem is causing you to feel a certain way. You should not blame the problem on others. Instead, be true to yourself and say: "This [issue] is making me feel angry/sad/fearful." Then, you can look into the issue as to WHY it is making you feel that way. Ask yourself: What is the trigger of this emotion? What are my action impulses? What did I do? What can I do to help reduce this negative emotion in my mind?

Once this feeling is gone, you will naturally stop suffering. The emotion itself is what causes the suffering.

Becoming independent emotionally

In addition to discovering what's your issue versus what's their issue, it's important to become emotionally independent. What do I mean by this?

I mean that your emotional well-being does not have to be dependent on anyone else's behavior, words, emotions or beliefs. As I said in the "preoccupation with interpersonal relationships" section, people with BPD tend to use others as a mirror of their own self-worth and as a facility to regulate their "systems" (mainly emotions and impulse control). Over time, Non-BPD's do the same thing.

A quote from the I-Ching helps illustrate this point:

Here the source of a man's strength lies not in himself but in his relation to other people. No matter how close to them he may be, if his center of gravity depends on them, he is inevitably tossed to and fro between joy and sorrow. Rejoicing to high heaven, then sad unto death-this is the fate of those who depend upon an inner accord with other persons whom they love. Here we have only the statement of the law that this is so.

Whether this condition is felt to be an affliction or the supreme happiness of love, is left to the subjective verdict of the person concerned.

If your emotional well-being is dependent upon your loved one's behavior, you are in a difficult and painful situation – one over which you have little control. This leads to a feeling of helplessness because you have no ability to direct your emotional life since your feelings are dependent on another person's words or actions.

Emotional independence is gained through a change in the way we approach loving others and loving ourselves. Children are naturally and understandably emotional dependent on their parents, because all of their emotional needs are (at first) supplied by their parents – and their siblings, peers, teachers, other family members and others in society. They have little ability to supply needs on their own. If you continue this pattern when you grow up, you're going to continue to be emotionally dependent on others to supply validation, etc.

Even competition with others is a form of negative validation for your emotional needs. Eros-type love of partners is rooted in desire and sees loves as an exchange of emotional needs. Love in this way is a transaction, in which each individual expects the other to fulfill their needs (and even to anticipate them) and the person is upset and (in some cases) feels like less of a person or judges the other person for failing to fulfill their emotional needs. This type of romantic (Eros) love is a dependent type of love in which there's an idea of possession of the other person, and that possession also breeds more dependence.

Even hatred of another individual can be the flip side of the same transaction-based and, when our desires and expectations are not met (or we don't win or we don't get revenge or whatever that requires the other person to be in relation to us to meet our emotional needs), we suffer. Our heart hurts because we are expecting something that we can't control.

We are basing our contentment and peace of mind (and of heart) on the behaviors, emotions, words, and intentions of the other person. The problem really comes into play when you start to realize that there's no end to suffering. No other person can live up to all of your desires, because your desires are a fire that constantly has to be fed, pacified and stoked. This is the way of black-and-white thinking and is a reason that when a person (BPD or not, although BPD people live this way a lot, because of the inability to self-regulate and looking to others to be that self-regulator) approaches relationships that way, they suffer.

You may not suffer in the "good times" but those good times are bound to go away (at least in certain moments) because you can't control 1/2 of the equation – the other person. This way of approaching love relationships is childish and emotionally immature – I'm not judging anyone, I'm saying that it is a child's way of approaching relationships because they have little self-efficacy.

I think that the Agape way of approaching love is all accepting and all appreciating for others in the way they actually are, rather than for what they can supply to us to keep the fires of passion burning. It is dispassionate and detached in the same way you might appreciate a beautiful sunset for what it is. You ask nothing of the sunset. It is as it is.

People can't be controlled. If you combine this way of loving and appreciating others with compassion, in which you can deeply relate to other's suffering, then you have a formula for emotional independence. It requires unconditional acceptance of others and compassion for other's suffering. It also requires an acceptance of your own self-worth.

Unpacking your emotional baggage

Most people have emotional baggage that they drag into relationships. Many people don't even realize that this "baggage" can drag down the relationship.

When many people first join my Internet list, I find that they have their emotions entangled in their partner's (or child's or parent's) emotions. The emotions of the person with BPD have a great effect on the emotions of the loved one. Also, many people are not really familiar with the language of emotions and often represent certain things as feelings that are not really emotions. People might say: "I feel disrespected" or "I feel used" or "I feel controlled." None of these "feelings" are emotions. When understanding your own emotional baggage it's most effective to stick with basic emotions – sad, angry and fearful.

Some people have deep emotional memories, some of them quite painful that can cloud their ability to see the moment for what it is. A person might associate a particular situation with a particular emotion. That is: "when I am in this part of the city I feel sad, because it's where my father died" or "when you yell at me I feel scared, because my father used to yell at me and hit me." Emotional memories can be very powerful and are timeless. When you are feeling something based on a current situation, ask yourself: "Is this an appropriate feeling for THIS situation? Am I feeling this because of an emotional memory?"

Performing an emotional inventory

The two most significant emotions related to our loved ones with BPD are anger (in the form of resentment) and fear. The single biggest factor that destroys marriages is resentment. The single biggest factor that destroys parent/child relationships is fear.

Both resentment and fear should be examined. You need to be thorough about this inventory. I suggest you start with your resentments against your loved one with BPD. You can say "I am resentful for…" and make a list of these resentments. The resentment list is a very powerful tool, especially for a partner/romantic relationship. Steven Stosny's latest blog post is entitled: "In Marriage, It's Compassion or Resentment"

This inventory is an attempt to get the resentments out into the open such that they can be examined, understood and, hopefully, resolved.

Here is an example of my resentment list concerning my wife:

I am resentful for…

- My wife not having sex with me enough.
- My wife spending all of our savings on travel.
- My wife not supporting me emotionally.
- My wife treating me like an employee.
- And so on.

The number of resentments and level of resentment I had for my wife at the beginning of my emotional inventory was historic. Once the resentments are listed, you should connect the resentment with the need that is not being met. What basic need is this threatening? These needs are:

- Your safety
- Your self-worth

- Your ambitions
- Your personal relationships
- Your financial security

While one can argue about the actual "basic needs" or about whether more or less should be on the above list, the list is a start. Clearly, my wife spending all of our savings on travel affects my financial security and it affects my personal relationships.

Lastly, we should list what emotion the threat triggers. It could be sadness, but more often than not it is fear.

I'll talk quite a bit about how fear feels in your body and what it look like on your face, but basic fear boils down to two things: 1) fear of losing what you have and 2) fear of never getting what you want.

Go on and make a list of your fears associated with your loved one with BPD. For example, a fear list for my now college-aged daughter was something like:

- I fear my daughter will fall apart at college and have to drop out.
- I fear my daughter will not have effective study habits and will fail out.
- I fear my daughter will never find any friends at college.
- I fear that my daughter will never find a partner or love.

While these fears might seem to be completely be about your loved one (i.e. fear my daughter will fall apart at college and have to drop out.), think about how the realization of that fear would affect you emotionally. Think also about the likelihood of that actually happening. Whether it is likely or not, it is always better to air out our fears, rather than to allow these fears to stew within us. Stewing causes the fears to grow and triggers other, related fears. If I fear my daughter will "fall apart" emotionally because of her BPD traits, I might further fear that she will attempt suicide or get addicted to drugs.

Because of these resentments and this fear, Non-BPD's spend much of our time either being mad as hell or scared out of our wits. That's no way to live.

A new voice inside your head

The voice you have inside your head can actually harm you emotionally. When we ruminate on feelings, resentments, fears and other emotional situations, we can reinforce the bad feelings and perpetuate the pain and suffering.

There are a number of things that you can do to change the voice inside your head. Later in this book I will explain ways that you can use these skills to improve your relationship with your loved one with BPD. First though, I will explain how you can apply these skills to make yourself feel better, more in control and less hopeless.

Be deductive

There are several ways to reason out situations. The two most common ways are inductive and deductive reasoning. Deductive reason is thinking like a detective (see later for more information on this way of approaching relationships). When you are deductive, you deduce (arrive at a fact by drawing a logical conclusion). You go from the general to specific case, not the other way around. Basically, you "narrow it down" based on your thinking.

If you're inductive, you go from the specific case and generalize about it. For example, if you're inductive you might say: "This dog has fleas, so all dogs have fleas." It's a sloppy way of thinking and keeps you locked into a particular world view that may not actually match the actually reality of the situation.

I often see people in the Non-BPD "community" use generalizations about what it is to be a Non-BPD. For example, someone might say: "All loved ones of people with BPD are co-dependent" or "All loved ones of people with BPD have low self-esteem." This kind of reasoning leads to stereotyping and missing the finer contours of a situation.

Many times, a difficult situation can be an opportunity for emotional growth. Yet, you have to understand the particular situation and not jump to the conclusion that it is the same as previous situations.

If you start generalizing your emotions, you can get stuck in them. If you say to yourself: "I feel sad now, so I'll always feel sad" that's inductive.

When used in combination with the next two skills, you can change the way you think about emotional situations by being deductive.

Ask yourself: "What is it about this particular situation that makes me feel [whatever]?" For that question to be effective, you must focus on the current moment and not bring in past issues or emotional baggage.

In other words, one must be present and aware of the current situation, rather than drawing conclusions about the situation based on previous emotional situations.

Trading Words

The language that you use inside your head can keep you emotionally frozen. My suggestion is that you change the words that you use to think about situations. By trading old words with new words, you can combat fear and shame within yourself.

Old Word – New Word

- Must - Prefer to, would like to
- Should - Choose to
- Can't - Choose not to
- Have to - Want to
- Ought - Had Better
- All - Many or most
- Always - Often or typically
- Can't stand - Don't like
- Awful - Undesirable
- Bad person - Bad behavior
- I am a failure - I failed at
- Anxious - Concerned
- Depressed - Sad
- Angry - Annoyed or frustrated
- Hurt - Disappointed
- Guilt - Have remorse
- Jealous - Concerned about relationship
- Never - Not often
- Is - Seems like
- Am - At this time

Examples:

- "I must do well" = "I want (or wish) to do well"
- "I shouldn't do that" = "I prefer not to do that"
- "I am a bad person" = "I did a negative thing"
- "I need love" = "I want love, but not need it to live"
- "I can't stand this" = "I don't like this"
- "I am a loser" = "I lost (or failed) at a task"
- "I am angry" = "That angered me"
- "I will always be sad" = "I feel sad at this time"

Tolerating Frustration

Pain hurts. Frustration is painful. It's bothersome but it is bound to be a part of life. Not getting what you want, or having what you like taken from you, not getting your way and the many others of life's disappointments can make you suffer.

Pain avoidance or the immediate cessation of frustration is one of life's biggest motivators. Unfortunately, some of life's frustrations don't have an immediate remedy. Sometimes you have to live in a frustrating situation for a period of time.

While you might start to believe "I can't take it anymore," I would encourage you to ask yourself, "Really? Can I not take it anymore?" One of the lessons we learn from our emotions is that they pass. Our painful and frustrating feelings are temporary.

Why do I mention frustration tolerance here? Because the process of healing can be a long one with steps forward and steps back.

Sometimes life is a little like quitting smoking. You may have never smoked in your life and that's great – however, the process of stopping smoking can be a difficult one. It's a "short term pain for long term gain" kind of process. Other situations can be like that as well – frustrating to the point of painful in the short term, yet rewarding in the long term.

There will be times in your life that you will have to endure frustration, whether it is related to your loved one with BPD or not. Understanding that you can and believing your ability to abide is important.

Grieving and Hope

Sometimes, when I look at my situation, I think about what "might have been" and worry about "what will be," especially with respect to my emotionally sensitive daughter.

I grieve for her and for her relationships with others, because I know that they will never be "normal" (which is really to say they will probably not achieve what I hoped for her). I think it is important to grieve for what might have been and to grieve for the "what ifs." However, once the grieving is completed, accepting the situation "as is" and moving forward from there is vital to your emotional health. I would encourage you to grieve first, and then accept.

Hope is a trickier situation. While this book is called *When Hope is Not Enough*, I do believe that there is hope for yourself and for the relationship with your loved one with BPD. If I didn't I wouldn't bother to write books or try to advise others.

Hope is, in some ways, the opposite of fear. Without any hope, you are worried about the impending doom of future situations. You're full of dread.

I think that hope comes through a sense of mastery over your environment both for you and for your relationship. This book intends to teach you that sense of mastery which, if it restores hope about your loved one for the future, is worth spending the time to learn, practice and master the tools and skills contained herein.

Doing the opposite of how you feel

Once when my wife was applying for a job, she expressed trepidation about having to face people. A friend hers told her: "Do the opposite of how you feel." It turns out that that is sage advice.

When someone feels bad, they are likely to do the natural thing. Earlier, I listed the natural action impulse that you get when you feel certain emotions. When you feel sad, you want to withdrawal and cry. If you feel really sad, you might want to hide from the world, pull the covers over your head and stay in bed all day.

Sometimes we all feel this way and retreating from the world is natural.

The next time you feel like that, do the opposite of what you feel like doing. Do the opposite of what is natural to do. It actually helps to change your emotions.

If you feel like withdrawing, engage the world. If you feel like screaming, laugh and rejoice.

If you behave in a different fashion, you feel differently. When you repeat the behavior again and again, it gets a bit easier each time.

Cultivating compassion for yourself

Compassion is not an emotion like anger, sadness, fear or shame. Compassion is an approach which can be cultivated and conditioned. The word compassion actually means "to suffer with".

When directed toward yourself, it is not self-love or narcissism. It is a deep feeling of affinity with the suffering that you have been through and a desire to salve that pain. It is an appreciation for the worth of yourself as a person. It is "self-worth" not "self-esteem."

There are a number of exercises available to cultivate and condition compassion. From the Buddhist tradition, one meditates on compassion for oneself and for others. One way to help cultivate compassion for yourself is to:

- Think about your suffering as if you were a child who is suffering and allow your heart to move and ache toward that child.
- Think about your worth as a person. All people have worth.
- Think about accepting the suffering and then letting it go.
- Think about what is left once the suffering is let go.
- Appreciate your own worth and vow to support that worth in each thing that you do.

Finding yourself

When you think: "I'm the kind of person who…." How do you finish that sentence? What is the story you tell yourself about you? What is the story that you tell other people about who you are?

96

In BPD, the self can be unstable such that a person with BPD might have trouble locating herself in the world. She might not really know who she is or what is most important to her. As a Non-BPD, you most likely do not have this problem. Yet, you can lose sight of yourself when you're subject to emotional upheaval.

To me, your self is like your window on the world. It's how you view and experience the world around you. It is not your emotions, your thoughts, your beliefs, your motivations, your desires or your dreams. These are mental features that pass through the context of yourself. These are clouds that pass through the sky of your mind.

Finding your window, your context is to have a ground from which to reach for the stars. That ground is based in your worth. All people have worth and, whether you feel like it or not, you are worthy.

All people are born with a level of worth and finding that worth and grounding yourself in it is vital. You can reinforce that worth and understand the context of yourself by conditioning your thinking and orienting your mind towards reaffirming your worth. Each day take a few minutes to reflect upon the following questions:

- What can I do today that will allow my worth to shine through?
- What can I do today to reaffirm my worth?
- What can I do today that shows compassion for myself?
- What can I do today that reflects my beliefs and values?
- What can I do today that would reinforce or enhance the connection with my worth?

Becoming goal-driven

At first when I began to consider goals and relationships, I was a bit disgusted over the thought. It seems manipulative and controlling to have a goal when relating to another person. Yet, after adopting a goal-driven stance with other people, I found that I was much calmer and better regulated myself.

Ask yourself: "What is my goal in this situation?" If you ask yourself this question, again and again, you can then follow up with the question: "How does doing [whatever] get me closer to that goal?" Sometimes you will find that doing [whatever] does not get you closer to that goal.

This same rationale applies to the person with BPD. After the emotionally dysregulated moment has past, it is valid and helpful to ask what their goal is and how doing [whatever] gets them closer (or further away) from that goal. Sometimes, however, the only goal is to feel better. Once they feel better, the problem is solved. Yet, you're still left with an empty and, at times, disrespected feeling. What can you do now to get you closer to your goal in a given situation? Does that goal conflict with your loved ones goal (which is usually to feel better)?

The one tricky thing about goals in relationships is to make sure it's your goal and not a goal you're assigning to the other person. Many parents come to my list with the goal of getting their child in therapy. Others come to the list with the goal of getting their love one to be accountable for her actions.

These are goals that the Non-BPD is assigning to the person with BPD. Instead, the goals have to be about you and your behavior and their goals have to be about them and their behavior. Otherwise, everyone is going to end up frustrated and controlled.

Make sure these goals are both effective and achievable. There's nothing more frustrating than setting a major goal and not feeling like any progress is being made. When I was in consulting, we used to say: "have many small, achievable goals. Celebrate success when you achieve each one."

Throw away the Scoreboard

This suggestion will most likely have the largest impact in your life. Although I just talked about "goals" in your relationship, in order to live a life and have a relationship without creating resentments and tallying up fears, you must throw away the scoreboard.

What's this about a scoreboard?

The scoreboard is the "what she does for me" vs "what I have done for her" measure. It's an accounting of transactions in the relationship. It's not just about marriage (and sex); parents have a scoreboard for their kids as well. How their kids with BPD don't appreciate the sacrifice they have made for them and blah, blah, blah.

This scoreboard results in more resentment (she's not meeting my needs) and more fear (I'm going to be the only one giving for the rest of my life).

Love is not a transaction. Love is an understanding. In love two people "get" one another.

Turn off the scoreboard and throw it away. Do it before you read the next chapter of this book. You will not be able to implement the attitudes in the next chapter when you have a scoreboard tallying every interaction.

Visualize smashing the scoreboard. The lights exploding. The timer falling to the ground. Never allow it to be reconstructed in your mind.

You don't need a scoreboard because you and your loved one with BPD are on the same team.

Chapter 7: Getting Ready for the Tools

Before you are ready to learn the tools and practice using them, it is vital that you examine your attitudes toward your loved one and your attitude toward life in general. This examination will not be easy; it takes time to understand one's own attitudes toward life and even more time to adjust them.

You may have to read through this section more than once to understand what I am saying, because I've found on my Internet list a great deal of confusion about these attitudes. Some of the attitudes tend to be counter-intuitive or run against attitudes that have been ingrained in us since childhood. Some members of my list have taken months to accept these attitudes and years to implement them in their lives.

The attitudes I present are the ones that allowed me to rethink my relationship with my BPD wife and emotional daughter. Once I adopted these attitudes in full, I felt a huge sense of relief about my relationship. Many Non-BPD's carry around a sense of dread about interactions with their BPD's. This feeling of dread can color the interaction and set you up for "failure." Many Non-BPD's feel that they have been emotionally abused by their loved ones with BPD.

I have found that by adopting the attitudes below, the equation of emotional abuse has been rewritten in my relationship. I no longer feel emotionally abused. I will explain how I got to this point in the chapters that follow. Just note that I didn't have to do anything to my loved one with BPD to arrive at this sense. Instead, I changed myself and my approach to the relationship which, in turn, changed the dynamics of the relationship for the better.

You are of worth and your feelings matter (even when it seems everyone tramples them)

Sometimes it feels like your feelings don't matter in a relationship, but they do. I find that many Non-BPD's think that their loved one with BPD doesn't care about their feelings. The Non-BPD's want to get to a place where their feelings matter.

When your feelings matter in a relationship you feel greater self-worth. I find that self-worth is one of the most important aspects of feeling good about yourself and about your life. Not self-esteem, self-worth.

When you feel like you and your feelings matter in the world, you feel better, happier and can more easily tolerate frustration. The first step in the process of becoming closer with another person is to accept that you have value and your feelings matter.

Use the exercises presented in the proceeding chapter to help increase your self-worth. Know that, even if it doesn't seem like your feelings matter to the other person, your feelings do matter because those feelings are intimately connected to your sense of worth.

Emotions are important (as important as rationality)

If you are anything like me (or like I was years ago), you place a lot of value on rationality. You are a solver. When you see a problem, you try to solve the problem rationality. You like to "think things out." I was just like that a few of years ago. Then, I discovered the power and importance of emotions.

I used to think that people who are emotional couldn't make sound decisions. I also used to shy away from making decisions when I was emotional. I labeled other people as being "overly emotional" or "overcome by emotions" when they made rash, unsound decisions. But I was wrong.

It turns out that emotions are required to make sound decisions. Earlier in this book, I mentioned the case of Phineas Gage, who, due to a brain injury, was unable to apply and integrate his emotions with his rational thinking. His life degenerated from one of responsibility into a boorish mess. While the case of Mr. Gage is an extreme one, everyday decisions also require integration of emotional and rational thinking. Purely rational thought or purely emotional thought does not allow us to make sound decisions.

The first worksheet for Dialectical Behavior Therapy shows a diagram of "emotion mind" on one side, "rational mind" on the other and "wise mind" as an intersection of the two ways of thinking. The idea behind this diagram is that when one is completely in either state (emotion or rational mind), one can make ineffective decisions. One must think and feel to be wise.

Additionally, the attitude toward emotions has to be, "emotions are not right or wrong, they just are." While some may say that some emotions (such as anger) are "impure thoughts," it is my belief that to understand the powerful influence that emotions have on a person, the emotions have to be accepted as existing and not be judged as right or wrong (more on this in a little while).

Emotions are built into each of us for survival. They are necessary to keep us safe and to help us make wise decisions. They are no more "right" or "wrong" as your breathing is "right" or "wrong." It just exists and is necessary for you to survive and thrive.

So, this new attitude, that emotions are not only important, but vital, to making wise decisions is vital attitude change you must adopt to help understand someone with BPD and to start learning the tools to make your life better.

Not all people think the same way you do (some are more sensitive, some are less)

This realization was another that astounded me. I always thought that my wife basically thought about things the same way as I did. I mean, who could be closer to me than a person I have spent more than twenty years side-by-side with? I could understand that my pattern of thinking might be vastly different that a New Guinea tribesman, even if Ekman showed they have the same basic emotions as I do. Again, I was wrong.

It turns out in this case that my wife thinks about things unlike I do. Even though we have been together for decades and have gone through many of the same life experiences, her reactions and inner thoughts are quite dissimilar to mine. Because of this, I have to be careful to assume the meaning of her reactions, even if I know what emotion is triggered. I might react one way and assume she would do the same. That is error I've committed many, many times much to my chagrin.

This is not to say that the way I think is "better" or "worse" than the way she does. It is just different. She is naturally much more sensitive than I am and likely to do things based on her emotions.

This attitude you have to adopt is that other people are not a mental "copy" of you. They think differently and, while you can use your own experience and thinking pattern as a general guide to what others are thinking, you have to stop assuming that others are thinking the same way as you are.

It's important to remember that your self is your window on the world. It's your frame of reference. Do not assume that your frame of reference is any more true than anyone else's. Do not let your frame of reference close your mind to alternative interpretations of events.

No one has a corner on the truth (even you)

Ok, now this is a biggie. I cannot even tell you how many times (hundreds?) the members of my list have argued and discussed this topic. This particular attitude is probably the most difficult to accept depending on who you are. If you accept the above attitudes, it will be easier to accept this one. "Truth" is different from "what happened," because truth must be filtered through the mind of the person perceiving the truth.

Since emotions are important (attitude #2) and people think differently (attitude #3), different people will feel differently about an event. The feeling is real and part of the truth for each person.

I know, I know – you're probably saying "Hey wait! What about what really happened?" Well, "what really happened" cannot be isolated from emotions that color it once the event is interpreted with your mind.

This is especially true for a highly emotional person, whether or not they have BPD. The memory of the event is more likely to be of the feeling that they got when the event took place rather than the event itself. And this type of memory is valid, because the feeling is real, albeit internal to the one who experienced it. What that person is recalling is the feeling, not the event.

This is not to say that feelings create facts in the real world. In other words, just because I feel scared, it doesn't mean that people are threatening me.

A person with BPD can be a very "effect and cause" thinker. Meaning, she feels angry and she must find a cause for the anger in the outside world. Something or someone must have caused this anger. Most of the time the cause is you, the attachment person.

The point of this attitude is subtle and key to understanding and interacting with a person with BPD. That truth, for them, is not the same as it is for you in certain cases. Remember however, that their truth is as real to them as yours is to you and that your truth is also colored by your emotions, beliefs and prejudices – your window on the world.

This is not to say that feelings can be used as evidence in a courtroom, but in the realm of human interpersonal relationships, feelings are as real and truthful as events.

Some things in life have to be accepted (and others can be changed)

When I think of acceptance, I am reminded of the serenity prayer that was "adopted" by Alcoholics Anonymous. It goes like this:

God, grant me the serenity to accept the things I cannot change, the courage to change the things I can, and the wisdom to know the difference.

I used to think that was a sappy little cliché, but now I realize that it contains much wisdom itself.

If you are anything like me, you are not happy that life is not fair. I used to walk around and think about how life is not fair and "why me?" Sometimes I still rail against the feeling that I never get a break and that things are always hard.

What I was doing though was protesting things I couldn't change. Trying to change things that cannot be changed leads to frustration. While certain things can be changed in life (like your attitude), some things cannot be changed. It really does take wisdom to identify the ones that can be changed and those that can't.

Once you're sure that something cannot be changed, it must be accepted "as is".

Otherwise, you are resisting a fact of life and that leads directly to frustration and suffering. As difficult as it may be to accept, any other path leads to frustration. Additionally, if you accept things over which you have the power to change you end up with helplessness.

One of the things that you will need to accept about your loved one is that she has a serious mental illness and that she may never be completely normal. It is perfectly natural to grieve for the "normal" child or "normal" relationship that you may never attain – so go ahead cry and mourn if you feel sad.

After the grieving, acceptance should make it easier. This is not to say there is no hope – little-by-little things can get better, but the choice to make things better is sometimes not completely yours.

Ways of thinking about change and acceptance

I have come up with four modes of thought that all of us are in at one time or another. These are:

"If only" thinking. "If only" thinking can be dangerous and it is often the thinking involved in BPD. The idea is that "I would be happy if only I had/lived/did something." It is conditional thinking. Unfortunately, with BPD, once the conditions are fulfilled, another condition comes to life.

That is, if your wife with BPD is thinking, "I would be happy if only we lived in New Zealand." Then you move to New Zealand and she'll find another "if only" to consider.

"What if" thinking. "What if" thinking can be helpful or harmful depending on what it is that you are thinking about. Sometimes "what if" can lead to great advances. However, with BPD, what if is usually the root of ruminating.

The person with BPD will spend hours in anxious "what if" thinking, worrying about what might happen and how they will feel when these things occur. "What if" can be positive or negative, effective and ineffective. Sometimes this way of thinking can spur you to change that which you have the power to change.

When "what if" thinking goes in a negative direction, the thinker can link a number of "what ifs," making a chain of ruminating and worry.

"As if" thinking. "As if" thinking is the mental state behind bullshitting (that is a term of art that I will explain later). It is pretending to understand something when in fact you could care less about whether the thing is true or not. As if thinking is often used to get someone out of your face.

You can also use as if thinking with yourself. Sometimes as if thinking is the key to beliefs that we can't definitively prove as true or false, like the belief in a supreme being. You can behave as if the Supreme Being exists, but you can't prove it. In these cases, as if thinking can benefit you.

"As is" thinking. "As is" thinking is accepting the world and conditions as they are in a given moment. Many times "as is" thinking can lead to peace and acceptance. A quote from the book *Alcoholics Anonymous* reads:

And acceptance is the answer to all my problems today. When I am disturbed, It is because I find some person, place, thing, situation -- some fact of my life -- unacceptable to me, and I can find no serenity until I accept that person, place, thing, or situation as being exactly the way it is supposed to be at this moment... Unless I accept life completely on life's terms, I cannot be happy. I need to concentrate not so much on what needs to be changed in the world as on what needs to be changed in me and in my attitudes.

I would encourage you to look carefully at your own thinking and see if you are in one of these four modes.

It is most important to be effective (rather than right all the time)

This particular attitude is one that has been the most controversial in my Internet group. Many people in life pride themselves on their morals and ability to discern right from wrong. Many people try to do the "right" thing in any given situation. Sometimes people will do what they think is right, even if that hurts another person that is close to them.

People are typically very judgmental. Before I started down this path, I also was very judgmental. Sometimes I can still be judgmental.

When I talk about judgmental, I am talking about judging whether other's behavior is "right" or "wrong" in your eyes. It is the act of labeling other people's behavior as "good" or "bad." The problem with being judgmental when dealing with someone with BPD is two-fold.

First, because of the shame involved in BPD, when a person's behavior is judged as wrong or bad, the person will expand that judgment to his or her feelings and further expand it to his or her self. Therefore, a judgment of the other person's behavior is essentially a judgment of the other person's self. I'm not saying this is "right" for the person to do – I'm merely describing the reality of what tends to happen in the mind of someone with BPD.

Secondly, the person is acting on their feelings and doing something that has, at one time in their life, been used to assuage negative feelings. They are acting in a way in which they will feel better. They are acting in a way that they have used to adapt to strong negative feelings in the past. While the behavior may be maladaptive, it is understandable behavior based on how the person feels.

You might not behave in the same fashion, but if you had their history, thought like them, had strong negative feelings as they do; chances are you would behave in the very same way. Thus, judging their behavior as "wrong" or "bad" is missing the objective of the behavior. Yes, the behavior may be self-destructive or nasty, but the behavior is a tool for adapting to how that person feels.

One of the biggest problems with being judgmental toward someone with BPD is that it denigrates their feelings and creates the "invalidating environment" that I spoke about earlier. If you judge another person's feelings (by way of their behavior) as bad, you are judging them as bad – at least for a highly emotional person.

It is extremely difficult to drop your judgmental attitudes. It takes time and practice. Being judgmental is taught to us from a very young age and it seeps into our language. In some respects, we are taught that being judgmental is a positive thing, a moral attitude. We are taught not to accept others and their behavior because their behavior is bad or wrong. This attitude helps keep us within our social group and helps keep us from risk.

In interpersonal relationships, particularly with a highly emotional person, it is corrosive. If someone feels they can't be accepted "as is" and "for what they are," that person will be either shameful or will fly into rage against the judge (or a combination of the two).

A sure sign of being judgmental is name-calling and labeling. If you find yourself, internally or externally (meaning to yourself or to others) labeling someone, you are likely being judgmental. I will talk about how to be less judgmental shortly.

I say, "It is most important to be effective." What does it mean to be effective? Before I could talk about effectiveness, I had to dismiss being judgmental, because it is a roadblock to effectiveness.

Being effective is doing whatever is necessary to gain a positive outcome in any given moment. In the case of emotions, it is doing what is necessary to feel better in any given moment. The major difference between effectiveness and mere adaptive behavior is that effectiveness takes into account the consequences that are associated with a given behavior, not just the immediate effects. That is where the idea of "positive" outcome comes into play. Being effective is doing the next required thing, regardless of the "score".

In the case of emotional situations, sometimes the most "conditioned behavioral" response is not the most effective one. An example of this is self-harm. Most often, self-harm – such as cutting, burning oneself or pulling at one's own hair – functions to reduce pain, not to inflict it. In other words, it is an adaptive response to internal (usually emotional) pain.

While you might not think that the behavior is "right," it is a valid response to internal pain, because it works to reduce pain. Although it is adaptive and "works," it is not effective, because of the significant negative consequences involved. It can lead to embarrassment, injury, infection or death. The potential negative consequences outweigh the effectiveness of the behavior. In Back from the Edge, a documentary about BPD, Marsha Linehan notes that while self-harm can reduce emotional pain, how can a person keep a job or function in society if the only solution to emotional pain is cutting oneself?

Doing what "works" is not always the most effective solution to a problem. Learning to identify the most effective solution is a skill itself, and I will discuss it at length later. One must adopt an attitude of doing the most effective action in any given situation. You have to be dedicated to being effective.

There's no need to be right all the time in relationships. If you have to prove you're right and the other person is wrong – if you have to stand on that point regardless of the consequences, you've resurrected the scoreboard. If you have to win at any cost, you're in for much conflict.

Now you might ask (as many of the people on my list ask), what if the most effective thing goes against my values? What if being effective is "wrong" in a particular situation? Well, my response to that is that emotions trump values. Emotions are immediate and primal, whereas values have been developed over time (sometimes over generations) and are more abstract than emotions. Again, this is not a case of "if it feels good, do it."

This is the accumulation of the first few attitudes I have directed you to take. If emotions are important, not all people think the way you do, no one has a corner on the truth, and some things have to be accepted, what we arrive at is the attitude that your values and judgments are not necessarily valid for other people.

If someone is overcome with powerful negative emotions, we find that: 1) it is important to them; 2) they are not thinking the same way you might; 3) your version of the truth in this situation does not match theirs; and 4) the fact that they are in this state is a truth and must be accepted.

Once those attitudes are applied to an emotional situation, you can start to be effective, even if being effective goes against the grain of what you deem is "right" or "good." I know this might be a difficult concept for you to understand at this point. It was extremely difficult for me to come to terms with it as well. Yet, in the case of emotional situations, it is essential.

I'd like to present an example of being effective versus being right. This example is not one that involves a person with BPD – it's just a regular, everyday example. Let's say my sixteen year old daughter has a curfew of midnight. At 12:30 AM, I haven't heard from my daughter and she is still out with friends. The phone rings and I can see that it is her calling from her cell phone.

What do I say to be effective in this situation? Well, the first question I have to ask myself is: what are my goals? Taking into account that it is already after her midnight curfew, there is nothing that I can do to enforce the midnight curfew rule. Meaning, the curfew has already been violated and we can't turn back time such that the curfew can't be broken. The rule has been broken already. I might be angry that she has violated a rule that I have laid down for her, but at this point there's nothing I can do to enforce the rule.

What are my goals? At this point, I'd say I have two goals in the interaction with my daughter. The first is to encourage my daughter to call me if, in the future, she is approaching her curfew and unable to get home. The second is to encourage her to respect the curfew and not to violate it in the future.

With those two goals in mind what should I say upon answering the phone? While it is perfectly within my rights to be angry with her and to say, "Why haven't you called? You know that your curfew is midnight and I am upset at you. You are grounded for a week," that approach would not be effective in supporting my goals. She would be disinclined to call me in the future when she is out late (goal #1).

Instead, if I want to be effective in this situation, I have to encourage her to call in the future. Upon answering the phone I instead say, "Hello, honey. I'm so glad you called. I was worried about you not being home yet." At this point, my daughter apologizes and tells me she went to a movie and it ran late and that she will be home in fifteen minutes. I then say, "Great, I look forward to seeing you."

If you are a strict disciplinarian, you may not agree with my approach to my daughter. However, being effective means keeping in mind what your goals are for a given situation. Since one of my goals is to see that she calls in the future, if I answer the phone with anger or immediate punishment, she will be less likely to call me in the future. Instead, she will be racked with dread about my anger and punishment and avoid calling just to delay the inevitable.

By answering the phone with, "I'm so glad you called," she is encouraged to call in the future. By telling her that "I was worried about you not being home yet," I express my feelings of worry, rather than those of anger and inform her that I am aware of her curfew violation.

While I can punish her for the violation when she returns home, it is more effective in this situation to reinforce the behavior that I desire (her calling) so that in the future she is likely to repeat it. Therefore, in this situation I decided to be effective (and reinforce the behavior I desire) and not be "right" by immediately punishing her for her rules violation.

110

If in the future, she finds herself in a more dangerous situation, such as being invited to ride in a car with a group of teens that have been drinking, she is more likely to turn to me and call for a ride. If I react with anger every time she calls, she is less likely to call, even when presented with a dangerous situation.

You can't solve anyone's (emotional) problems (except your own)

I used to be a "fixer." I used to believe that when I saw a problem, the first thing to do was to immediately work toward a solution. Unfortunately, I have learned that my approach to problem solving does not work with emotional situations. In fact, it can make the situation much worse. Usually an emotional person just wants to be heard and needs to know that the emotions that they feel are warranted.

You may think that, if the person with BPD is your spouse or child, "who else, other than me, is supposed to solve my loved one's problems? Isn't that what being a loved one is all about?" The short answer to those questions is: they have to solve their own emotional problems and no, that is not what being a loved one is all about.

Your job as a loved one is to listen and empathize, but not solve. I will tell you ways that you can increase your ability to both listen and empathize later in the book. At this point you must adopt the attitude that it is not your job to solve other people's problems. You can only solve your own. It is a hard lesson to learn, but it is also a necessary one.

It's not about you (or IAAHF)

This concept grew out of the evolution of me and a friend of mine as Nons. When I first discovered that my wife had BPD, I joined an Internet group and began reading the experiences and advice of others. This was in October of 2005. I noticed that I had an affinity to another member of the group and began corresponding with him via private email and via the Internet group.

What we concluded was that his wife had PTSD, not BPD, but still an emotional disorder. My wife had more symptoms and they were more acute, but his also had many of the symptoms you see in BPD. He was also a "fixer," and together we tried to puzzle out why our wives acted in the manner that they were acting toward us. The first question we asked was: "What about me?" We just couldn't understand why our supposed beloved wives would act in this fashion toward us. What about my feelings? Why is it that everything is about her feelings? Why is it that every situation is about how she feels?

The breakthrough came in the late fall of 2005 when my wife became emotionally dysregulated and went to a high-priced mall and spent thousands of dollars that we didn't have. After that experience, I was left with the feeling that she had done this to hurt me and, at one point, she said that she had done it to hurt me specifically.

After probing the situation with my wife and, after discussing it via email with my new friend, he suggested something different. My wife didn't spend the money to hurt me; she spent it to make herself feel better. She spent it because she felt bad. It helped ease her pain.

I was quite surprised at the implications of this revelation. What it meant, and what the idea of "what about me?" evolved to, was "it's not about you." In other words, my wife's motivations were not to hurt me, in fact, I was not even considered when she acted upon her "action impulses" and shopped for those items. Instead, she was doing it to stop her (emotional) pain, pure and simple.

My friend and I began to look at an even more complex dynamic at work which was that my wife felt she deserved to spend the money, even though she knew we didn't have it. Because of her strong feelings of shame, she often feels undeserving of acceptance. When someone feels undeserving of acceptance, there is quite often a "flip-flop" in that feeling. That is, feelings go from feeling undeserving to feeling over-deserving.

My wife went from feeling she didn't deserve anything (including acceptance) because she was such a shameful and broken person to feeling over-deserving - that she deserved even things that she couldn't afford. Her worth vs. her worthlessness swung from one to the other and helped motivate her spending. This wild swinging between one polar opposite and the other is a common pattern of thinking among people with BPD. This back-and-forth swing was all about her feelings toward herself and not about me. The idea of "it's not about you (the Non)" still applies to the BP's rapidly cycling self-image.

When my friend and I shared this concept of "it's not about you" with the group, it was met with derision. The other members of the Internet group could not accept that their loved one's behavior was not directed at them, that their loved ones did what they did to make themselves feel better and not to specifically hurt their spouses or parents. It was especially difficult to accept for those members at whom the person with BPD had raged, had manipulated or had belittled. How could hurling insults at me possibly be "not about me"?

While it is a difficult concept to accept, it makes more sense in its current incarnation. We decided to reiterate the concept again in the form "it's all about him/her." Maybe because other Nons view their loved one with BPD as selfish that concept (instead of "it's not about you") became more accepted.

To further clarify the concept once again, the formulation was changed to "it's all about his/her feelings" or IAAHF for short. When your loved one behaves in a manner that is seemingly destructive toward you (or someone else this person supposedly loves), it is important to keep in mind: IAAHF. Nine times out of ten, they are acting specifically to halt emotional pain, which is why I called my Internet group "Anything to Stop the Pain." They will do anything, including hurt you, to stop their own painful negative feelings. It's all about his/her feelings.

I found that some people bristle at the idea that it's "all about" the borderline's feelings. Sometimes this formulation makes the Non-BPD's ask: what about my feelings? (which, in a way, is a reformulation of "what about me?").

The intention of this concept is for you to understand the motivation of behavior, not the entire landscape of the relationship. There will be times in which the context of the relationship is about your feelings. Yet, when the "crazy" behavior takes place, it is most often motivated by dysregulated feelings and emotions. The purpose and intent of the behavior is to quell those feelings, even if it seems as if it's your fault that those feelings exist. To understand and use this attitude properly, you have to remember that it's (the behavior) is all about (motivated by) his/her feelings (dysregulated emotions that require calming/quelling of pain).

Chapter 8: Tools for the Relationship

Now begins what I call the "how-to" section of the book. Personally I think this section is the most important section. If you have skipped forward to this section without reading the last two chapters, I would suggest you go back and read those sections before continuing on to this one. I will go through these tools in the order that I believe that you need to learn them and apply them to your loved one and to yourself. Some of the tools are complex and all of them require practice. Just like with a physical tool, such as a saw, you must use the tool again and again for the correct purpose for you to gain mastery of the tool.

Some time ago I found a quote on the Internet from a woman with BPD that was posted on a previous version of the "Crazy Boards" (which was a support forum in which people with mental illnesses posted their opinions about various issues). Unfortunately, that version of the board is now defunct and the archives no longer exist on the new version. It was however preserved for some time in Google's cache (which preserves historical Internet pages), and I was able to obtain a copy. The reason I point out this method of discovery is that I am unable to attribute appropriate credit to the author of the quote.

I don't think that, in most cases anyway, that the "manipulative" behavior is deliberately so, despite appearances - thus it cannot be truly manipulative, by definition. These behaviors DO have function and an objective, as do all behaviors (including brushing one's teeth), but we do not describe ALL non-disordered people's attempts to find or maintain love or get attention or avoid pain manipulation - only when it truly is just that.

I think a new word is called for.

More accurately, the behaviors in question are more like "tools." Lacking a circular saw, I may try a hatchet to cut my board so I can cover my window and keep out the chill. It is not as effective, and is potentially damaging and will make a pretty ratty and half-assed covering, but it is the only tool I have to do what I need to do.

Granted, those with loved ones [of BP's] need to find ways to protect themselves, but applying such language ideas as "manipulation" does not give the "other" proper tools, either.

The overall effect is two people standing around with hatchets trying to make a straight cut down the length of an oak plank. Ain't gonna work.

This quote is specifically responding to being called manipulative and it is important in that respect, but I actually placed it here to reinforce the idea of tools. Each task has an appropriate set of tools and, with practice, the tools can be mastered. Once they are mastered, the tools can be used time and time again, with you honing your skills until each can be used without thinking about it.

The tools then become conditioned behavior themselves. I like to compare it to an athlete who practices a sport – say, basketball – and how, with practice, a person becomes better and better at shooting, running, jumping and rebounding. With enough practice he might be able to be a professional basketball player. Some skills, like athleticism, bring natural talents and individual characteristics into play. It is unlikely that someone who is five-foot-five could make it to the NBA, regardless of his skills. It's possible, but unlikely. Just like one's natural talents for basketball (height, jumping ability, speed, hand-eye coordination), one's natural ability to deal with these tools come into play.

Some people are naturally better able to utilize these tools than others. Some people have been taught other "tools" that interfere with the acquisition of these. In some sense, you may have to "unlearn" some conditioned behavior and replace that behavior with these more effective skills. It's not whether your current skills are better or worse than the ones I am introducing here – it's just that doing certain things can be ineffective with people who have BPD.

As I said in the previous chapter, there are some things that you can change and some things you have to accept. I recently had a conversation about this with one of the members of my list.

ME: You also have to understand - I changed ME - not her. She has changed in a response to my changes - but I changed ME.

MEMBER: I wonder what the literature would call this. You got therapy, counseling, and became an expert to treat HER condition by changing your own self... when there was nothing wrong with you to begin with. (Yes, I know that these skills and techniques are something you feel are a big improvement... I see their usefulness and applicability, and how they can help you in other relationships as well...) but was there something 'wrong' with you before you did all this? Was your journey undertaken because of serious defects in YOU? Or just shortcomings in specifically needed skills to assist another in overcoming THEIR problem? Your learning wasn't to correct defects in yourself, but to aid ANOTHER (actually, your daughter as well) in THEIR therapy. "Caregiver" is the term that comes the closest I can think of, but obviously that term doesn't include all you've done here.

- Conversation from ATSTP List

You see, what you have to do is change yourself, not the person with BPD. In changing yourself the relationship is bound to change in some fashion. The only thing you can change is yourself and the only person the BPD can change is his/herself.

The First Tool: Recognizing Emotions

Since I believe that the foundation for BPD is emotional dysregulation, most of the day-to-day conflicts, issues, rages and manipulative behavior spring from this feature of BPD. Emotional dysregulation is the engine that powers the train of BPD. Shame and impulsiveness also contribute no doubt (maybe as fuel and throttle respectively), but the engine itself is emotional dysregulation.

In that way, BPD is much like a traditional mood disorder, such as bipolar disorder. The main feature that separates BPD from bipolar disorder is the length and frequency of the "mood" swings. Emotions are more fast-acting than moods and they can come and go quickly. In the DSM-IV, which until very recently was the mental health diagnostic manual used in the United States (now replaced by the DSM-V), the diagnostic guidelines refer to this quality within the BPD diagnosis guidelines this way:

Affective instability due to a marked reactivity of mood (e.g., intense episodic dysphoria, irritability, or anxiety usually lasting a few hours and only rarely more than a few days).

The key to that and what distinguishes BPD from other mood disorders is the "usually lasting a few hours and only rarely more than a few days" part. Since emotions are short-lived, they will pass quickly through the mind of someone with BPD. They will be intense (all emotions are) and may last longer than yours do, but emotions are immediate and normally will not last more than "a few hours" and more likely last only a few minutes. The intensity will typically be stronger than a "normal" person.

116

If we return to the example of a wife with BPD being angry with her husband when he arrives home late, you can see that she cycles through several emotions rather quickly. She starts with shame and then in a matter of seconds that shame morphs to anger and she acts on it. In the case of the husband, he is surprised by the anger and its intensity. Since he didn't see it coming and knows that it doesn't match reality, he doesn't know how to react. He reacts in a natural way to a display of anger – he defends and fights back.

Learning to recognize emotions within yourself and in others is the first tool. It is a skill that takes practice, but it is indispensable when dealing with someone with BPD. They are all emotions and most of the time those emotions are negative and painful. I call this skill "taking the person's emotional pulse." You need to see where the other person is emotionally right away so that you're ready for the behavior that comes naturally from that emotion.

There are many books on recognizing emotions within yourself and others. I would recommend Ekman's *Emotions Revealed* which does a great job of showing how emotions are displayed on someone's face. The key point here is that you can learn to recognize your own emotions, and I will provide three sub-tools that can aid you with that. Remember these sub-tools are for recognizing your own emotions, not for recognizing those of the person with BPD.

Since the publication of the first edition of this book, Ekman has released several emotional training tools. According to Ekman, once an emotion is triggered and experienced, it will be expressed on a person's face for at least $1/25^{th}$ of a second. Most people can't suppress emotions as quickly as that ($1/15^{th}$ of a second is more typical).

If after reading this book, you would like to gain knowledge into other people and their emotional expressions, I would encourage you to take his online course (called the METT – micro expressions training tool) to learn this valuable skill. I'm not about to teach you something of that level of detail.

Ekman has spent forty or more years working and researching in this area. He even put electrodes in his face (and his research partner's face) to generate every possible permutation of facial expressions and coded these in the "Facial Action Coding System" (FACS). One of the interesting side-notes of his research is that when he and his subjects displayed the emotion on their faces, they felt the emotion, regardless of the trigger. Meaning, if they used a sad expression, they felt sad, even if they felt perfectly fine beforehand.

I have used Ekman's tools myself and have learned to read micro-expressions. It is a powerful skill when dealing with women and emotionally labile men. It is also one in which you don't have to wait until the "Impulse and Behavior" phase of the BPD dynamic to understand how the person with BPD is feeling.

First, however, we will start with recognizing how YOU are feeling with some sub-tools.

Sub-tool: Mindfulness

Mindfulness is a method of being "in the current moment" and examining one's thoughts and actions carefully. It is a complex skill to learn. Mindfulness comes from the Buddhist tradition and is particularly emphasized in Zen Buddhism.

Mindfulness is also emphasized in Dialectical Behavior Therapy, which is a treatment for BPD. DBT calls it "Core Mindfulness" and it is the first of four modules that a person learns to help to manage their behavior and emotions.

Entire books for thousands of years (because of the Buddhist connection) have been written about Mindfulness. I will be unable to explain the entire tool of Mindfulness here. However, I can explain the basics and how Mindfulness can help you learn to watch and understand your emotional reactions.

Mindfulness is based on the idea that all feelings, cognitions, thoughts and experiences are filtered through one's own mind. It is the opposite of "mindlessness" in which one is inattentive to the reactions within one's own mind. In Buddhism there are basically six sources of sensory input: the five "regular" ones (sight, sound, hearing, touch and taste), plus an additional source from mental input which is from your mind itself. Very basically, your mind can provide feedback to itself and in that way it becomes a "sense organ."

The "true mind" is uncluttered by these sensory inputs (including thoughts) and is analogous to a clear blue sky over which pass the clouds of sensory inputs. In the "unmindful mind," these sensory inputs can be like waves that wash you this way and that, and, in a person with BPD, can be more like a tsunami that carries the person's mind away with them. The key to mindfulness, when it comes to emotions, is to stand your ground and let the tides pass you by.

When I think about this I am reminded of my childhood in which my grandmother had a beach house not far from the ocean. My father and I (after I got over the trauma of *Jaws*) would wade out in the water until it was up to my chest and we would ride the up and down motion of the passing waves. I also remember feeling the motion of the waves long after they had passed, and I had left the ocean.

Emotions are like this as well. They have the power to wash you away, and you can usually feel them for a period of time after they pass. I learned to keep my feet firmly affixed in the sand and not let the waves wash me away.

Mindfulness is about the current moment. It is not about the past or the future. Memories, hopes, fears and dreams are part of the past or future and are simply sensory input from your mind. The only thing that you are assured of having is the present moment and the only moment in which you can live is the present moment. Mindfulness suggests living fully in the present moment and not dwelling on the past or hoping for (or fearing) the future.

One of the simplest, yet difficult to master, exercises in mindfulness is being attentive to a single "object." Buddhism (and DBT) suggests that you start with your breath. The reason behind this "object" as the focus of mindfulness is three fold: 1) we all breathe, 2) breathing is the "interface" between the external world and the internal world and 3) breathing is one of the few (if not only) physical process that can be both autonomic and conscious. Your breathing takes place whether you are aware of it or not, and you can control it if you want to.

The exercise for becoming mindful is to sit and concentrate entirely on your breath as it leaves and enters the body. I usually focus on it right below my nose. The idea is to focus completely on that one physical process and let all other thoughts pass out of your mind. Once you have "cleared" your mind of the noisy thoughts and feelings, you can learn to watch the clouds of the emotion pass through the sky of your mind. I would encourage you to try it, but, be warned, it takes practice. Quickly the cacophony of worries, judgments, feelings and concerns flood back in. One must focus and refocus over and over to remain mindful.

Sub-tool: Attentiveness

Dr. Paul Ekman suggests in his book *Emotions Revealed* a similar technique to mindfulness, but one that is less difficult to master. Mindfulness is a powerful tool and not limited to the emotions. Ekman uses the term "Attentiveness" for his technique.

Ekman worked with the Dalai Lama and other Buddhist monks along with Western scientists at the "Mind and Life" meeting on the subject of "Destructive Emotions." This summit is chronicled in Daniel Goldman's book *Destructive Emotions*. From *Emotions Revealed*, Ekman describes attentiveness:

I have not been able to find a single term to describe this type of consciousness; the best I have been able to come up with is attentively considering our emotional feelings. When we are being attentive, as I mean it, we are able to observe ourselves during an emotional episode, ideally before more than a few seconds have passed. We recognize that we are being emotional and can consider whether or not our response is justified. We can reevaluate, reappraise, and if this is not successful, then direct what we say and do…

Most people are rarely so attentive to their emotional feelings, but such attentiveness is possible to achieve. I believe that we can develop the ability to be attentive so that it will become a habit, a standard part of our lives. When that happens, we feel more in touch, and better able to regulate our emotional life. [31]

In the case of Attentiveness, as Ekman has outlined, one must practice it for it to become a habit and part of our regular lives. More information on attentiveness can be gathered from Ekman's book, but the basic idea is quite similar to the tool that I am currently presenting. When you become familiar with emotional feelings, you can recognize them earlier and earlier as they arise, and you can keep your feet on the ground as the emotional waves pass.

---

[31] Ekman, Paul, *Emotions Revealed*, Page 75.

Sub-tool: Felt Sense

Another psychological researcher, Dr. Eugene Gendlin, created another technique to help someone recognize emotional responses. Actually, Gendlin's technique, called Focusing, is more aimed at using your emotional and bodily reactions to help you make sound decisions about issues or problems in your life.

Part of the process in Focusing is becoming aware of (what Gendlin calls) your "felt sense." The full technique also led Gendlin to what he called "the philosophy of the implicit" and to another technique called "thinking at the edge." He spent the latter half of his career developing these two techniques and tools.

For the purposes of this book, I'd like to concentrate on steps in Gendlin's basic Focusing technique and how it applies to my current subject. In his book *Focusing*, Gendlin outlines "six steps" to achieving his entire process. This is a brief summary of Gendlin's technique and is not intended to be a replacement for training, practice and mastery – nor is it an exhaustive explanation of Focusing. The steps of Focusing are as follows:

1. Clearing a Space – this basically means that you look inside yourself and ask yourself what is there. You are not supposed to "go inside it," only recognize it is there and acknowledge its existence. You step back and create space in your mind and wait to sense what is there inside you.
2. Felt Sense – after seeing what is there, you focus on a single issue or problem that is there. You are to get a sense of what the problem feels like to your body and your mind. It is mainly a physical feeling, like tightness in your chest or throat.
3. Handle – the "handle" is a succinct word or phrase that arises from the felt sense. It might be a descriptive word like heavy, sticky, overbearing, jumpy, tight, etc.
4. Resonating – in your mind you go back and forth between the felt sense and the handle to make sure that the handle clearly and fully describes the felt sense of the problem.
5. Asking - you ask the handle/felt sense, "why does it feel [handle]?" and wait for an answer from deep in your mind/body.
6. Receiving – the receiving is when what Gendlin calls a "shift" comes in. The felt sense may provide an answer, however slight, because you recognized and labeled the feeling. The feeling can then shift and help release some of the problem. [32]

As with Mindfulness and Attentiveness, this technique is complex and takes practice. Most people feel that they need a teacher or guide at the beginning.

My interest in Focusing is not so much for problem solving or "shifting" (steps 5-6) but for an accurate identification of how you feel about a particular situation. Steps 2-4 do provide a strong "felt sense" of what is going on inside your mind and body, especially emotionally. You can learn more about Focusing by reading Gendlin's book of the same name or visiting www.focusing.org.

Once you have learned to recognize your own emotions, you can start to recognize emotions in others. This tool can be more difficult to master, because you don't have direct access to the other person's mind or body and can't feel what they are feeling directly. People are hardwired to recognize some basic emotions, even if only to protect themselves or to reproduce.

In day to day life, we usually experience four basic emotions - anger, sadness, happiness and fear. I am not planning on spending much time on happiness because it is not a problem. I do, however, want to include one additional complex emotion that is important when dealing with someone with BPD which is shame or embarrassment.

When someone feels one of those emotions, telltale signs appear on their face and in their voice. These displays may only last a brief moment, sometimes a tenth of a second or so, but they will be there. It is impossible for a "normal" person to suppress these signs.

In Daniel Goldman's book *Destructive Emotions*, which is something of a journal of the Mind-Life meetings between Buddhist monks (including the Dalai Lama) and western scientific researchers, the researchers found an experienced monk that could suppress the startle reflex at a loud sound, but he was the only one who could accomplish this. [33] I doubt that your loved one with BPD can accomplish the same and becoming a master meditation yogi is out of the question. So, if they feel something, you can learn to detect it through listening and watching carefully.

---

[32] Paraphrased from www.focusing.org

[33] Goldman, Daniel, *Destructive Emotions*, Page 35

One of the interesting features of BPD is that, although the sufferers feel emotions more intensely and more often than others do, they have trouble actually identifying the emotions within themselves. The emotions take over and they are unable to differentiate one feeling from the next. They become their emotions. Buddhist Monk Thich Nhat Hanh describes anger taking over a person's mind in this way:

When we are angry, we are not usually inclined to return to ourselves. We want to think about the person who is making us angry, to think about his hateful aspects - his rudeness, dishonesty, cruelty, maliciousness, and so on. The more we think about him, listen to him, or look at him, the more our anger flares. His dishonesty and hatefulness may be real, imaginary, or exaggerated, but, in fact, the root of the problem is the anger itself, and we have to come back and look first of all inside ourselves. It is best if we do not listen to or look at the person who is the cause of our anger. Like a fireman, we have to pour water on the blaze first and not waste time looking for the one who set the house on fire... [34]

I want to briefly describe what your loved one will display when he/she is in the grips of a particular emotion. I will describe the physical effects and likely action impulses for four emotional responses: Anger, Sadness, Fear, and Shame. Since your loved one with BPD is likely to have a strong negative emotional reaction about many things, you can quickly "take their emotional pulse" when you first interact with them to infer what the main emotional component is at the current moment.

Anger

Anger is one the most powerful emotions that a human being can experience. Anger can completely take over a person and cause fighting, raging, screaming and other destructive behaviors. Anger is like a freight train rolling down the tracks; it is difficult to stop because it has such powerful momentum. Anger usually arises from your wishes, plans or desires being thwarted or blocked in some way.

Here is what Buddhist monk and author Thich Nhat Hanh says about anger:

Anger is an unpleasant feeling. It is like a blazing flame that burns up our self-control and causes us to say and do things that we regret later. When someone is angry, we can

---

[34] Hanh, *Peace is Every Step*, Page 121

see clearly that he or she is abiding in hell. Anger and hatred are the materials from which hell is made. A mind without anger is cool, fresh and sane. The absence of anger is the basis of real happiness, the basis of love and compassion. [35]

Anger can be triggered by what someone else does, what is said to you, other feelings and many other things. Typically, in someone with BPD, anger is triggered by a perceived slight on the part of the loved one or friend. Anger may be triggered, for example, by someone saying something mean about the person with BPD or by even looking at them in a way that they interpret as threatening. Anger is generally a reaction to a perceived threat, although it can also be a reaction to other emotions, such as sadness or fear.

What does anger look like in someone else?

Anger can make the body feel some combination of these things, depending on how angry the person is and what other emotions are associated with the anger:

- Hot face, flushing
- Tightening muscles
- Narrowing of the mouth, with a downturn at the corners
- Glaring, with eyebrows compressed tightly over the eyes in the middle
- Narrowing of the eyelids
- Fists balling
- Jaw clenched and thrust forward
- Gritting teeth
- Yelling, raising voice
- Throwing things
- Complaining about how bad things are or how the person is not appreciated or treated well.
- Stomping, slamming doors or walking heavily.

These feelings in the body are caused by chemical changes in the brain that interplay in the body. These feelings are normal when a person is angry.

---

[35] Hanh, *Peace is Every Step*, Page 120

In yourself, sometimes adrenaline is released in your blood stream from your adrenal glands (on top of your kidneys in your lower back), so you might feel a tingling sensation come from your lower back and feel energy flow through your body. If adrenaline is released you can also become stronger, swifter or more violent than you ever imagined you would.

Sometimes people have directed anger to a positive cause, like woman's rights or civil rights. That type of anger is really resentment and comes from reinforcement of the anger over time; it is not really the anger of which I am speaking. Remember emotions are immediate and short-lasting, so that kind of anger must be revisited over and over to become "productive anger."

The behaviors that occur after someone becomes angry can be extremely destructive. When you are angry it is natural to want to strike back at (or run away from, if fear is involved too), the person (or object) with whom you are angry. Unfortunately, that behavior such as swearing at, yelling at, hitting, kicking, etc. can be regretted later and can have results that are irreversible. I would guess that most domestic violence and "crimes of passion," like murdering one's spouse impulsively, take place because of anger.

One member of the ATSTP group related a story in which a person he knew discovered his wife in an extra-marital affair and killed both the wife and her lover. This individual is now in prison and the others are obviously dead. Anger can have lasting effects and must be handled properly and delicately. My point is that most anger is destructive and negative to the person experiencing it, and to those in their immediate vicinity.

Still, anger is a natural emotion and arises naturally like the others. It is virtually impossible to go through life without getting angry. That also means it is impossible to have a human relationship (at least one that is long-lasting) without anger appearing in the picture from time to time. Your BPD loved one is probably angry a lot. Now, by studying the "symptoms" of anger, you can easily identify anger and that skill will come in handy a little later.

Sadness

Sadness is also a powerful emotion, but not as powerful as anger. While depression can be overwhelming and can significantly impact one's life, normal sadness usually passes after a good cry. That is exactly what you feel like doing when you're sad, and it is completely normal, even for big strong men. You might also want to retreat from the world, hide under the covers and sleep all day. Sometimes with strong sadness or depression, you might contemplate hurting yourself or even suicide. The reason for this is that extreme sadness is painful both to the body and to the mind. However, typical, run-of-the-mill sadness will not usually trigger suicidal ideation in someone without BPD or other mental illnesses. If you find that you are having suicidal or self-harm ideation over life's "little" disappointments (or for no reason at all), please go to see a mental health professional.

Sadness is most often triggered by loss or disappointment, and everyone experiences both loss and disappointment from time to time. Even little disappointments can have a large effect on a person with BPD. They can go into a tailspin for hours or days on the slightest disappointment because it sets off a deep emotional reaction.

Like anger, sadness can completely take over one's life. Losing a loved one usually triggers grief and can last for a long time. Again, like "productive anger" the sadness in this extended period is triggered again and again when something reminds you of the loss. An anniversary of a loved one's death is an example of how you can be retriggered into sadness.

Every year my wife gets extremely sad around the anniversary of her mother's death even though it's been over twenty years since my mother-in-law died. Sadness can be mild or strong, and when it is extremely strong we usually call it depression.

What does sadness look like in someone else?

- Mouth going down at the corners and frowning
- Eyebrows making a tent-like shape above nose and forehead wrinkling
- Eyes "pinched" or droopy toward the nose
- Tears welling up
- Use of a low, monotone voice
- Expressions that life is not worth it
- Retreating, sleeping, withdrawing
- Slumped posture or shoulders

Sadness is a strong feeling, and it is painful. The natural thing to do when a person feels sad is to retreat, withdraw and cry. Crying helps release tension and produces hormonal changes that help us feel better.

Fear

Being scared is a natural state to (generally) external stimuli. It is an unpleasant feeling. My daughter is scared of needles and of thunderstorms. When she has to go to the doctor she will worry about shots for weeks ahead of time. When summer comes along and big thunderheads amass over our town, she will sometimes go into the closet to hide from the sounds. Her reactions are completely normal to what she perceives as a threat to her.

There are many things that can trigger fear. Sometimes the feeling of fear comes when you interact with the person with BPD – you fear her reaction will be one of anger. Sometimes you might fear that you will never get through a situation intact. In some ways, that is the heart of fear – the fear of bodily, emotional or mental harm will be done to you. The natural reaction to fear is to run away and hide, or to morph the feeling into anger and attack back. It is the "fight or flight" response.

What does fear look like in someone else?

- Eyes widening
- Mouth slightly open
- Sweating
- Being jittery or jumpy
- Eyes darting or looking around
- Shaking or quivering
- Muscles tense
- Running away from or being frozen in fear
- Screaming or shouting in fear
- Goosebumps

Fear is a very basic and primal emotion and everyone experiences fear at some point. Fear is one of the things, like anger, that keeps us safe from enemies and threats. If you have no fear at all, you are likely to get into threatening situations that could do you harm. You are likely to run unnecessary risks. Fear is useful, but unpleasant.

Shame

When you are dealing with emotional situations, especially with highly emotional people, there are some emotions that are generally only triggered through social means. These emotions are also extremely important in BPD and are interrelated. Those emotions are Embarrassment, Guilt and Shame. All of these are painful emotions. Shame is the most important because it is a core component to BPD as I earlier explained.

What does shame look like in someone else?

- Blushing, flushing in face
- Crying
- Withdrawing
- Looking away
- Lowering one's eyes
- Bowing one's head
- Criticizing oneself
- Apologizing

Now, you might say, "My loved one with BPD never apologizes to anyone, especially me." I can certainly understand. Shame is one of the most difficult emotions to identify. It is a complex emotion and not one of the "base" emotions that most emotion researchers include as universal.

That is because the sense of shame comes from social interaction, not directly from the "animal brain." You have to have to think of yourself in the context of other people to have shame. You have to make a judgment about yourself (i.e. "I am a bad person") to feel shame, and that judgment is typically gleaned from the reactions of other people. Richard Moskowitz says this about the body language and attitude of feeling shame:

We feel shame about anything about ourselves that we would prefer others not to see. The body language of shame is about being invisible or not acknowledging being seen by others. We become small in posture by slouching or turning away. We avert our gaze from that of others, which is reminiscent of a baby covering its own eyes and imagining that it has become invisible to others. As adults, however, failing to meet another's gaze is also a sign of submission. [36]

The second reason that shame is so difficult to identify is that the person that experiences it finds it difficult to tolerate. Shame is usually very quickly morphed into another emotion (typically anger or sadness) because it is so self-invalidating and painful. It is difficult for someone to apologize for who they believe that they are (shame), rather than something that they have done (guilt).

Finally, shame is difficult to identify because the natural reaction to shame is to hide it and to cover it up. However, if your loved one does indeed have BPD, they are bound to have shame, since it is one of the building blocks of BPD. I will get to what you can do about that shame shortly.

The Second Tool: Being Non-judgmental

Being judgmental is something that is ingrained in us from a young age. It is probably a hold-over from a "local group adhesion" urge – that is, that our local group (whether it is a family, tribe, nation, religion or ethnicity) needs to be protected against "others" who are dissimilar to us. When I use the term "judgmental" I am speaking of deeming something or someone as good or bad, or right or wrong, not in a sense of exercising strong or poor judgment. That is something completely different and is not the subject of this section. I will use the term "judgmental," rather than "judgment" to differentiate the two concepts.

As members of society we all have values, morals and beliefs. These attitudes help inform our choices. Every day (often hundreds of times a day) we are judgmental toward other people. We might think that another person is a jerk or that their religious beliefs are not correct (since ours are, of course) and both are a form of being judgmental. Being non-judgmental is extremely difficult, because we are rarely taught how to do it. In fact, our culture reinforces judgmental thinking at just about every turn. Unfortunately, that creates an environment of "us versus them."

When we begin to think more and more in that fashion, we are ourselves suffering from a form of black-and-white thinking that is common to BPD. People with BPD can be very judgmental, and the reason is related to this black-and-white, us-versus-them attitude that characterizes BPD. It creates a fear of judgment in them and, in turn, a "get the person back"

---

[36] Moskowitz, Richard, From URL: http://www.soulselfhelp.on.ca/drm10shame.html

mentality that translates into judgment and blame by the BP toward the Non-BP.

There are benefits of being non-judgmental in this context. While your first reaction to someone with BPD might be to "give them a taste of their own medicine" and be judgmental toward them, this behavior is counter-productive and sends you down the same black-and-white road that the BP so often travels. Sometimes I use the analogy that the BP is actually allergic to judgment and if it is sensed, the BP will become emotionally dysregulated and all hell breaks loose.

I'm not saying you have to set aside your morals or values in order to be non-judgmental. I've gotten into numerous (heated) discussions with Nons about this concept. In the case of the BP, what I usually answer is that emotional dysregulation will trump values and morals every time. It's difficult to do what is right if you feel awful and believe that doing what is wrong will stop that feeling. As for you, sticking to your values is essential, yet emotional situations are not value-based.

Emotions just exist and they are not right or wrong. Behavior spurned on by emotional dysregulation can be dangerous and (in your mind) "wrong." But the emotions themselves are real, actually felt and exist – it is not wrong to feel a certain way about something. Being non-judgmental is the first step toward compassion for another person.

How does someone become non-judgmental?

Observe

First one must learn to observe the situation without immediately judging it as either good or bad, right or wrong. Just look at the behavior or listen to the words spoken and observe it or hear them. Notice the experience and the emotions that are in play. Do not let the emotions actually rise in you. Watch and wait. Focus your attention on what is happening around you and be "in the moment," not linking the current moment to future events or past ones.

Describe

Describe the situation to yourself without being judgmental about it or calling names. Say to yourself, in your mind, this (whatever it is) is happening. If we use the example of someone driving (what you feel is) too fast and you are in the car, say to yourself, "he is driving seventy miles an hour in a forty mile an hour zone." Not, "he's an out-of-control jerk." Describe what is happening as precisely as possible, with as much detail is possible. Notice the environment around you and the other person's actions and reactions. Again, do this without judging the situation as good or bad, right or wrong.

Find Your Feelings

Notice your own feelings, but do not let them run away with you. Sometimes another person's emotional dysregulation will spur dysregulation within you. I recently had an experience with my son in which he was angry and sad about something that I felt was minor. He was frustrated and upset for more than an hour. I got angry and frustrated myself and punished him by putting him in time out repeatedly during this hour. I let my anger get the best of me and didn't take a step back to find my feelings.

We are all human and that was a very human experience. I did feel remorse over repeatedly punishing my son, because his dysregulation was real to him and punishing him for his feelings is not a positive experience for him. It is invalidating (see more about invalidation in the next section) of his emotions.

In this interaction with the other person, find your feelings and try not to act on them immediately, as much as you feel compelled to do so. In the example of the car, you can say to yourself, "I feel scared that we are going to get hurt."

Learn to Do the Most Effective Thing

This particular point is one of much debate on my Internet group. Acting effectively is sometimes extremely difficult because, at times, it might go against your long-term feelings and values about a situation. Acting effectively means doing what must be done in a given moment to get positive consequences from the action, rather than negative ones. You must deal with the situation that you actually are in, not the one you wished you were in.

Deal with it directly and don't avoid. One must let go of "shoulds," "ought tos," and "unfairness" in a situation. One must face the situation as is.

Often, we in the group go around-and-around on this point. The reason is that sometimes, as I have said, the most effective action is not the one that "proves us right." When someone is obviously lying to you about something or wants you to do something that you find goes against your wishes, sometimes the most effective thing is not to battle it out over what is true and what is false. You see, emotional reality has its own sense of truth. What is true to the person at that time is how they feel about the situation and not the situation itself. They may completely "believe" what they are telling you because it matches their feelings. Remember, that Ekman says:

For a while we are in a refractory state, during which time our thinking cannot incorporate information that does not fit, maintain or justify the emotion that we are feeling.

When someone is emotional dysregulated (in the refractory state in his words), they can't "listen to reason" when confronted with facts. If you try to use "the truth" to fix the situation, you are not behaving effectively, even though you may be "right" in a given situation. Emotions are not about right and wrong.

Context is more important than Content

When someone communicates emotionally, the context is more important than the content.

What does that mean? It basically means that one has to understand the emotional context of a conversation, instead of focusing on the actual content of the conversation. What does that mean? That means that when someone is emotional, they may talk about one thing when they are really trying to express something else.

For example, I have a close friend who has an emotionally sensitive wife (not diagnosed with BPD though). When they were renovating their new home, his wife became quite upset about the bathroom faucet fixtures. She flew into a rage about how these fixtures were not the right ones and how they didn't match the towel racks. When he related this story to me he just couldn't understand how she could become so upset and thoroughly enraged about something as trivial as that. He couldn't understand how the whole situation got so out-of-hand and how he ended up being to blame for the fiasco. I simply told him, "It wasn't about the faucets."

Why did I respond that way? Because, as I said above, the issue was emotional – it was about emotional context, rather than concrete content. His wife was upset, frustrated and angry that the faucets didn't match. If she had not had these emotions, she wouldn't have expressed the rage and blamed her husband for the error.

Focus on the Consequences, not your Opinion

Rather than inserting your opinion into the situation (e.g. "this guy's nuts and out of control for driving so fast"), focus on the possible consequences of a particular behavior ("we could get into an accident or get a ticket"). Focusing on the consequences of an action should not proceed to more judgments. That is, just the facts, not the good or bad. If you say, "we could get into an accident and that would be bad," this, while true, has inserted another judgment. It would be bad, but the consequences of an accident might be getting injured or totaling a car. There are few positive consequences of a car accident, so I will leave that example and move to another one that is more relevant to BPD.

Many people with BPD engage in self-injury. It is impossible for you, as a Non, to stop someone from cutting themselves. You may feel that it is a bad (or wrong) thing to do, which is, of course, a judgment of the behavior. When I first discovered my wife's cutting, I felt the same way. I didn't understand why she would do something so bad to herself.

Self-injury is effective in the reduction of emotional/physical pain. It seems strange, but it is true. People usually cut themselves to actually reduce pain, not inflict it. It is sort of like scratching an itch. So, self-injury is effective in reducing pain. At the same time, self-injury has some major possible negative consequences. There's infection, possible uncontrolled bleeding, possible death or a visit to the emergency room, where, I can assure you, the medical staff is unlikely to treat you kindly.

(While this is a side point, most people in the medical community – doctors and nurses included – have little or no training in dealing with people who self-injure and, for the most part, feel that they want to deal with other patients first, since the patient caused her own issue. Also, they will likely send the person to the psyche ward, which is usually not effective because the person was using a tool for pain reduction. They're not crazy, just engaging in a practice that has significant negative consequences.)

Rather than focusing on whether cutting is bad or wrong, focus on the negative consequences of the behavior. When combined with the other tools in this book, you can actually help discourage self-injury in your BP, especially when combined with identifying feelings (last section) and validation (next section). Focusing on the consequences is explained in greater detail in the next section; I only included it here because it encourages you to be less judgmental.

An exercise in being Non-judgmental

One way to become non-judgmental is to become aware of your (often) unconscious and conditioned judgments. I often hear Non-BP's say, "My BP is acting crazy" or some such. The labeling of anyone's behavior as "crazy" is a judgmental label. The behavior makes sense (even if it is emotional sense) to the person at the time they are doing those actions. Certainly, a person with BPD might perform certain actions that someone without BPD would find objectionable or "crazy." However, because of a number of symptoms of BPD, especially shame and fear of judgment, labeling another person's actions as invalid or crazy can undermine the trust that you are trying to build.

In this exercise, I would encourage you to take a specific time-frame – it could be an hour, two hours or a full day – and identify your judgments of other people's actions, attitudes and interactions. In other words, if you find yourself thinking about another person (whether with BPD or not), "that person is an idiot," that is a judgment and should be counted as one.

Continue to practice this exercise such that you can become more aware of the judgments about others and about life that you make, even if those judgments are ingrained and unconscious. By making the unconscious biases conscious, you can more easily slip their grasps and become less judgmental of others, including your loved one with BPD.

Keep and mental or written tally of these judgments to see if, after time, the number of judgmental thoughts is reduced.

The Third Tool: Validation

Validation (or emotional validation) is an extremely powerful tool when it comes to emotional situations. It is complex and multi-stepped and it takes a lot of practice to master. On my Internet list, I talk a great deal about validation because it is essential to managing a relationship with someone with BPD. If you learn to master validation, you can see a marked change in the way your BP loved one interacts with you.

As I said earlier, one of the causes of BPD is the "invalidating environment." Now, it could be that it is not an actual "cause" (and that all the real causes of BPD are biological), but more a reinforcer of BPD. An invalidating environment reinforces the idea that a person's feelings are wrong, and, in the case of BPD (with the twenty rules in mind), reinforces shame which, in turn, leads to anger. If you invalidate a BP's feelings, you are likely to fuel more shame, because they actually feel those emotions, whether or not they seem right or appropriate to you.

Validation is a tool that verifies that the other person's feelings are valid, but doesn't necessarily condone or agree with their behavior. Remember, the behaviors come from feelings, beliefs and "action impulses." Those can be separated from behaviors. You are not "giving into" the BP if you learn to validate their feelings. And, if you master validation, you might eventually receive validation back from your BP, which is a remarkable improvement over IAAHF. Don't expect it right way, but after some time, it can happen.

With validation, you are basically saying, "Your feelings matter. It is OK to feel that way. It is normal to feel that way." The way in which you validate someone else's feelings is important.

Many people believe that saying "It's OK. I love you" or "You are safe with me" is a form of validation, but it is not. Those statements are about your attitudes toward the other person, not about his/her feelings.

Validation is always about the OTHER person's feelings, not about our own feelings. In some ways, this can get frustrating for us, because everything always seems to be about the other person's feelings – and in the beginning, that is true. I will later explain another tool that gets your feelings on the table, but for now we need to focus on the other person's feelings and how to validate them.

Validation is not giving advice. In fact, if you do give advice when the other person is emotional, they are likely to get angry with you. People don't like to feel that they are being told what to do about an emotional situation – that is quite invalidating. It feels like you are telling them how they should feel and they can't control the emotions.

135

So, right away I'd like to list some of the most invalidating things a person can say to someone with BPD. I didn't create this list myself but found it on another Internet list. Unfortunately, the author is unknown to me. (Since the first edition of this book, I have discovered this list on the Internet site http://www.eqi.org which is a site about emotional literacy and is written and researched by Steve Hein).

Invalidating Phrases

"Ordering" the BP to Feel Differently

- Smile.
- Be happy.
- Cheer up.
- Lighten up.
- Get over it.
- Grow up.
- Get a life.
- Don't cry.
- Don't worry.
- Don't be sad.
- Stop whining.
- Stop laughing.
- Don't get angry.
- Deal with it.
- Give it a rest.
- Forget about it.
- Stop complaining.
- Don't be so dramatic.
- Don't be so sensitive.
- Stop being so emotional.
- Stop feeling sorry for yourself.
- Stop taking everything so personally.

Ordering the BP to "look" differently

- Don't look so sad.
- Don't look so smug.
- Don't look so down.

- Don't look like that.
- Don't make that face.
- Don't look so serious.
- Don't look so proud of yourself.
- Don't look so pleased with yourself.

Denying the BP's Perception, Defending

- But of course I respect you.
- But I do listen to you.
- That is ridiculous (nonsense, totally absurd, etc.)
- I was only kidding.
- I honestly don't judge you as much as you think.

Trying to Make the BP Feel Guilty While Invalidating the BP

- I tried to help you.
- At least I …..
- At least you….
- You are making everyone else miserable.

Trying to Isolate the BP

- You are the only one who feels that way.
- It doesn't bother anyone else, why should it bother you?

Minimizing the BP's Feelings

- You must be kidding.
- You can't be serious.
- It can't be that bad.
- Your life can't be that bad.
- You are just … (being difficult; being dramatic, in a bad mood, tired, etc.)
- It's nothing to get upset over.
- It's not worth getting that upset over.
- There's nothing wrong with you.

Using Reason

- There is no reason to get upset.
- You are not being rational.
- But it doesn't make any sense to feel that way.
- Let's look at the facts.
- Let's stick to the facts.
- But if you really think about it....

Debating

- I don't always do that.
- It's not that bad. (that far, that heavy, that hot, that serious, etc.)

Judging & Labeling the BP

- You are a cry baby.
- You have a problem.
- You are too sensitive.
- You are over-reacting.
- You are too thin-skinned.
- You are way too emotional.
- You are an insensitive jerk.
- You need to get your head examined!
- You are impossible to talk to.
- You are impossible.
- You are hopeless.

Turning Things Around

- You are making a big deal out of nothing.
- You are blowing this way out of proportion.
- You are making a mountain out of a molehill.

Trying to get the BP to question himself/herself

- What is your problem?
- What's wrong with you?
- What's the matter with you?
- Why can't you just get over it?
- Why do you always have to ....?

- Is that all you can do, complain?
- Why are you making such a big deal over it?
- What's wrong with you, can't you take a joke?
- How can you let a little thing like that bother you?
- Don't you think you are being a little dramatic?
- Do you really think that crying about it is going to help anything?

Telling the BP how he/she "Should" Feel or Act

- You should be excited.
- You should be thrilled.
- You should feel guilty.
- You should feel thankful that…
- You should be happy that ….
- You should be glad that …
- You should just drop it.
- You shouldn't worry so much.
- You shouldn't let it bother you.
- You should just forget about it.
- You should feel ashamed of yourself.
- You shouldn't wear your heart out on your sleeve.
- You shouldn't say that about your father.

Defending the Other Person

- Maybe they were just having a bad day.
- I am sure she didn't mean it like that.
- You just took it wrong.
- I am sure she means well.

Negating, Denial & Confusion

- Now you know that isn't true.
- You don't mean that. You know you love your baby brother.
- You don't really mean that.
- You are just … (in a bad mood today, tired, cranky)

Sarcasm and Mocking

- Oh, you poor thing. Did I hurt your little feelings?
- What did you think? The world was created to serve you?
- Do you think the world revolves around you or something?
- What happened to you? Did you get out of the wrong side of bed again?

Laying Guilt Trips

- Don't you ever think of anyone but yourself?
- What about my feelings?!
- Have you ever stopped to consider my feelings?

Philosophizing or Clichés

- Time heals all wounds.
- Every cloud has a silver lining.
- Life is full of pain and pleasure.
- In time you will understand this.
- When you are older you will understand.
- You are just going through a phase.
- Everything has its reasons.
- Everything is just the way it is supposed to be.

Talking about the BP when she can hear it

- She is impossible to talk to.
- You can't say anything to her.

Showing Intolerance

- This is getting really old.
- This is getting really pathetic.
- I am sick of hearing about it.

You're probably thinking "Wow! That's a long list!" It is a long list. I think it is important that you understand what invalidation is before I teach you how to validate.

You're probably also thinking, "I've said some of those things so many times to my loved one with BPD." I certainly thought that when I saw the list.

You might also be thinking, "I thought this book was about Nons and for Nons. Why so much talk about the BP?" or "Are you telling me I've been doing something wrong for so long?"

This is where things get interesting. You see, I believe that since BPD is a very relationship-oriented disorder, changing the way in which you interact with the BP will in turn change them. Mostly, the point is to make your life easier. If you learn and apply these tools, you will have less raging, less acting out and more peace in your life.

I'm also not saying you have been doing the "wrong" thing for a long time. I don't believe in human emotional relationships there is a wrong or right thing to say, only an effective and ineffective one. What I am saying is that what you have been doing has been (unknowingly) reinforcing shame and anger in your BP.

If you're not dealing with someone with BPD or a similar emotional disorder, the approaches mentioned may be effective in a given situation. Unfortunately, BPD is an emotional disorder and, when dealing with emotional situations, it is more effective to shy away from using emotionally invalidating responses.

Like I said validation is a multi-step process and you can validate someone's feelings in a variety of ways. I will now explain exactly how to do it and give some examples.

Since I published the first edition of this book a very kind, organized member of my Internet support group codified the steps of the validating process that I presented into a mnemonic device.

Here is an explanation of the device and how it relates to validation. The device is I-AM-MAD and I will first present it and then explain it in detail.

I – identify the feelings

A – ask a validating question

M – make a validating statement

M – make a normalizing statement

A – analyze the consequences of proposed or past actions

D – don't solve the problem for the other person

This device provides a simple road-map for how to validate a person and how to have a validating conversation.

Step 1: Identifying the Feelings

I dedicated an entire "tool" to recognizing feelings in others so that you can accomplish step one properly. What you must do is look at the person with BPD and say to yourself or to them how they seem to you to be feeling. As I said before, people with BPD are typically so overcome with negative emotions that they have difficulty sorting these emotions out inside themselves. I also indicated before that this has to be done with certain attitudes in mind. I want to list those attitudes again here so that they will be easily remembered. If you want the details, go back and read through that section again. The attitudes are:

- You are of worth and your feelings matter (even when it seems everyone tramples them)
- Emotions are important (as important as rationality)
- Not all people think the same way you do (some are more sensitive, some are less)
- No one has a corner on the truth (even you)
- Some things in life have to be accepted (and others can be changed)
- It is most important to be effective (rather than correct all the time)
- You can't solve anyone's (emotional) problems (except your own)
- It's not about you (or IAAHF)

With those attitudes in mind and with the tool of a non-judgmental attitude in hand, you can identify the feelings of the other person. The most effective way to do so is to use "sensing" words, rather than "knowing" words. That means using words/phrases like:

- Look
- Seem
- I can hear that...
- I can see that...
- It must feel [whatever]...

142

Rather than words/phrases like:

- I know that...
- I understand that...
- I know you...
- I understand you...

So, you can say, "Wow! You look so sad!" or "How angry you seem to me."

When someone with BPD is emotional dysregulated, she has trouble identifying her own feelings. She may feel completely jumbled inside and awash with strong negative feelings. She is unable to think rationally and that is part of the problem in self-identifying her feelings.

Additionally, she may feel fearful to communicate even what emotions she can identify, because, if in the past she has felt invalidated by others, she doesn't trust her emotions with others and may not trust her emotions even inside herself. If you learn to use the skill of identifying the feature of a feeling in your BP, you can use this part of the validation process to identify those feelings for her. It takes practice, but it is worth it.

By hearing that her feelings have been noticed, the person with BPD is likely to calm down a bit. She feels heard.

Most people believe that remaining calm in the face of strong emotions expressed by their BP loved one is the best and most effective course of action, but in reality, it is not. A study of BPD patients using functional MRI technology "found that the level of amygdala activation to the Fearful, and Neutral faces in BPD patients is significantly correlated with diagnostic measures of emotional liability."[37]

What does that mean to you? Well, although clothed in scientific language, what that means is that a person with BPD is more likely to view a "neutral" (or calm) face as a threat and become fearful. If you go

[37] Donegan NH, Sanislow CA, Blumberg HP, Fulbright RK, Lacadie C, Skudlarski P, Gore JC, Olson IR, McGlashan TH, Wexler BE, "Amygdala hyperreactivity in borderline personality disorder: implications for emotional dysregulation", Biological Psychiatry, 2003 Dec 1, 54(11), Pages 1284-93

"calm" on her, in the face of her emotional dysregulation, she will see you as a threat and, if she sees you as a threat, she will do one of two things: fight or flee. The tenor and tone of your voice matters in this area.

Ambiguity and unpredictability are two of the most difficult situations in which a person with BPD finds herself. Because of the shame and the dread, an uncertain future is doom. An uncertain, neutral or ambiguous expression is assumed to be angry.

The purpose of someone coming to you in an emotionally dysregulated (or close to one) state is to communicate the emotions that she feels. She may have difficulty expressing these emotions and may use other means for expressing them such as blame, sobbing, cutting, raging or other behaviors that are difficult for you to deal with.

The underlying point however is one of communication – she is trying to tell you something, but she doesn't have the language for it. Therefore, if you respond to an emotional communication in either an invalidating fashion (using one of the many, many invalidating phrases above) or in a way that doesn't match the emotional distress, the BP will feel unable to communicate. She will think "I'm going off the deep end here and you are so calm! You don't understand anything! You'll never understand me!" and not trust you.

The tenor of your voice is more effective if you express your emotional identification with emotion in your voice as well, but with slightly less emotion than the BP is feeling. In other words, express distress in the identification, but less emotion than if you are actually in distress yourself.

So, when you say something like "Wow, you look so angry," do so in a forceful, emotion-filled and confident manner. The BP may respond with "I'm not angry. I'm so depressed," but that is OK, because you now have your foot in her emotional door. You are now communicating with her on an emotional level and that is the only level she will be able to understand in her current state. One thing that you can say when you guess incorrectly about the other person's emotional pulse is: "That's how I would feel, tell me more about what you feel." That allows go to validate and listen more carefully to the emotions.

Of course, it is also likely that she will respond with "you're damn right I'm angry!" If this is the case, you have correctly identified the emotion, and she has taken a small step towards linking her inner emotional states with the emotion felt. That is a step in the effective direction, because, after repeating it, the BP can do it for herself, without your intervention.

Now you might be asking, "Hey, wait a minute! Do I have to be a mind reader?" Unfortunately, in the case of BPD, the answer is "yes" (at least partially). You have to become (at least temporarily) an emotional mind reader.

Step 2: Asking a Validating Question

Step two in the validation process is to ask a validating question of the BP. There are many forms of validating questions, and I will give some examples below. The most effective question for a BP who is emotionally dysregulated is the question: "What happened?" Remember this question in your next interaction with your BP. The emotional identification (step 1) and the validating question (step 2) can be combined.

Most of us tend to ask, "What's wrong?" However, if you look back into the invalidating phrases, you will see that "What's wrong..." is the start of several invalidating questions.

A person with BPD tends to personalize the environment and to believe that other people's feelings toward a particular situation are all about her (IAAHF). She is sensitive to judgment and links (through extreme personalization) other people's actions, statements and questions with a judgment of her. This is a natural feature of BPD even if it is annoying to you. Unfortunately, this feature goes against your natural reaction to someone in distress; if you ask her "what's wrong," she is likely to hear "what's wrong with you?" Of course, that is invalidating and contributes to the disorder. It is more effective to ask, 'What happened?"

On a brief side note, when a BP asks you "What's wrong?" she is much more likely to be fishing for an answer to the question "Are you mad at me?" because of the intense personalization of the thinking. My wife often expresses that "everyone hates her" and that other people's behavior and statements are an expression of their "hate" for her. While it is possible, it is much more likely that others are just going about their own lives without considering her at all. This line of thinking arises from shame and the dread of being punished, even if she is not sure what she is being punished for.

If you already know what happened you can say, "How did that make you feel?" If you already know how she feels about that, proceed to step three. However, it is often useful to get the information about what happened directly from the BP, because her distorted and emotion-influenced thinking might have "colored" the truth about the actual events. What you're trying to discern here is how she saw/felt about what happened.

Some other validating questions (especially in following up on the first one "what happened") are:

- How did you feel about that?
- What did you do (say/feel/think)?
- What would you like to do (or feel like doing) about it?
- How could you take that?
- When did it happen?
- Where did this happen?
- What do you think caused you to feel that way?
- What do you think caused the problem?
- Did that hurt your feelings?
- What do you think was meant by that?
- Oh?
- Yeah?

Step 3: Making a Validating Statement

Now you will want to make the validating statement about the other person and not about you, because, remember IAAHF. It might be best to avoid starting a sentence with either "you" or "I" and make it more generic.

A validating statement should be a response to the validating question, but, as I have said, if you already know what happened, you can make a validating statement first. This step in the process of emotional validation is probably the most important, but it is also the most difficult.

People on my Internet list find this step the most unnatural of the steps, and it requires the most practice. What it involves is speaking to the feeling of the situation, to the emotions, rather than to the event, facts or truth of the matter. In the case of BPD, the feelings are the truth. One must find the grain of truth in the feelings and speak to that grain of truth.

In the beginning, it is easiest to follow a simple planned response. Although when you initially begin to practice this technique, it is likely to feel forced, fake or patronizing. Because the BP has opened up to you emotionally, it is less likely to feel that way to her, because if you do and say this validating statement as naturally as possible (and speak to the truth about the feelings) it can often hit the nail right on the head.

What you say when making a validating statement is something like:

"Wow, it must be really hard to feel that way."

OR

"That must have made you feel…"

Again, this statement should be made with emotion in your voice to indicate that you heard the expression of the feeling and how it really must hurt. The anatomy of this validating statement can be dissected and many validating statements can come out. The basic model is stated above.

Again, avoiding "you" and "I" at the beginning of this statement is most often more effective than using these words. "You" can trigger the dynamic I wrote about before – that is, that the BP will feel blamed for their feelings. "I" can make the conversation about you and this conversation is not about you – it's about the BP's feelings about the situation.

Before I dissect the validating statement to make other statements and help provide a guide for them, I'd like to say that avoiding judgment is particularly important at this point. Often, this is where the conversation with a BP goes awry, and she "flies off the handle" into deeper and deeper emotional dysregulation.

Remember, emotions can fuel other emotions and that can trigger rage or shame or numerous other emotional states. Sometimes a BP might state how she behaved because of how she felt and you may not agree that the resultant behavior was appropriate. By responding to inappropriate behavior you can interject judgment into the conversation, and that judgment is almost guaranteed to cause additional dysregulation.

For example, I will present a conversation with my daughter (who at the time was too young to be officially diagnosed with BPD, but shows the biological signs of emotional dysregulation), when she came home from school looking upset. Here is the basic outline of a real conversation between us in which I use these tools and with which I will try to illustrate my point:

My daughter enters the house looking upset and sheepish. I look at her and gauge her emotional pulse. To me she looks both angry (small mouth with compressed lips) and sad ("tented eye-brows").

(1) ME: Wow, you look upset. Are you angry or sad? (Identify the emotion and show that you recognize something is going on emotionally)

HER: I don't want to talk about it.

(2) ME: What happened? Did something happen at school to make you feel sad? (Ask a validating question, without any judgment or statement of right/wrong or good/bad)

HER: Yeah, that jerk Sarah didn't want to play the same game as I did. She was being so mean. I hate her and her annoying friends.

(3) ME: That must have made you feel pretty angry, huh? (Ignore the "jerk" statement and the "hate" statements, if you speak to those she will feel that you are judging her or admonishing her for her feelings. She will exit the conversation and no longer share emotional statements. This conversation is about getting over the current emotional moment, not about teaching her your values or about scolding her for her language. There will be time for that later. Instead, make a validating statement about her emotions).

HER: Yeah?! I can't stand when she acts that way! I ran over to her at recess and hit her with my book bag!

OK, this is the point of the conversation about which I was speaking. You probably believe, as I do, that hitting a schoolmate with a book bag is wrong. Any level of violence at school can lead to punishment by school personnel, suspension, expulsion or other severe consequences. In this litigious age, you can be sued or punished for the actions of your children at school. Believe me, I realize that. However, this is not the point in the conversation to extol your values. I can't emphasize this enough.

Many people of my Internet list get excited about this statement, thinking that once a "boundary" is crossed, punishment needs to be immediate. Actually, what is at work here is not that my daughter crossed a boundary (except one of her own perhaps) – no, she broke a rule of the school and of society that "you do not strike other people." Of course there are consequences and punishments for breaking rules – that is the very nature of rules (and laws).

As for my daughter, the most effective course of action is to understand why she broke the rule – why she hit the other girl. She did it because she was angry and, as I've said, the natural thing to do when you are angry is to attack.

Now before you think that I am excusing her behavior, you must read to the end of the tools section of this book. I will deal with the behavior before the end of this conversation or, if more appropriate (depending on the level of emotional dysregulation) in a later conversation. When someone is emotionally dysregulated is not the time to teach values, punish behavior or judge the person. Depending on the type of person you are, this concept may take some time to sink in. I will cover when it is time to teach and how to do so later in this chapter.

These tools represent a road map to understanding how to be effective with a person with BPD, and you have to be patient and follow the trail until the end.

To help illustrate why this is not a "teaching time," I want to use an extreme example. Usually I don't like using extreme examples or exceptions to illuminate a point, but in this case I saw something in the news that caught my attention. It was an interview with the mother of a teen age girl (Megan Meier) who had killed herself because a "friend" on MySpace had been mean to her. Here is a clip about the story from ABC News:

Megan was distraught. Tina [her mother], angry about the nasty online exchanges, insisted that Megan log off the computer.

"Megan got upset with me and yelled — not yelled, but was crying and said 'You're supposed to be my Mom and you're supposed to be on my side,' and then took off running upstairs," said Tina.

Twenty minutes later, Tina went to check on her daughter and made a horrible discovery. "I went upstairs and opened the door and saw her hanging in the closet," she said. "And I screamed and ran over and tried picking her up." [38]

Admittedly using a young girl's suicide is an extreme case; however, I am bringing this up here because of the reaction of her mother. She knew Megan was distraught (which is a strong form of sadness). Megan was crying which is a sure sign of sadness. Instead of being validating toward her sadness, her mother scolded her from nasty messages she had written on MySpace and insisted that she log off the computer.

Megan felt invalidated and that her mother was not on her side. Her mother was being judgmental and trying to teach her a lesson about watching her language (even on-line). Megan was emotionally dysregulated and needed validation, not lesson-teaching.

I am not blaming her mother for her daughter's suicide. I am merely pointing out that invalidation and judgment at this point in the conversation can spur further emotional dysregulation, and that further dysregulation can lead to impulsive reactions, including hanging oneself in the closet.

This is not the time to give advice and, in fact, unless you are asked for advice, there is never an effective time to give advice in an emotional situation. The person who is emotionally dysregulated doesn't want advice; they just want to be heard and to be sure that you are "on their side."

In the past, before I learned and practiced these skills I would have reacted completely differently to the same conversation.

My daughter comes into the house like a storm.

ME: What's wrong with you? What did you do this time?

HER: Shut up. I don't want to talk about it!

ME: Listen here, young lady, you don't say "shut up" to me. I'm your father. Drop the attitude right now!

[38] Quoted from http://www.abcnews.go.com/2020/story?id=3958937&page=1

150

HER: You never listen to me. (Glaring) I just want to go in my room and be alone.

ME: No, you will tell me what happened. Am I going to get a call from the school about what you did? Again?

HER: Who cares? Nobody ever listens to me! I don't care about any of you! (Stomping around) I hate you!

ME: Hey, don't use that word! Never use that word! You tell me what happened or I'm going to take away your computer privileges for a week!

HER: Fine! Go ahead! I don't care about the stupid old computer anyway!

She exits and stomps off to her room, slamming the door.

Then, I have to ask her sister what happened at school and her sister tells me that she hit her friend with her book bag. I ask why and I get a run down on how she got mad because she wanted to play some stupid game that nobody wants to play anymore and how she started yelling and running at the other girls.

Now I'm worried that I will get a call from the school and that my daughter will be suspended. I end up calling the mother of the girl she hit to apologize for my daughter's behavior. Then I go into her room and pry the behavior out of her and yell at her for doing what she has done, tell her she can't hit other girls at school, that it is unacceptable and ground her for a week.

Sound familiar?

Anyway, while that scenario is as likely and as "right" as the previous one (with which I am not yet finished), it is not emotionally effective for her. You might say, "Well, she was sassing you. She told you to shut up. She disobeyed you directly."

I often have certain members of the group that are more "authoritarian" in their approach that say such things. My point is that she is angry and my responses in this interaction caused more anger. The most effective reaction in this situation (if you accept my previous premises) is to help her get out of her anger, to help her return to baseline. Then real teaching and the imparting of values can begin.

Now let's look at the validating statements in their constituent parts. The subject should be either the situation or a statement from you about the situation. You can use the "feeling" words again (such as sounds like, it seems like, etc.). The end of the sentence should generally be the feeling that is felt. You should not use the word "you" unless you say something like "that must make you feel" or "that must have made you feel."

Examples of validating statements:

- That must have made you feel really angry.
- What a frustrating situation to be in!
- It must make you feel angry to have someone do that.
- That's so difficult for you.
- Wow, how hard that must be.
- That's stinks!
- That's messed up! (or stronger language if you are so inclined)
- How frustrating!
- Yeah, I can see how that might make you feel really sad.
- Boy, you must be angry.
- What a horrible feeling.
- What a tough spot.
- That must be really discouraging.
- I bet you feel disappointed.
- Rats, I know how much that meant to you.
- That's so painful for you.
- Tell me more. (shows interest)
- Wow, she must have made you really angry.

And, of course, many, many more. If you want a validating statement to feel "true" make it about the truth of the situation for the other person. That truth is the way they feel about the event.

When you make a validating statement you should not:

- Make it about you. "I hated it when that happened to me."
- Try to one-up the person. "Oh, you think you have it bad..."
- Tell them how they should feel. "You should feel blessed..."
- Try to give them advice. "What you really should do is..."
- Try to solve their problem. "I'm going to call that girl's parents and..."

- Cheerlead (there is a time for this, but not now). "I know you can do it…"
- Make "life" statements. "Well, life's not fair…"
- Make judgmental statements. "What you did was wrong…"
- Make "revisionist" statements. "If you had only…"
- Make it about your feelings. "How do you think that makes me feel?"
- Make "character" statements. "You're too sensitive…"
- Rationalize another person's behavior. "I bet they were just…"
- Call names. "You're such a baby."
- Use reason or the "facts." "That's not what happened…"
- Use "always" or "never" statements. "You always get yourself into these situations…"
- Compare the person to someone else. "Why can't you be like your sister?"
- Label the person. "You're nuts."
- Advising to cut ties or ignore the situation. "Just ignore him."

Remember, the current problem is not what happened; it is what the BP feels about it. So, the problem that must be addressed is her feelings, not the situation. To address her feelings, you must do so using emotional language, not rational or judgmental language.

Step 4: Making a Normalizing Statement

As crazy or out-of-whack as you might see the BP's feelings to be, she is feeling them just the same. If you were in her shoes and if you had the biological make-up and experiences that she has had, I expect you would feel and behave in a similar way. One of the things that a BP needs to feel is that she is not crazy or broken.

Since shame is such a vital part of BPD, feeling "different," "crazy," "messed up" or "broken" is akin to having to wear a scarlet letter across her chest. She believes that everyone can see through her to her shame and, when she is overcome by strong emotions and acts out on the emotions, she is likely to feel embarrassed by her behavior later. This dynamic fuels more shame. This problem is assuaged by "normalizing" the feelings.

In its most basic form normalization of feelings communicates to the BP that it is perfectly normal and natural to feel the way that she does.

Normalization is chiefly about the feelings, but it can also be about the behaviors that the feelings trigger. What you have to do is relate the feelings or behaviors to "normal" people. This can be done with a group of people, with the BP's own experiences and with yourself. I use this technique often with my son who doesn't have BPD (he's only in kindergarten) but is extremely emotional at times (because he's only in kindergarten). Let's examine some normalization statements and techniques:

Using a "normal" person or group to normalize.

- "Anyone who felt that way would want to do that."
- "I think most everyone feels that way when…"
- "Yes, feeling that way is perfectly natural."
- "Most people would be so angry if that happened."
- "That's so embarrassing." (Implies to everyone)
- "A lot of people react that way."
- "Anyone in that situation would be frustrated."
- "I think it's perfectly normal to feel that way…" (Implies normal people feel that way)

Using the person's own experiences to normalize

- "After all that you've been through, I can see how you would feel that way."
- "Wow, you've experienced so much heartache. No wonder you feel that way…"
- "Boy, and after that person did that before… You must be furious."

Using your own experiences to normalize

- "I think if I felt that way I'd…"
- "I know I'd do the same thing…"
- "I'd feel embarrassed too…"
- "I don't blame you. I'd feel that way too."
- "Boy, that'd make me mad…"
- "I feel so sad too."
- "You know, I felt exactly the same way when…"

- "You know what I used to do when I was your age and felt that way?" [for use with younger children]

Normalization is extremely important because it gets to a place where you can actually help facilitate the BP solving her own problem, which occurs in Step 6 of the validation process. The BP will not be able to generalize problem solving in a "normal" fashion if she thinks she is either the only one on earth who feels this way or that her problems are because she is messed up in the head. Instead, she is likely to give up or, worse, to kill herself. If the problem is not a normal one, it is an unsolvable one, and unsolvable problems lead to more desperate solutions. The nuclear option is suicide.

My wife has told me that suicide is always a solution that lurks in the back of her mind. She thinks, "Well, I can always kill myself and that will stop this pain." Now that we have children, suicide is less of an option for her, she admits, because she had a relative that committed suicide and she saw the long-term detrimental effect on this woman's children.

Since BP's are impulsive, suicidal gestures may appear anyway. These are born in pain, hopelessness (because they don't feel "normal") and impulsiveness. While a greater percentage of BP's kill themselves than the general population (it is estimated that 8-10% of BP's kill themselves, which is about 400 times the rate of the general population), relatively few BP's successfully complete suicide versus the numbers that attempt it (some estimates say 50-75% attempt suicide at least once in their lives).

This is probably due to the impulsive nature of the suicide attempts; these attempts are not planned and utilize whatever is at hand that may not be completely lethal. They might take every pill in the medicine cabinet or cut their wrists with a dull knife. This is the reason that you should never have a gun in the house with a BP, or, if you do, the BP should not have access to it. Self-inflicted gunshot wounds are most often fatal. I will talk more about suicidal gestures in the last section of this book and whether they are a "cry for help," real, or attempts to garner attention from others.

A quick note: The above steps may have to be repeated if more emotions come out or if the BP dwells on the current emotion. The main purpose of the proceeding step is to return the BP to baseline. Only from baseline (and, according to DBT, from "wise mind") can the BP make sound decisions about what to do next.

These steps are not to solve long-term problems or to solve anything at all. They are to get the BP out of the emotionally dysregulated state, to "reel them back in," so to speak. If you do steps 1-4 without the BP returning to baseline, either you haven't completed the steps effectively or the BP is so far into emotional dysregulation that nothing will help, and they will just have to return to baseline naturally.

Unfortunately, the "unrelenting crisis" aspect of BPD sometimes means that they will go from one dysregulated state to the next without returning to baseline. If they do not return to baseline after the above steps are complete and repeated, it might be time for you to apply a boundary of your own and leave the situation. I will talk about effective boundaries in a little while.

Do NOT go on to step 5 until the person with BPD returns to baseline or is close to baseline.

Step 5: Analyze the Consequences (of behavior not feelings)

This step can be taken in conjunction with step 6, depending on whether you are analyzing the consequences of the past behavior (do this first) or the consequences of future behavior (step 6 and then this). Sometimes you will have to go back and forth between these steps.

Analyzing the consequences differs from finding out what the "right" thing is to do. If you try to discover the "right" thing, you are applying your own values and standards to the other person. What is "right" according to your value-set may not be "right" according to hers. This is not to suggest "moral relativism," rather that, given the situation that this other person is in and what their biological and environmental factors are, her choice needs to be based on consequences, not morals or values. Otherwise, the "perceived judgment" card will be played, and the BP might do the exact opposite of what you think is right, just to strike back at her judge.

Consequences can be real or perceived, based on fact or on future feelings, but the consequences analyzed are always those of behaviors. This means that a negative consequence can be a feeling, but this feeling is the result of (or the consequence to) a particular behavior. I'm going to provide two examples of analyzing the consequences, both based on actual events – one based on past behavior, the other based on possible future behavior.

156

One thing you will have to do before you can analyze the consequences with your loved one is to "bridge the gap" between the first part of validation and the second half. You do this by using a "connecting phrase." Connecting phrases can be invalidating as well. Here are some connecting words and phrases and my comment on the level of invalidation each implies:

"But.." This would be used to connect the normalizing statement with the analyzing the consequences step. Unfortunately, the word "but" is probably the most invalidating word that you can use at this point. "But" implies that what you have just said is not really true.

An example: "I think anyone would feel that way if that happened to them, but...", or "I can see how you would want to do that, but..", or "Yes, but...."

My wife's mother was a very "yes, but..." kind of person and that tendency was so invalidating to my wife that she suffers from it to this day. It makes the other person feel like "you're good, but you're really not that good" or "it's OK to feel that way, but it's really not OK to feel that way." Don't use "but" as a connecting phrase.

"However..." This is also used to as a connecting phrase, and it is less invalidating than "but." It does have some level of invalidation implied, but not as much as "but." When I floated the idea of replacing the word "but" with "however" on an Internet board (not my own) a few years back, at first I got a maelstrom of dismissals. Then, after people tried it, I got heaps of praise over this simple word change.

"On the other hand..." This one is even more effective and less invalidating than "however." It does have a tinge of invalidation in it though.

"Yet..." This one is about the same as "on the other hand."

"And..." This one is less invalidating, but may be difficult to work into the conversation smoothly, especially if you are disagreeing with the BP's proposed actions.

"At the same time..." This one is so far the most effective and least invalidating connecting phrase that I have found. I have noticed that my daughter's therapist uses this one all the time. It reinforces that everything that has happened in the conversation thus far is true, yet pushes the conversation in a new direction. I try to use this one when I can without appearing to be a broken record.

Now, let's return to the conversation with my daughter:

My daughter enters the house looking upset and sheepish. I look at her and gauge her emotional pulse. To me she looks both angry (small mouth with compressed lips) and sad ("tented eye-brows").

(1) ME: Wow, you look upset. Are you angry or sad? (Identify the emotion and show that you recognize something is going on emotionally)

HER: I don't want to talk about it.

(2) ME: What happened? Did something happen at school to make you feel sad? (Ask a validating question, without any judgment or statement of right/wrong or good/bad)

HER: Yeah, that jerk Sarah didn't want to play the same game as I did. She was being so mean. I hate her and her annoying friends.

(3) ME: That must have made you feel pretty angry, huh? (Ignore the "jerk" statement and the "hate" statements, if you speak to those she will feel that you are judging her or admonishing her for her feelings. She will exit the conversation and no longer share emotional statements. This conversation is about getting over the current emotional moment, not about teaching her your values or about scolding her for her language. There will be time for that later. Instead, make a validating statement about her emotions).

HER: Yeah?! I can't stand when she acts that way! I ran over to her at recess and hit her with my book bag!

ME: Wow, she must have made you really angry.

HER: Yeah, no joke! She totally pissed me off.

ME: Yeah, I can see she did. I think if my friends wouldn't play a game that I wanted to play that would make me frustrated and annoyed with them as well. At the same time, hitting your friend doesn't really get you closer to your goal, you know?

158

HER: But I was angry!

ME: I can see that you were angry and understandably so and when you're angry you feel like hitting - everybody does. If you hit your friends though, they will be afraid of you and you will have fewer friends. I don't think that is what you want, right? You seem to want to have closer friends. Hitting them will push them away. And if you push them away, that will make you feel sad...

HER: I guess so...

First, you can see that I used the validating statements and normalizing steps multiple times with her during the conversation. You can also see that I did most of the talking in this section of the conversation. With children, sometimes it is necessary for you to do the talking; it is less necessary with adults as you will see later.

You might also notice I didn't say "I love you" or "I support you." I didn't say either of those things because both of those statements are about me and my feelings for her. That makes the conversation about me instead of about her feelings about what happened. This is a common misperception of what validation of another's feelings is all about.

By listening to her feelings and identifying and normalizing them I have communicated to her: I am listening and hearing how you feel. That alone communicates that her feelings matter and that I care about them.

I used several devices to help examine the consequences. One is whether the behavior gets her closer to her "goal." This is a powerful device that you can use to get the BP back on the track of critical thinking. I point out that my daughter's goal is to have closer friends (which is exactly correct, since BP's put a lot of weight in relationships and fear losing them) and that her behavior, while natural and understandable, is ineffective and counter-productive to reaching that goal.

Secondly, you will notice that I don't say that hitting her friend with a book bag is wrong and unacceptable behavior, even though it will get her into trouble with the school (I could have said that as a negative consequence, but I'd rather focus on how these consequences are out-of-line with her goals.)

While it may be true that she broke a school rule and that hitting other people is against our family values, this statement will be taken as judgmental and shame-producing and will be resented. She would shut down the conversation and not hear the most important parts. That is how "analyzing the consequences" differs so much from "extolling your values" or "punishing improper behavior." (I will talk more about improper behavior and how to deal with it later in this chapter.)

Finally, I used her future possible feelings – that she would feel sad if her friend didn't want to be friends anymore – to help her weigh the consequences of her actions. See, when in the moment, a person who is emotionally dysregulated (as my daughter was when she hit the girl with her book bag) will act impulsively and "naturally" to get rid of the negative emotions. The negative emotions are painful and disturbing and someone with BPD feels them with more intensity than you and I do. They act without thinking.

I think that this explains many of the "crazy" behaviors of a person with BPD. She is just trying to get out of the painful emotional state. She is not considering the consequences or whether her actions are right or wrong. She is not considering the rules that you or others have laid down for her to follow. She lets her emotions run away with her.

By using her future possible feelings as a consequence, I am laying down the framework for her to consider thinking about feeling sad in the future. So, rather than saying "the school will punish you" (which will be ignored in the future if she is dysregulated), she is more likely to consider the consequences, especially if these consequences are emotional (her feeling sad) and personal (her losing friends).

The second example of analyzing the consequences is with my wife. She's an adult and can more easily see the consequences of her actions, but she might not care about them when she is emotionally dysregulated. This example involves self-injury.

I get a call at work. It is my wife.

ME: Hello?

HER: Hi.

ME: Wow, you sound so sad! What happened?

HER: Oh, nothing... I'm just really depressed about everything.

ME: That feels awful.

HER: Yeah, it does. And I'm anxious. For the first time in a long time I really want to cut.

ME: Well, I can see why you might want to cut yourself. I never realized until recently how it can help reduce your pain. I think anyone with the pain you feel might want to do that.

HER: Yeah.

ME: At the same time cutting has some negative consequences.

HER: Like what?

ME: Well, there's scarring and possible infection.

HER: I've already got scars.

ME: And there's the treatment of the hospital staff if you have to go. You know how awful they can be to someone who has hurt themselves.

HER: I never cut deeply enough to go to the hospital.

ME: Well, maybe not... still, if others see the marks, you will feel really embarrassed and who knows what they will think of you.

HER: Yeah, you're right about that.

OK, in this case I came right out and said the word consequences because I know my wife can understand it. As you can see, I didn't judge her desire to self-injure as "wrong" or "bad." No matter what your opinion of self-injury, even if you think the practice is repellant, if you judge it, you are sure to spur on more shame. Here is a clip from an Internet site regarding self-injurious behavior and your reaction to it:

Ultimatums do NOT work. Ever.

Loving someone who injures him/herself is an exercise in knowing your limitations. No matter how much you care about someone, you cannot force them to behave as you'd prefer them to. In nearly two years of running the "Bodies Under Siege" mailing list, I have yet to hear of a single case in which an ultimatum worked. Sometimes self-injury is suppressed for a while, but when it inevitably resurfaces it's often more destructive and intense than it had been before. Sometimes the behavior is just driven underground. One person I know responded to periodic strip searches by simply finding more and more hidden places to cut. Confiscating tools used for self-injury is worse than useless -- it just encourages the person to be creative in finding implements. People have managed to cut themselves with plastic eating utensils.

Punishments just feed the cycle of self-hatred and unpleasantness that leads to self-injury. Guilt-tripping does the same. Both of these are incredibly common and both make things infinitely worse. The major fallacy here is in believing that self-injury is about you; it almost invariably isn't (except in the most casual ways).

Accept your limitations. [39]

In fact, I noted that it can be effective for self-soothing – which is true. It is effective for self-soothing of emotional pain, but it has significant negative consequences which I enumerate to my wife in this conversation. I actually went down the road of counting out some of the downsides to cutting in a specific way.

The first statement (about scars and infection) is the most practical of the consequences and the least likely to sway her opinion. I used it first because she is still dysregulated at that point, and she would be unlikely to "think through it" anyway.

The second consequence (of the treatment of the hospital staff) is also true, and it plays on her anger about other people not treating her well. BP's don't like to go to the hospital after self-injury because it induces more shame (about people knowing about their cutting) and anger (about being treated with less compassion than the other patients there). My wife's counter to that argument is a way to avoid going to the hospital and face that shame and anger.

The final consequence (about others seeing the marks) is the most compelling in this case. Why? Because it plays on her future feelings. She

[39] Quoted from http://www.palace.net/~llama/psych/injury.html

162

wants to avoid feeling shame at almost all costs. I know that the shame is there and I also know that she would feel additional shame if others (other than me and her therapist) were to know that she cuts herself. So, like my daughter's possible sadness over losing friends, this consequence is both future-looking and based on emotions.

Emotional consequences are the most relevant to the BP, and avoidance of future negative emotional states the most convincing.

Step 6: Don't Solve the Problem (not giving advice)

Now that the emotions have been identified and validated and consequences have been analyzed, it is time for the "redirecting the choice" phase. You shouldn't provide a solution. You should instead empower the BP to solve the problem.

Keep in mind that most of the time no practical problem will be solved, even in this phase, because the "real" issue to the BP is that she feels bad.

Once the emotional validation steps (steps 1-4) are complete, she is likely to return to baseline and not feel bad anymore. In her eyes, the problem is solved. In your eyes the problem has not been solved because there is still a question of her inappropriate behavior and the possibility of future inappropriate behavior that can put both you and her at risk. Step six is the "teaching time" (sort of).

A person in emotional crisis cannot be told what to do and you can't solve her problems. I know that you love her and you would love to solve her problems, but, if you remember my "attitudes" in the previous chapter, one is that you can't solve another person's emotional problems – you can only solve your own. The same is true for the BP.

She must solve her own problems; that is the only way that the solution will hold. Professional help, mental health workers, therapists, social workers, friends and family members can help facilitate change, but the ultimate solution has to come from the person with the problem. Step six is not actually a "teaching time" – it is a time for you to facilitate the BP in solving her own problems.

As I said above, most of the time nothing will get solved, because once the emotional crisis is complete (and emotions are fast-acting – albeit intense) the crisis is complete in the mind of the BP. She may even go on as if nothing has happened, which can be particularly disturbing and "Jekyll-and-Hyde-like" for you.

If the BP has raged at you and called you names and then, as if by magic, she is suddenly fine and dandy and acts as if nothing has happened to hurt your feelings, it is likely that the emotions have passed. Forgetting about it is natural for her, although it can be quite unsettling for you. I've had situations in which my wife was loving and amorous one minute, angry to the point of throwing things the next and back to loving a few minutes later – such is the nature of swinging emotional states.

Still, the point of step six is to try to influence future behavior and to try to have the BP make more effective choices the next time she feels angry or sad or whatever. When she behaves inappropriately it is in response to the intense emotions that she feels. She will either do what is natural (such as attack when angry) or do what she has learned to do to adapt to the painful emotional tides.

A behavior can be natural for the BP even if the behavior is inappropriate for a given situation. My daughter's hitting the other girl with her book bag was natural in that it was an outlet for her anger; the entire point of the interaction in my daughter's mind was to get rid of her anger. The attacking behavior was the catharsis of the emotion.

Yet, the behavior was inappropriate for the situation. As I have said, the main "goal" in the mind of an emotionally dysregulated person is to self-soothe and release the negative emotion. She will not consider the consequences naturally, which is why we analyzed them in the last step.

What we are doing now is trying to have the BP come up with a more effective solution for self-soothing. I can't reiterate enough that a solution might not come immediately. That's OK, because the solution must be arrived at in little steps.

The problem you are trying to get them to solve is essentially, "What can you do to make yourself feel better when you feel so angry (or sad or anxious or whatever) that has less negative consequences?" In the case of my daughter, I am trying to get her to think twice before hitting her friend. In the case of my wife, I am trying to delay her desire to cut and, with delay, her desire might subside.

This part of the conversation is about asking the BP what she thinks can be done in the future that is more effective than what she has done in the past. Returning to the end of the conversation with my daughter:

ME: Wow, she must have made you really angry.

HER: Yeah, no joke! She totally pissed me off.

ME: Yeah, I can see she did. I think if my friends wouldn't play a game that I wanted to play that would make me frustrated and annoyed with them as well. At the same time, hitting your friend doesn't really get you closer to you goal, you know?

HER: But I was angry!

ME: I can see that you were angry and understandably so and when you're angry you feel like hitting- everybody does. If you hit your friends though, they will be afraid of you and you will have fewer friends. I don't think that is what you want, right? You seem to want to have closer friends. Hitting them will push them away. And if you push them away, that will make you feel sad...

HER: I guess so...

ME: What else do you think you can do to help you feel less angry? Something that will not make you lose your friend?

HER: I could yell at her... and force her to play the game.

ME: Yes, you could do that. However, that might still make her feel angry at you or scared of you... Is there anything else you can think of?

HER: I could ignore her.

ME: You could... yet you might still feel angry... Do you think you'd still feel angry if you ignored her?

HER: Yeah, probably. I guess I could go and play with someone else.

ME: Do you think that would work?

HER: I think so.

ME: Ok, well the next time you're angry with a friend at school why don't you try that and see if it works?

HER: OK, I will.

Now we have gotten to the end of the conversation. I asked a series of questions that put the onus on her to come up with an answer for herself. A person with BPD is a human being and can figure out things for herself. She just has to be out of the emotionally dysregulated state in order to make wise decisions. You can't tell her what to do or solve her problems for her. You will also notice I didn't say any of her solutions were "bad" – I only analyzed the consequences of the first one and asked if the second one would work. This approach is non-judgmental.

What I did was ask her for a solution to facilitate her solving the problem. I also "redirected" the solution until she came up with one that was more effective than the first two. If you continue to ask for solutions, at some point the person will come up with a solution that is more effective than her previous behavior. It takes practice.

Don't worry if the first few attempts at such a conversation go awry. Like any other skill you must do it over and over until it can be done without thought, as if by habit. At first it might seem clunky and faked. Everyone who tries a new skill experiences this feeling. You might also feel that it is forced and patronizing. Once you have grown accustomed to speaking to an emotional person in this way, it will become more natural and more effective with the person. It is not a "magic trick" or "Jedi mind-trick;" it is merely the most effective way to communicate with someone who is emotional.

My wife has learned some of these techniques and has used them with our children and with other people. They work whether or not the person is emotionally dysregulated. My wife recently used the techniques on a bill collector who had called us. We were going through some tough financial times, and she decided to validate HIS emotions by saying something like: "I know we are late on this bill. It must be frustrating for you to call people all day and ask for money…" He immediately became friendlier and less threatening.

It left a bad taste in my wife's mouth because she felt she had used a "trick" on the guy. It wasn't that she didn't want to use the "trick" that made her angry about the situation; it was that what she really wanted to do was say, "What kind of jerk you must be to have this job? Do you enjoy being an asshole all day?" Of course, if she had said that he would have felt judged and insulted and likely gotten more threatening. So, being effective is difficult, especially when you feel compelled to be judgmental and express how you "really" feel.

Some examples of validating and facilitating questions are:

- Do you think that will work?
- I never thought of that, maybe you could try it?
- Why don't you try it and see?
- What do you think will work?
- What do you think you can do?
- Is there anything you can do?
- Is there anything else you can think of?
- What would you like to do?
- What do you want to do?
- How do you think you'll feel if you do that?
- Are there other things that you can think of?
- What do you think might work?
- What do you think about that?
- How do you feel about that?

Levels of Validation

Validation can be done on several levels. I mentioned many of the levels in the proceeding text without noting them as separate levels. Now I will outline these levels and you can pick-and-choose what you think might be most appropriate for any given situation. Also, if one level doesn't work, you can always try another.

Level 1: Show an interest in the person's situation.

Showing interesting in a person's situation and not thinking "Oh no, here we go again." Look directly at the person. Maintain eye contact. Listen and respond accordingly. Ask prompting questions like "What happened?" and "What happened next?" Responding with "Uh-huh" and

"Tell me more" also helps to indicate that you are interested and listening to the other person's issue.

Level 2: Reflect back the person's emotions

Reflect back what the person said so that she can be sure you heard her: "You are frustrated because your boyfriend won't go to the dance with you. Right?"

Summarize the situation and focus on the feelings. Use feeling words like "sounds like" or "it seems like." You don't have to agree with the assessment.

For example, my wife will say, "Everyone in town hates me." And I can respond with, "Sounds like you're feeling that everyone hates you." I'm not agreeing with her assessment, just reflecting back what I hear her say and putting it in the context of feelings.

Level 3: Try to "read" another person's desires and feelings

This is similar to the "identifying the feelings" step described above, except you can also extend it to wishes and desires. You can say, "I sense that you want me to take you to the mall." If the person is asking for some need (emotional or physical) you can identify that request in this way. This also should be non-judgmental. Don't resort to, "but I'm not taking you to the mall because you haven't behaved well lately." You can deny their request, depending on your feelings; however, you should do so in a validating way.

Level 4: Validate her feelings based on past experiences

I spoke extensively above about how to validate her feelings. However, using past experiences can make it even more effective. "Since that person is like your abusive father, I can see why you are frightened of him" or "Since you were in a terrible car accident, I can understand how you would be afraid to drive."

Using what you know about her can strengthen the statement. This level of validation can also be done in a positive way. You can say, "I remember when you were in this situation last year. You did a great job of getting through it then."

Level 5: Normalize

I also explained normalization. While normalizing, communicate that the person's feelings and behaviors are "reasonable, normal, effective or meaningful." You can say, "I think it is quite normal to be nervous before a blind date," or "Everyone gets angry when someone calls them names."

Level 6: Treat the other person with respect and don't be condescending or judgmental

Respect the other person. Listen and respond with your feelings. Know that the other person is a person with strengths and weaknesses. Believe that the other person deserves respect. Have hope that the other person will be able to get through the crisis.

Advanced Validation

After you have practiced the basic validation techniques that I presented above, you may come to notice that your BP begins to "catch on" to these techniques and finds them "patronizing," less than sincere, or "a trick."

What I suggest is that you use the levels of validation to create new validating phrases that respect the truth of the situation and still validate the BP's feelings. You will have to experiment with different approaches to validation. I can't tell you exactly what to say in any given situation; however, if you master the basic validation techniques, I suspect you will feel comfortable enough with the process of validation that you can come up with validating phrases and questions that suit the situation and don't come off as "pat responses."

The most important note about validation is that it has to be done with some level of truth behind it. Putting yourself in the shoes of the other person can help you understand the truth as she sees it. If validation is done with truth and honesty, it is almost always effective. If it is done as a rote response to the other person's dysregulation, it will not ring true and most likely be dismissed as forced or fake by the other person.

Remember, people with BPD are extremely sensitive people and their lie detectors are quite well honed. They can sense a lie from you very adeptly and if you try to accomplish validation without believing the truth in your statements, it might not be effective. The essential point here is that you have to find the grain of truth in the other person's statement and emotion.

Even if the reaction seems completely out-of-whack with what you are feeling, finding that grain of truth and responding honestly and in a validating way toward it can make the difference between effective validation and ineffective validation.

Unlike the last edition of this book, I have decided in this edition to include some Advanced Tools for a relationship.

You can use these advanced tools when you have mastered the basic tools. Some of the advanced tools touch on validation. I would implore you to make sure you have become familiar with and have practiced the basic tools before attempting to implement the advanced ones in your relationship.

I-AM-MAD: a summary of Validation

When the school year started a year into my daughter's DBT therapy, I got a call from my daughter's social worker. She was worried that my daughter had gotten extremely angry about having to retake a math test.

My daughter had not done well and made numerous careless errors. The social worker was confused and concerned that my daughter's reaction to the work was out-of-proportion with the task at hand. The social worker called my wife, and my wife and I discussed it on the phone. This occurred about six weeks into the school year.

I knew immediately what was going on. My daughter had a moment of emotional dysregulation while with the social worker. The trigger for the emotional dysregulation was probably her shame for not being good at math and that translated to her believing that she would never be able to be a good student (or a good person, since that is the nature of shame).

She then got angry about having to redo something that she would never be good at. I'm sure her frustration level was very high at the time. That's the "bad news" part of the story. The "good news" part is that this event occurred six weeks into the school year. Two years before, my daughter experienced moments of emotional dysregulation at school almost every day.

170

My wife asked me to craft an email to the social worker explaining what we have done with our daughter and how much she has improved. She also asked me to lay out the skill of emotional validation, essentially as I have in this book. I didn't want to cut-and-paste portions of this book for her; I mean, after all, I spent many pages on validation and problem resolution here.

What I did instead was write a one-page summary of the emotional validation technique that I describe in this book. After I sent it to the social worker via email, I posted a sanitized version of the email to my Internet list.

One of my wonderful members reformatted my email into an easy-to-remember "tool" called the "I-AM-MAD Communication Tool." Now that you have gotten this far through the validation tool, you're ready to understand the summary in this form:

I-AM-MAD

1. Identify the emotions.

It's best to do this with "feeling" words, like "look", "see", or "sound", rather than "know" or "understand".

Examples:

- "I see that you are frustrated."
- "You sound aggravated."
- "You look really upset."

2. Ask a validating question.

This encourages them to share their feelings about whatever triggered them. Do not use "what's wrong?" If you use "what's wrong?" they will hear "what's wrong with YOU?" Also, don't assume you did anything wrong. Remember, IAAHF (It's All About His/Her Feelings).

Examples:

- "What happened?" (most effective because it is open-ended, requires more than yes/no answer)

- "Did something go wrong at work [school] today?"
- "Want to talk about it?"

3. Make a validating statement about their emotion.

Validate the feelings expressed in step 2. This helps reinforce that it is natural and valid to feel what they are feeling in the situation. Again, remember: "It's all about her emotions."

Don't defend against blaming or projecting. And don't apologize at this point, even if you are guilty. (Apologies for things you are actually guilty of can come later... after they have returned to their emotional baseline.)

Examples:

- "Wow, it must have made you feel awful to have done poorly on that test."
- "You worked so hard on that. It's got to be disappointing when the teacher gives you a poor grade."
- "Yes, it is frustrating when it seems that someone is taking advantage of you."
- "Yeah, that's really disappointing."

4. Make a normalizing statement about their emotion.

By relating the situation as common to all people or "normal" for them, this helps alleviate their stress about feeling judged or unaccepted.

Examples:

- "I think anyone would feel angry if they had to do that"
- "I would feel the same way if that happened to me."
- "I can see why you feel that way."

5. Analyze the consequences of their behavior.

By analyzing the consequences of both negative and positive behavior with the person, you help them to separate their emotional reaction from their behavior. The behavior may need to be changed, but the emotions are natural and should not be punished for.

Examples:

- "When you don't ask questions about something that confuses you, I don't realize that you are struggling, so I can't help you. When you do ask questions though, I can either give you the information you need to solve the problem yourself or we can work together to figure out the best solution to the problem."
- "When you yell at me, I feel disrespected and become upset too. However, when you speak calmly to me, I know you have respect for me, so I am able to listen to you better."
- "When you refuse to talk to me, I don't know what else to do except give you space. When something is bothering you, it's best to be open and honest with me so I know what's going on and don't make the wrong assumptions about what you need."

6. Don't solve the problem for them.

Solving one's own problems helps to build self-confidence. Empower the person by getting them to come up with a solution themselves. When given the opportunity in a non-judgmental setting, most people will find that they can come up with solutions to their problems. You can guide them through this process by asking helpful questions to ascertain what they need or want.

Examples:

- "How would you like to handle this?"
- "What would help you make a better choice next time?"
- "Is there anything I can do to help?"

(Note: Sometimes you have to go back and forth to help them find the most effective solution. They may say, "I don't know" or "I don't care." This can be tough. Go back to step one to deal with any additional emotions that become apparent.)

Validation for Beginners

Validation is probably the most important tool in the tool set that I provide. Emotional invalidation can reinforce shame and make the person with BPD behave in a more erratic fashion. It has even been suggested by some researchers that invalidation can lead to mental illness, self-injury and anxiety. Dr. Thomas Lynch writes this about invalidation:

...a history of emotion invalidation (i.e., a history of childhood psychological abuse and parental punishment, minimization, and distress in response to negative emotion) was significantly associated with emotion inhibition (i.e., ambivalence over emotional expression, thought suppression, and avoidant stress responses). Further, emotion inhibition significantly predicted psychological distress, including depression and anxiety symptoms.) [40]

You can see that the dangers of emotional invalidation are great, which makes the tool of validation hold even more importance. Unfortunately, validation is a difficult tool to master, especially in the complex, multi-step form that I have presented here.

One of the main reasons that it is so hard to start being validating is that most of us are taught to be invalidating. We're taught that the world is a difficult place, that you shouldn't get too emotional about things, and that life is not fair. Often, we're told to "suck it up" or "get over it" or told to "cut it out."

I know that before I discovered the power of validation, I said some of the same things to my emotional daughter. I have heard my wife's relatives say similar things to her when she is emotional about an event.

The habit of invalidation is difficult to break. Invalidating responses can often become conditioned, just like the conditioned behavior of which I wrote before. Breaking that conditioning requires reconditioning and then validation can become a habit.

Like I said, validation is an extremely difficult tool to start using. Sometimes it seems that people don't know where to start when it comes to validation. When I get "newbies" (new members) on my Internet list, they frequently state that using this tool is quite difficult, and, after writing the first edition of this book, I thought it would be vital to indicate how one can start with the tool. With the help of several of my list members, I came up with a "validation for beginners" tool.

---

[40] *Treatment of Borderline Personality Disorder Using Dialectical Behavior Therapy,* Thomas Lynch, Ph.D. and Clive Robins, Ph.D., The Journal, March 1, 1997, Vol. 8/Iss. 1

Before I go over what is involved in the tool, I want to list the steps in my full validation tool again with a comment on how difficult each step is:

Step 1: Identify the Emotions. This step can be quite difficult and awkward at first. You probably haven't been doing this with your loved one and many Non-BP's find this step challenging. Sometimes even the BP's can find this step invalidating if it is done in a judgmental fashion. (i.e. "You're angry again?!").

Step 2: Ask a validating question. This step can be easy. Practice asking "What happened?", but not "What's wrong?" or "What happened this time?"

Step 3: Make a validating statement. This step is moderately hard. It can be much harder if you're a "fixer" and you want to give advice right away. Resist the temptation to fix the problem or give advice. Advice is not validating.

Step 4: Make a normalizing statement. This step can be quite hard, because often it is not done with honesty. You might end up thinking, "normal people wouldn't react this way" which makes it hard to normalize.

Step 5: Analyze the consequences. This step is next to impossible at first. Some amount of validation and trust is required before this is possible. Many times, at the beginning, this step feels like advice or judgment. If you say, "you shouldn't do that," you are being judgmental.

Step 6: Don't solve the problem. Again, this step can be very difficult, especially when you're dealing with a child or teenager. Parents sometimes feel compelled to solve their children's problems or "lay down the law".

OK, on to validation for beginners. Since some members of my list found the full technique difficult to utilize at first, I have decided to break it up and let you know what to do at the beginning.

When you start validating, the first thing you have to do is identify the invalidation that you have been, unknowingly, doing thus far. Listen carefully to what you say to others. If you have to, write down what your responses were (or going to be) when a loved one comes with an emotional issue. Compare those responses with the invalidating phrases list and look at it from your loved one's perspective. You have to eliminate invalidation before starting to validate.

Next, start with step one (Identify the Feelings) just to yourself. If you feel uncomfortable saying the emotions out loud at first, keep the identifications to yourself. Then compare those internal identifications with your loved one's behavior and words. It is important to listen to the emotion, but, initially, you don't have to say what you think the emotion is until you gain a more complete emotional lexicon.

When you feel more comfortable that you can make an accurate assessment of the person's feelings, start verbalizing using "general" emotion words such as "upset" or "stressed".

Step two is important and it is pretty easy to do. Like I said about, practice asking open-ended validating questions, such as "What happened?" or "Did something upset you at work/school today?"

Step three is difficult at first, but I think it is helpful to do even in the beginning.

Wait to start using step four until you've gotten a better handle over steps 2 and 3. Once you're able to effectively articulate a validating statement, you're ready for step 4.

Steps 5 and 6 need to wait until you get a handle on steps one through four. Even though there's a tinge of "enabling" in using only the first few steps of the validation process, you have to walk before you can run. So, in summary, validation for beginners is this:

- Remove invalidating phrases.
- Don't make it about YOUR feelings.
- Ask on open-ended validating question: "What happened?"
- Make a generic validating statement: "That's stinks" or "That's must have made you feel pretty bad."
- Listen and let your loved one talk.

You can start using the rest of the steps little-by-little until you've mastered the tool completely. It takes time, practice and effort — at least it does for now.

176

An Exercise in Validation

I sometimes like to assign homework assignments for my list members. I don't do it very often, but I think it's easy to learn from one another's experience if you are all having a very similar experience. One of the exercises we worked on last year was one to help us learn the benefits of validating another person.

My suggestion to the group was to make a validating statement to someone with whom you have a temporary interaction. This person could be a server at a restaurant, a clerk at the grocery store or an acquaintance at work.

Here is an example conversation that I had with a co-worker who I knew by sight, but with whom had never really had a conversation. Before I provide the text of the conversation, I have to provide a bit of background.

This woman had attended a company conference a couple of months before. After her plane landed, she met a driver that was to take her to the hotel. He asked her to wait by the curb while he picked up the car and then picked her up. After he was gone for a time period, she found out that he had returned to the car, got into the driver's seat and had a heart attack and died.

I had heard the story from a mutual acquaintance and knew that this woman had this particular experience. I spoke to her in the elevator on the way up to our common floor.

ME: Hi, aren't you the one who had your driver die at the conference?

HER: Yes, that was me.

ME: I heard about it from [our shared acquaintance] Wow, what a disturbing experience that must have been for you!

HER: Yeah, really. It was.

ME: It really must have been. I mean, how scary for you. What if he had died with you in the backseat? You could have been killed!

HER: Yes, I know. You're totally right. It was pretty scary.

177

ME: I bet. I think anyone would find that experience frightening.

HER: I guess so. Thanks.

OK, as you can see in this brief conversation, I made several validating statements. The main point is that I focused on her feelings about the experience, not about his death. While the driver's death was tragic in itself, she wanted to hear that it is OK for her to feel frightened and disturbed by it. I validated her feelings effectively. The result of that conversation was that she and I are close friends now.

I would suggest that you select someone who has been or is going through an emotional experience, even if it is just a frustrating one, and practice making one or more validating statements to him or her. See what happens. Experiment. Don't solve the problems, just focus on the emotion that the other person must have felt or is feeling.

A server in a busy restaurant is a good person to use. I once used validation with a used car dealer who was intending to buy one of my cars. I said, "It must be pretty annoying to have people come in here and haggle with you all day long." He responded, "You have no idea!" He then proceeded to give me an additional $1,000 for my car. While you could argue that I manipulated him, I just made him feel that his emotional frustration was noticed and that alone can make someone feel good.

The Fourth Tool: Boundaries

Now you may ask, "Why are boundaries included in both the 'what doesn't work' section and the 'tools' section?" Well, the reason that I have included the idea of boundaries in both is that most people don't understand what effective boundaries actually are. If you do understand boundaries, they can be an effective tool in dealing with someone with BPD.

Boundaries are for you and what you do when someone has behaved in a way that is inappropriate. Boundaries are not for the other person. Many books, texts and Internet resources say that boundaries are what you impose on the BP, but that is not the case.

Those impositions are rules and, with respect to BPD, rules are made to be broken. Some respected sources call these types of "boundaries" ether "limits" or "communicated expectations." Whatever they are called, in my experience, boundaries like this are not effective.

Many books encourage you to "strengthen your boundaries" and become less "co-dependent" with your loved ones. What they are really suggesting is creating rules for other people and those rules, whatever they are called, usually don't continue to be effective when someone is emotionally dysregulated. They may work at first, but they will "wear off" with time.

When someone has BPD, one of the lingering questions in their mind is "Will you still love me if…" The reason can again be linked back to the shame. She often feels worthless and unlovable. She might behave in a way that is decidedly unlovable just to reinforce that "he will love me even if…"

If you demonstrate that you can love her as she is, even if her behavior is erratic, then you have passed the test. I'm not saying that any of that is done with malice – actually the situation is quite sad and comes from a feeling of worthlessness.

In the book *I Don't Have to Make Everything All Better*, Gary and Joy Lundberg write that there are three emotional needs in life. They call these needs together "the universal need":

The Universal Need

Every person needs to feel that
I am of worth,
My feelings matter,
And
Someone really cares about me [41]

I agree that those needs are universal and human. They are emotional needs.

In the case of BPD each of those needs can get distorted. Shame causes the person with BPD to feel worthless (need #1). Invalidation can cause the person to feel their feelings don't matter (need #2). Relationship

[41] Lundberg, Gary and Joy, *I Don't Have to Make Everything All Better*, page 14

conflict can make the person feel that no one really cares about them (need #3).

Compare these needs to the BPD "schemas" (or basic beliefs) that Beck and Freedman found when researching BPD. These are:

The world is dangerous and malevolent.
I am powerless and vulnerable.
I am inherently unacceptable. [42]

I bring this up here because I believe that it is relevant to explaining why a person with BPD will desperately and annoyingly violate rules that are set down for her. It might appear to you that she has no personal boundaries of her own and that she consistently violates what appear to be her values. She does this in a frantic attempt to get those three needs met when she feels the needs are not being met and in contrast with the schemas that she believes about herself.

Boundaries come into play when a line is being stepped over. Boundaries are about what you will and will not do should certain situations arise. You make boundaries for yourself and you abide by them for yourself. Earlier in this book I related a member of my group's take on boundaries and I believe it is worth re-telling:

"In essence, boundaries are what you do with YOURSELF — AFTER the line's been crossed. And eventually, they become what you do to put yourself in a position so the line CAN'T be crossed. They really have nothing to do with the "perpetrator.""

If that's confusing, think of it this way:

1. The law says: Don't go over 55 mph. (That's a rule, not a boundary.)
2. A speeder goes 85 mph. (That's breaking a rule, not breaking a boundary.)
3. You're a passenger in a car while the speeder is driving. (You're in a dangerous situation. Boundaries still aren't a factor.)
4. You tell the driver they should slow down. (That's a plea, not a boundary.)

[42] Beck, AT and Freedman, A, et al. *Cognitive Therapy of Personality Disorders*, 1990, general concept.

5. They don't, so you yell at them that they should. (That's still a plea.)
6. You tell them if they don't slow down, that they'll get a ticket. (That's a threat of consequences, not enforcing a boundary.)
7. Next time they ask you to ride with them, you don't. (THAT'S a boundary.)

See, the thing is — Boundaries can't be enforced, because they're not rules. You either do them, or you don't.

The idea even works in the traffic parallel. What's a boundary on a road? A concrete divider. Cars CAN'T go over that. On the other hand, yellow lines are just rules that say "Don't drive over this." So they have to be enforced.

So, how can you tell a rule from a boundary? If you have to enforce it, it's not a boundary."

- an ATSTP member on boundaries

So, in this example, the boundary is your choice not to accept rides from this person anymore.

I have created a personal boundary with my wife. She has a tendency to over-medicate on prescription anti-anxiety drugs. Many BP's over-medicate, and I explain more on this in the Frequently Asked Questions chapter in the back of this book. It's difficult for me to cover every situation involved in BPD in this book, but I try to cover the most pressing in the FAQ section.

Back to my boundary – I have created a boundary for myself that I refuse to go out of the house if she has over-medicated. I used to go with her places when she was in that state, but now I have decided to no longer do so. The last time she over-medicated and wanted to go out and do something (have dinner I believe), I told her flat-out, "I will not go anywhere when you are in this state." Of course, that made her angry and she stormed out of the house anyway. I couldn't stop her from doing so – she is an adult and makes adult choices.

She may have to suffer consequences (including legal ones) if she does that, but I can't stop her with rules. I can try to convince her to make a more effective decision with the tools in this book, but in this case it was not possible. The point I am driving at is that the boundary is for me and it is followed by me. I chose not to go and there was no level of convincing that she could do to make me cross my own boundary.

I should also note what my wife's reaction was to me "enforcing" my own boundary: rage. I think that you need to expect a strong emotional reaction from your BP when you create and use a boundary for yourself.

Many people think that boundaries will help calm the waters in a relationship with someone with BPD. This is usually not the case.

In my case, the boundary was about what I would and would not be comfortable with, and I used the boundary to avoid something I would not want to engage in (going to dinner with my over-medicated wife). I certainly was not comfortable with her rage at me, but I have come to expect that when I use that particular boundary. Basically, I choose to trade one extremely uncomfortable situation (going out with her) with another (getting yelled at), but I cannot do anything about her reaction to my saying "no."

Remember, boundaries are for you. They are what you will and will not do in a given situation. Some can be based on your personal values, others can be based on what you do and do not feel comfortable with.

The Fifth Tool: Don't Dexify

In the first edition of this book, this tool was "Don't Defend." I have changed "Defend" to "Dexify". What the heck is Dexifying?

Dexify is a made-up word that encompasses defending, explaining and justifying. In addition to the idea of defending, the ideas of explaining WHY you did something and justifying your words and behavior to a person with BPD is generally not effective.

When you are being attacked it is natural to defend yourself. This is especially true when the attack has no basis in reality, when the attack is based entirely on the feelings of the BP. I'm sure that you have experienced this kind of attack before. BP's are famous for coming up with "crazy" notions and attributing them to you.

She can ruminate on a situation and gradually work that situation into one in which she believes is threatening to her. The example I gave earlier in the "BPD Dynamic" section is such an example – the wife accuses her husband of having an affair when none actually exists.

Sometimes the attack will have some basis in reality. She may take something small and blow it up into a crisis. She may judge you or blame you for something that has nothing to do with you. She may use what I like to call the "what about you?" tactic – that is when she senses that you are criticizing her behavior (and therefore her feelings), she turns it around into an attack on your behavior.

My wife uses this tactic quite a bit. In order to get the spotlight off of her behavior, she will tell me that I am angry all the time and that the kids are frightened of me. She will dredge up things from the distant past (sometimes fifteen years ago) to defend her current behavior. The "what about you?" tactic is annoying, and it begs to be negated and defended against.

I have learned that it is more effective to not defend against false accusations, paranoid blame and the "what about you?" attacks. This skill is difficult to accomplish because, as I said, it is natural to defend yourself when being attacked. It is also natural to justify your behavior or to explain why the BP has it "wrong" about you.

Rather than defending, explaining or justifying my words or behaviors, I just ignore the attack and focus on the true problems at hand, which are the BP's dysregulated emotions.

This skill will take lots of practice on your part, but once you drop the defensive stance, you should see this area improve. If you don't fight back or reinforce that a particular tactic is "getting to you" the tactic will eventually be dropped, because it becomes an ineffective one for the BP.

If you continue to defend or to attack back – like saying "I'm not the one who…" or "Oh yeah? Well, what about the time you…" – then the cycle of emotional dysregulation goes back and forth, feeding itself, until it is a huge bonfire of anger.

One other related issue is that of apologizing. I generally do not recommend apologizing, especially for events for which you have no responsibility. One of the problems with apologizing is that apologizing puts the spotlight on your involvement in the event and takes the focus away from the BP's feelings. If you apologize for something that you had no hand in (like "I'm sorry that you feel that way") then the conversation is likely to get derailed.

While the BP may want for you to apologize, particularly if she is accusing you of creating a situation in which you caused the negative feelings (like "You always make me feel this way!"), apologizing for things that are not your responsibility can create a difficult dynamic for you.

In the future, you will be more often asked to apologize for conditions that are not your creation or responsibility. One of the goals of these tools is to encourage the BP to be responsible for her own feelings and behaviors that arise from those feelings.

That being said, if the situation is one in which you have contributed to the pain or you have done something yourself that is ineffective, apologizing is fine and warranted. Yet, rather than saying "I'm sorry" I recommend saying "I was wrong, when…" Admitting that you were wrong is much more powerful and candid than saying you're sorry.

In the advanced tools section of this edition, I cover "relationship maintenance," an important part of which is knowing when and how to properly apologize for your own behaviors, words and actions.

That tool is understandably difficult to master and, in some cases, a simple apology will do. I once drank too much and became angry with my wife and argued with her about her feelings. This situation was one in which I behaved in a dysregulated fashion. The next day, I apologized for my actions and explained my behavior using my feelings (anger) as an "excuse." I cover this technique more fully in the "relationship maintenance" section of this book.

The Sixth Tool: Inserting your feelings

You might now be asking (or have asked previously in reading this book), "What about me and my feelings?" Here is where you and your feelings come into play.

People with BPD instinctively understand the language of emotions, so if you insert your own feelings into a conversation with a BP, she is likely to understand what you're going through. The big problem comes in when she believes that you are saying she is to blame for your feelings. Your feelings could very well have been triggered by her behavior; however, it is most effective to present your feelings in a certain fashion. I will describe the steps for presenting your feelings and what to do and say when she responds to them.

Step 1: Say what happened

Tell the BP what happened in your eyes. However, like I said in the non-judgmental section, you should do this by sticking to the observable facts.

Do not insert your judgments of the situation in this part of the conversation. Just say what happened exactly. Say, "I came into the house and found you bleeding from cutting yourself," not "Look at this bloody mess! Are you nuts?"

This is a difficult step to master. Everyone has built-in and learned judgments and reactions to a particular situation. Separating the actual event from the thoughts and feelings that the event evokes takes practice and time.

One thing that can help you master this step is to create a running dialog in your head for a short period of time. Walk down the street and observe everything you see, without judging it. The dialog may go: "I see a blue car... Now I see a big brown building... I hear a car horn... I see a woman with a blue business suit on... Now I see a teenage boy with his pants down around his thighs..."

I put that one in because if you are in my generation (or near it) you probably believe that the current style (where boys wear their pants around their thighs and down past their boxers) is ridiculous and that belief can evoke a judgment. That is, if you say to yourself, "Look at that idiot – how ridiculous he looks!" that is a judgment of the boy's chosen style of dress. While I am likely to make the same judgment in this case, if you just observe what is going on around you, you can sever the relationship between the observation and the judgment.

Step 2: Say how you feel about what you observed

Tell the BP how you feel, simply and without judgment. Don't blame your feeling on the BP or on the behavior of the BP. You can say, "That made me feel scared" but not "you're always trying to scare me." You should always try to use emotional words. The main four emotions are angry, sad, scared and happy. They can come in combination and in sequence. I have also included some shameful words because BP's understand shame and if you feel that way you can use some of those terms. What you will want to do for this step is state, "I felt [emotion word]." Here are some emotion words in categories:

Angry

- Mad
- Furious
- Pissed off
- Annoyed
- Frustrated
- Irritated
- Outraged
- Resentful
- Bitter
- Upset

Sad

- Disappointed
- Displeased
- Dejected
- Glum
- Hurt
- Defeated
- Unhappy
- Depressed
- Lonely
- Miserable
- Isolated

Scared

- Afraid
- Fearful
- Anxious
- Apprehensive
- Edgy

- Uneasy
- Jumpy
- Tense
- Panicked
- Overwhelmed
- Terrified
- Desperate

Happy

- Glad
- Joyful
- Content
- Amused
- Cheerful
- Optimistic
- Satisfied
- Hopeful
- Excited
- Thrilled
- Delighted

Shameful

- Embarrassed
- Guilty
- Ashamed
- Mortified
- Regretful
- Humiliated
- Belittled

So, you can say, "I feel/felt [insert emotion word here]." Make sure that you use an emotion word. Many people tend to say something like, "I felt disrespected" or "I felt like you were trying to control me." Neither of those are emotions. Here are some words and phrases that are typically used that are not emotion words:

Non-emotion Words (do not use)

- Tired
- Worn out
- Exhausted
- Controlled
- Disrespected
- Cheated
- Trapped
- Hated
- Imposed Upon
- Wronged
- Manipulated
- Unappreciated
- Unnoticed
- Mistreated
- Abused

As you can see, except with the first few (e.g. tired), most of these are words that require the presence and action of the other person to exist. Meaning, you can't feel "cheated" without someone "cheating" you. You can't feel "unnoticed" if you didn't expect someone else to "notice" you.

True emotion words are statements about how you feel inside without needing the other person to feel that way. That is, you can feel sad without the other person doing anything. You can feel controlled, but you can't be controlled without another person doing the controlling.

If you use an emotion word and are non-blaming and non-judgmental, you can't be argued with. How can a BP argue with you if you are stating how you felt? Once you have accepted the fact that emotions exist and they are not wrong or right, then stating how you felt is a statement of fact. The BP will not normally say, "You shouldn't have felt that way" (although they might), because that has been subtly said to her throughout her life through emotional invalidation. So, if you state the way you felt simply, there is no argument.

Stay away from "you made me feel…" or "you're just trying to make me feel…" Stay away from "always" and "never" statements – you're talking about a specific event here, the one you described after observing it. That is what is triggering your feelings, so stay on point.

Step 3: Say what you want to happen

188

State what you want to happen specifically and concisely. Don't accuse or call names in this step either. Sometimes, if it is appropriate, use your statement about your feelings as a counter-point to what you'd like to happen. What I mean by this is that if you had said, "That makes me feel scared" you can say in this step, "I would feel much less scared if you…"

Sometimes recognizing the BP's goal in the conversation, which is typically "let me tell you how badly I feel," can help facilitate assent to the requested behavior.

If the person with BPD continues to change the subject or rages or whatever, go through steps 1-3 again. This tool is about YOU and about you being heard by the BP. This is about how to get your needs met. It is a road map for asking for what you want and inserting your feelings.

Step 4: Express gratitude if they choose to do what you want

If the person with BP does what you requested in step 3, you should immediately thank them and back up what you said in steps 2-3. You can say, "Wow, I really appreciate you saying that. That will definitely make me feel less scared."

Example Conversations

Below are two example conversations. Both are real conversations that have been paraphrased by me. The first involves a serious and dangerous situation that occurred with a friend of mine who has a diagnosed BP adopted son. The second involves a situation from one of my Internet board members and, while the situation is real, I have made-up the conversation, supplying what the member could say if he was using this tool.

In the first conversation, we will have to use validation to calm the situation and this tool "inserting your feelings" to get a resolution to the dangerous circumstances.

A Non-BPD father comes home after traveling. He arrives home about 9 PM and his BP nineteen year old son is in the house. When he arrives his son is in the family room downstairs brandishing a kitchen knife and sobbing. His son has been cutting himself with the knife and is clearly upset.

189

FATHER: You look so sad! What happened?

SON: I got fired today.

FATHER: Wow that must have made you feel really sad...

SON: Uh-huh.

FATHER: Yes, I can see how you would be sad about that. Losing a job can be stressful on anyone.

SON: I just want to go away...

FATHER: You feel sad about yourself and embarrassed. I felt the same way when I got fired from my job at your age. It hurts.

SON: Yeah.

[OK, now here is where this tool kicks in]

FATHER: You're holding a knife.

SON: Yeah, so?

FATHER: It makes me frightened when you hold a knife like that.

Son says nothing.

FATHER: I would like for you to put the knife down so that I won't feel so frightened.

SON: I don't want to.

FATHER: I can see you don't want to. However, I don't like feeling this scared. If you put the knife down I will feel less scared and we can talk about how you feel about losing your job.

Son puts down the knife.

FATHER: Thank you. I really appreciate that. I feel much less scared now.

190

The father went through the validation tool briefly and then started inserting his feelings. The son and father have different goals in this conversation. The son's is to talk about how badly he feels about losing his job – that is, he wants to have someone reinforce to him that his feelings matter. There's nothing that can be done about getting fired, although in a later conversation the father can find out what happened to get the son fired and work on that so that his son will make more informed choices in his future jobs. BP's get fired a lot and quit jobs a lot as well. I cover the reasons for this in the FAQ section.

The father's purpose in this conversation is to have the son put down the knife so the implied violence in the situation can be defused. This goal is accomplished by using the "inserting your feelings" tool.

BP's understand feelings quite well. By using feeling words ("frightened" and "scared"), the father can more effectively communicate with the son. He stays on target even when the son replies, "I don't want to" about the knife. By saying on point with his request and reiterating steps 2-3, he is able to link the request (put down the knife) with the alleviation of his feelings (fear). The father inserts a request that speaks to his son's goal in the conversation ("we can talk about how you feel...") such that his son sees a benefit from complying with his father's request. Of course, when the son complies, the father is appreciative.

The second conversation occurs between a Non-BPD husband and his BP wife.

The phone rings at the husband's office. It is in the afternoon and he sees by caller ID that it is his BP wife.

HIM: Hello?

HER: Hi. What are you doing?

HIM: Just preparing for a meeting.

HER: Meetings! You and your meetings! You know, you should quit that stupid job!

HIM: You sound upset about my job.

HER: I am! That dumb job keeps you away from home all the time. And you have to travel… what about me? I'm left at home when you go gallivanting all over the country. I want a husband who works at home.

HIM: It must be lonely to be left alone when I travel.

HER: It is. Why won't you just quit your job?

HIM: I guess everyone feels lonely when their spouse has to be away. You want me to quit my job.

HER: Yeah!

HIM: I would be frightened for my future if I quit my job.

HER: What do you mean?

HIM: Well, it scares me to be without a job.

HER: It does?

HIM: Yes. I would appreciate it if you could stop asking me to quit my job. I can see that you're lonely when I travel, at the same time, I would be less stressed if you would stop insisting I quit.

HER: I'll have to think about it. Maybe we can talk about it when you get home.

HIM: Yes, I think that would be helpful. Thanks.

HER: Bye.

In this case, nothing gets solved completely, but the husband has been able to get the wife to stop asking about quitting his job for the time being. She will probably ask again later. The husband does three things that are skillful in this conversation. First, he focuses the attention on his wife's feelings of loneliness. This is the real reason that she has made the request. She feels lonely when he travels and when he is at work. This loneliness (or emptiness) is very common feature of BPD. People with BPD have trouble being alone.

The second thing the husband does is insert his feelings of fear and uneasiness about not having the security of a job. Again, BP's are all feelings, so linking something with an emotion is necessary and skillful. She is likely to listen more intently when feelings are being discussed.

The third thing the husband does is not to respond to the judgmental attacks on the nature of his job. He could have said, "My job is not dumb! It is important to me!" He could have attacked her back saying, "At least I have a job! You just sit around the house being lazy!" By not defending, he helps halt the situation from getting out-of-control. If he had attacked, it would quickly become ugly. Maybe you have been in similar circumstances and defended or attacked back. If so, ask yourself: what happened next?

The Seventh Tool: The I/YOU Switch

This tool was one that was developed by me and a member of my Internet group. If you start to research BPD, you will find out a lot about "projection." Projection is a term that was coined by Sigmund Freud, and it means that one's own thoughts or feelings are so unacceptable that one has to attribute those thoughts and feelings to others. The idea of projection is applicable to BPD, even if not in its "classic" form.

The thoughts and feelings of a person with BPD are so unacceptable to her that she must do something with these feelings. Sometimes this "something" is attributing the feelings to other people. You have probably experienced this in your relationship with your BP loved one.

What this tool entails is basically reversing the projection by switching the words "I" and "You" in a statement made by the BP and re-interpreting it in your mind. You see, most of the time, the "crisis" is NOT what you've done or what you are – it's not about you, remember? No, most of the time it is all about his/her feelings (IAAHF).

Even if the BP is blaming you for the feelings or for being unappreciated or whatever, it is still most often about how she feels. These feelings are unacceptable and have to be off-loaded onto you. It's an emotional dynamic similar to the "what about you?" argument I explained earlier.

Now, let's use some examples of the I/YOU switch and reinterpretation. I will supply what the BP says to you and then interpret it with the I/YOU switch. Some of these might sound uncannily familiar to you:

- "You are a terrible father and the children hate you!" (I feel like a terrible mother and I am afraid that the children hate me)
- "You treat me like crap!" (I am afraid that I treat you like crap and that you will leave me)
- "I want a divorce. I'm out of here!" (I am afraid that you will think I am not a lovable person and want to divorce me)
- "You are a horrible person and I hate you!" (I am afraid that I am a worthless, horrible person and you will find out and hate me)
- "You are always angry and yelling at me!" (I feel angry all the time and feel compelled to yell at you)

I think you get the idea here. Much of the reason for the projection on the part of the BP is due to shame and the desire to cover that shame. She is dreading that you will find out that she is broken, crazy and worthless, and she has to protect against that ever happening. If that does happen, you are guaranteed to leave her or not love her anymore.

The most effective way to react to these types of projections is to ignore the accusations and to use the previous tools, particularly identifying feelings and validation, to keep the conversation focused on the real problem, which are her negative feelings. If she says, "You treat me like crap," you can say, "Wow, it must feel awful to feel like you're being treated like crap."

What this does is refocuses the conversation on the feelings, and does not accept the responsibility for actually treating her in a certain way. Sometimes it is most effective just to ignore these statements and keep in your mind that such statements are about her feelings and not about your actual behavior. Like most emotion-driven beliefs, these usually subside as the underlying emotion subsides.

My wife will threaten divorce several times a year (it used to be more often), and she will try to pin the blame on me for her desire to end the relationship. However, once her anger and frustration subsides, she will no longer want to divorce, and she may be affectionate towards me within hours of declaring that our relationship is over. In fact, she might not even remember her previous proclamations, because, once the emotion is gone, the desire to divorce is also gone.

Now you might then ask: which is "true" then – the desire to divorce or the expressions of affection? Actually, they are both true, depending solely on how the BP feels at the time. Since feelings can "create" facts for a BP, each scenario is equally as "real" to her at the time. Each feeling is felt strongly and completely. At the same time, if you can practice using the tools in this book, and can set an example for the BP of emotional modulation, the BP will learn to moderate her own emotions, self-validate and self-soothe. That is the point at which real healing can begin.

The Eighth Tool: Reinforcement

Reinforcement, especially positive reinforcement, is a powerful teaching tool. You could more accurately say "training" tool. You have probably used reinforcement in your life without even realizing it.

Consider potty training. If you have ever potty-trained (or as many modern texts call it "toilet taught") a toddler, you know how difficult that task can be. However, all kids eventually learn to use the potty – I don't know of a case of a kid going into high school without knowing how to use the potty.

Potty training provides an excellent example of positive reinforcement and the ignoring of "backsliding." That is the essence of this tool. When you teach a child to use the potty, you make a BIG positive deal about it when it is successful. The first time you see the poop in the potty, what happens? Typically, the parent praises the child, positively reinforcing the behavior in a way that is out-of-proportion with the accomplishment. You may say, "Yeah! You did it! That's fantastic! Good Job!" and clap your hands and cheer. You also will tend to do it within seconds of the completed behavior.

That is where positive reinforcement differs with general praise. Praise can be given much after the fact and can be bestowed for a number of reasons, including character traits. That is, you could say, "Wow, you are so smart" after your child receives a 100% grade on a math test. That is praise. (Although I'm not sure it is effective, but that is not the topic at hand).

Positive reinforcement is for behaviors and should occur right when the behavior is completed. That is how animals are trained. The positive reinforcement (feeding, for example) occurs within seconds of the completed behavior so that the two can be connected in the mind of the animal.

If I return to potty training, you will notice that you also naturally ignore and don't punish behaviors that don't match the desired behavior. That is, if the child has an accident and poops in his/her pants (while not wearing a diaper) you don't say, "You are a naughty little boy/girl!" No, that would be damaging to your child's self-worth and cause shame. No, instead, you say, "Everyone has accidents at first. You can try again next time. It's OK."

This is an accurate corollary to emotional regulation and reinforcement and punishment. Since the BP naturally has difficulties regulating her emotions, the idea of her "messing up" or "backsliding" is analogous to child pooping in her pants (even if this is more the "rule" than the "exception" in the BP's life).

It is not effective to punish her for behaviors that (at first) she can't control. The behaviors are conditioned and the purpose of this tool is to help recondition a BP to behaviors that are more desired and effective. After conditioning, the child is able to control (or at least sense) when she has to go potty. After conditioning a BP is able to control (or at least sense) when she is becoming dysregulated.

The way to approach this is through what DBT calls "just noticeable progress." In other words, if the BP makes a choice of behavior that is more effective and on the road toward desired behavior (desired by you), you magnify it and reinforce it positively.

If she behaves in a way that is not desirable you don't punish that behavior; you ignore it or use the validation skills to consider other alternatives in step 6 of the validation process. This method of approaching behavior modification is tested and proven effective with animals and athletes. You positively reinforce a small success toward the goal and let the failures extinguish themselves.

I would like to provide an example from my own interaction with my wife. As I said previously she does over-medicate at times and she also (used to) drive in that state.

A few years ago she drove while overmedicated and was asked for her keys by restaurant security, who felt she was too impaired to drive. Rather than getting angry with them (which she would have definitely done in the past and has a history of doing), she handed over her keys and took a cab home. I positively reinforced this choice, even though it was one effective choice among several ineffective ones. The next time she over-medicated, she didn't drive at all. Today, she no longer overmedicates, and she hasn't for several years.

Many parents believe that punishment is the best way to deal with unwanted behavior. Actually, it's not. According to Karen Prior in *Don't Shoot the Dog*, there are eight ways to modify behavior. The following list is based on Prior's text and that I have commented on regarding BPD:

Method One: Shoot the animal (in the case of BPD this would be to divorce the spouse or to "disown" a child)

Method Two: Punishment (punishing the BP for emotional behavior.)

Method Three: Negative Reinforcement (removing something negative when the BP does something right. That might be taking off a restriction when the BP behaves in the fashion you desire)

Method Four: Extinction (Letting the behavior go away by itself. Unlikely to work with BP – although some studies suggest BP might be "outgrown")

Method Five: Train an Incompatible Behavior (Positively reinforce something that makes it impossible for the BP to participate in the previous behavior)

Method Six: Put the Behavior on a Cue (Putting a cue on the desired behavior and then removing the cue)

Method Seven: Shape the Absence of the Behavior (Reinforce everything that is not the undesired behavior. This, in combination with method eight, is the method that I am suggesting in this book)

Method Eight: Change the Motivation (Solve the root of the problem. In the case of BP it would be addressing the emotional dysregulation directly. If the BP is not emotionally dysregulated, the behavior will cease)

Prior goes on to say about punishment:

One reason that punishment doesn't usually work is that it does not coincide with the undesirable behavior; it occurs afterward, and sometimes, as in courts of law, long afterward. The subject therefore may not connect the punishment to his or her previous undesirable deeds; animals never do, and people often fail to. If a finger fell off every time someone stole something, or if cars burst into flames when they were parked illegally, I expect stolen property and parking tickets would be nearly nonexistent.

[Additionally], the subject learns nothing. While prompt punishment may stop an ongoing behavior, it does not cause any particular improvement to occur. Punishment does not teach a child how to achieve a better report card. The most the punisher can hope for is that the child's motivation will change: The child will try to alter future behavior in order to avoid punishment.

With BPD punishment can be damaging in addition to ineffective. Since the emotions are felt so strongly and behavior is almost automatic (it's not and can be severed from the emotions and retrained – which the very nature of behavioral therapies), if you punish a BP for emotion-fueled behavior, it is likely to result in more shame and invalidation for the BP. That makes the condition worse, because she senses that you are punishing her for "who she is" (leading to anger and isolation) or indicating that she is a "bad person" (leading to intense shame).

In order to use this tool in the proper way, you will positively reinforce the desired behavior and ignore the undesired behavior – providing no reinforcement at all.

The Ninth Tool: Cheerleading

Unfortunately, the concept of cheerleading is something that I mention in the first edition of this book, but I left out as a tool for a Non-BP/BPD relationship. I mention it when talking about what NOT to do in when a person with BPD is emotionally dysregulated (or experiencing an emotional dysregulation moment). Cheerleading is new to this second edition, although it has appeared in some of my other books.

Not all interactions are appropriate for cheerleading; in fact, many interactions are not. If you tell someone "you can do it" when they deeply believe that they can't, this could lead to a mistrust of your opinion of them.

In the case of dealing with an emotional person, typically, "positive mental attitude" statements are unhelpful and invalidating. Saying there's "no need to be sad/scared/angry" for example just serves to invalidate the emotion that the other person is already feeling.

Many people think that effective cheerleading statements involve saying that one person is "proud of" the other, "believes in" the other or "loves" the other. The problem with each of these is that 1) those statements are about how YOU feel and 2) Those statements don't necessarily foster effective behavior.

At www.dbtselfhelp.com (which is a wonderful resource that I highly recommend) the worksheet on cheerleading states that there are four types of effective cheerleading statements. Mainly, that site is for self-cheerleading, I will try to adapt these to relationship cheerleading. The types are:

- Statements that provide the courage to act effectively
- Statements that help in preparing for the situation, getting ready to be effective, to focus on what works
- Statements that counteract myths about interpersonal behavior.
- Statements that congratulate and reinforce effective behavior.

Later in this book, I suggest a tool that can help with #1, which is the tool to "Be Brave." While a person's inclination may be to avoid an uncomfortable situation or to behave in a conditioned or ineffective manner (because of lack of courage or self-assurance about the situation), being brave in the face of uncomfortable situations reinforces itself and serves to support type #1.

Some examples of #1 might be:

- "You can do hard things." (which is my favorite and can apply to both #1 and #2)
- "Remember the time you did [whatever]. That was so brave of you in that situation."
- "I'm impressed with your courage in the face of that." (stay away from using "I'm proud of you..." statements)
- "Yeah, that is really hard. At the same time you have faced something like that before..."

If you combine "Be Brave" with "You can do hard things," you go a long way to being more effective, because these two concepts help counteract the idea that you are "walking on eggshells" around someone else and that your feeling that avoidance of an emotional situation is the best route to take. I believe taking on an emotional situation head-on is more effective than letting it fester – both for you and for the person with BPD.

In type #2, the focus should be on effective behavior for a future task. #2 is quite important and, in some ways, is the most difficult type to effectively navigate. Because of conditioned ineffective behavior and the sway of negative emotions, a person might be tempted to repeat ineffective behavior, based on the emotions that they are feeling.

A work (or school) situation is a good example of this dynamic. If someone is having a problem with their boss, they might, in anger, have the urge to quit the job or lash out at the boss (or the customers). Work situations can be especially frustrating for a highly emotional person. Work that they consider menial or "beneath them," overbearing bosses, long periods of downtime in which a person can ruminate or become paranoid that others don't like them, all contribute to frustration at work.

Some examples of #2 might be:

- "You have every right to be angry. Still, the last time he said that sort of thing, you reacted positively. I think that worked out pretty well."
- "Bosses can be a real pain. I know when my boss gets on me; I try to do [something effective]. I've seen you do that in the past, so you know you're capable."
- "You had a similar situation when [whatever] happened and you handled that well."

In type #3, you are debunking deeply-held beliefs about interpersonal behavior. This technique can be tricky, because a person who is overcome with emotion might not be able to see the other side of the coin. In this type, you are basically reiterating that a person has the rights to their feelings and emotions and helps counteract the idea that other people might not like them just because of an emotional situation.

Some examples of #3 are:

- "It's hard when your co-workers are angry at you. I know I don't like that either. Yet sometimes it's about their anger more than your behavior."
- "I think you have the right to state your feelings about the situation."

- "You have every right to ask for what you want, even if you think that will annoy them."
- "I think there's a lot of validity in how you feel, certainly as much as how they feel."
- "Sometimes people get annoyed when you don't do exactly what they want. However, you have rights and feelings too."

Some examples of #4 are:

- "I was very impressed with the handled that situation."
- "That was fraught with difficult feelings, yet you navigated that well."
- "I think your approach to that difficult situation was very effective."
- "You worked hard on that and it showed."

The Tenth Tool: Being Brave

If you have learned to identify your own feelings toward your BP, you probably have discovered that you are, in some sense, afraid of him or her (or at least afraid of what he/she might do or say to you). After repeated rages and other undesirable behavior, you may find yourself avoiding certain subjects, dreading others and not being completely honest with yourself.

This reaction to dysregulated emotions and behavior is quite normal. I used to feel this way all the time. I dreaded going home to her if I knew that she was dysregulated and "on a tear." I know my kids felt the same way because they told me that they did. My daughter said that she was afraid to come home for fear that mom would be "acting crazy." Both my children and I avoided talking to my wife when she was in that state.

In this tool I am suggesting being brave about talking about emotions, not necessarily about behavior. Some of the previous tools can help you be brave about talking about behavior, because they provide a road map for such a discussion. When you are dealing with a BP, you might tend to shy away from identifying the emotions and feelings – especially shameful ones. I used to believe that I shouldn't point out my wife's shame because it would spur on more shame. Instead, I found out that, once I did point out obvious shame, my wife was actually relieved that someone else had noticed and validated her feelings of shame. In that case the shame was the elephant in the room that no one talked about, but everyone was worried about. Once I finally said, "there's an elephant in the room," everyone was relieved that they were not the only one who saw it.

Being brave means mentioning the elephants in the room. It means "going where angels fear to tread" and stating the obvious, yet avoided, subjects. It means being willing to talk about those things that you have problems with – but it also means doing it utilizing the effective tools I have described thus far. Be brave and be confident when you speak of these things.

The Eleventh Tool: Words, Thoughts and Attitudes

I sometimes try to point out the language in my Internet list member's posts as betraying their true feelings about their BP loved one. The words that you use, even inside your own head, to characterize someone or something do help shape your underlying beliefs about these subjects. In this tool, I am encouraging you to examine your language and see what the language you use about your BP encourages you to believe about him or her.

Let's take some words that are very negative about someone with BPD:

- Crazy, nuts, nutty, insane, loco, Out of her mind
- Bitch, troll, princess, witch, jerk, asshole
- Worthless, hopeless, impossible, insensitive
- Overly emotional, cry baby, too sensitive
- Pathetic, sad, pitiable
- Incompetent, useless, inadequate, lazy

Using these words and words like them is judgmental and forms an opinion about your BP in your head. Even if you never express these words to the BP, the opinion is still there and can color your interactions with the person.

The Twelfth Tool: Taking Care of Yourself Emotionally

Taking care of yourself emotionally is not really a tool per se. It is a basic foundation for operating the other tools. On certain medications the pharmacist will affix a label saying, "do not operate machinery while taking this medication."

If you are emotionally dysregulated or under the influence of strong emotions, you will be unable to effectively use these tools. Use the emotional identification tools to become aware of your emotions and your emotional triggers. Sickness, tiredness and a poor diet can contribute to dysregulation.

Isolation also can foster emotional ill health. I recently had a consulting client of mine thank me at the end of session just for "finally having someone to talk to about these issues." Non-BPD's are typically very isolated and secretive. They are embarrassed about what goes on in their household. They feel like there's no one to share these experiences with. Connecting with a community of like-minded people (such as my email support list) can help to reverse some of the isolation. Consulting with a knowledgeable and understanding person can help as well. Alcohol and mood-altering drugs can definitely contribute to emotional dysregulation.

Learn the skills I have set forth in this book and practice, practice, practice. Once you have mastered these tools, you are much less likely to get emotionally dysregulated yourself. Do things for yourself and by yourself if possible. Do things that you like and desire doing.

It takes time to develop an emotional awareness and a mastery of the tools in this book. Patience is required.

Relax. Breathe.

Carrying the Tool Box

Now that you have reached the end of the tools, I'd just like to say that this is not an all-inclusive list. It will get you started though. Once you have mastered these tools, you will be able to go on to other, more complex ones in the next chapter of this book.

Today is the day you can start using these tools. I might suggest that you practice the tools on someone else besides your loved one with BPD first to see what happens.

You can practice on anyone who is emotional. If the server at a restaurant is extremely busy (and probably frustrated), you might say, "Wow, you look really stressed. It must be tough to have so many customers." See what happens.

Also, until you get a handle on reading other people's emotions accurately, you might use more generic emotion words like "stressed," "upset," or "frustrated." You can also use more generic validation words like "difficult," "hard," and "tough."

The purpose of having a tool is so that you can use it to build a better life for yourself. You have to use the tool, practice with it and eventually obtain a complete mastery of it. Once you are comfortable with the tool, you can use it to build toward your goal.

I often have people ask me, "What do I do now?" after their loved one is diagnosed with BPD or they realize that their loved one has BPD. My answer is: do what is effective and use these tools to be effective. The follow-up answer is: what is your goal?

Think carefully about what the goal is – what the desired future state is. To get to that goal, you will have to take many small steps, but, as they say, a thousand mile journey begins with a single step.

You cannot cure BPD in your loved one. In fact, she can only recover from this debilitating mental illness with her own efforts, in conjunction with professional mental health assistance and her acquiring the skills that have been shown effective for overcoming this condition.

What you can do is work to make your life calmer, easier and less out-of-control. As I said in the preface, unlike other books for Non-BPD's, I have just told you how.

Try these tools out and see how they function. It might take some time to get acclimated to them, but with practice, you'll be fine.

On a final note about tools, one of the members of my Internet list asked me to summarize all of these attitudes and tools in a list of "four rules." When I did, I came up with this:

Four rules for dealing with someone with BPD:

1. It's not about you (or it's always about his/her feelings).
2. Validate his/her feelings (this takes practice).

3. When it is about you, speak in a non-judgmental fashion and express how you feel.
4. Let the other person solve his/her own problems.

Four rules for dealing with yourself in this relationship:

1. Do no harm.
2. Be brave.
3. Some things have to be accepted and others can be changed – learn which is which.
4. Stick to your values while being effective.

Chapter 9: Advanced Tools

Unlike the previous edition of this book, in this edition I have decided to include some advanced tools. What I found was that some of the readers of the first edition outgrew certain tools and needed some additional guidance about where to go. I have a certain member that has synthesized my methods with another self-help author and, because of this, he was asking questions about advanced tools. While I initially intended this book to be an introduction to emotional tools and their application, some readers require more information about what and how to implement these tools in their lives.

These advanced tools are intended to be used when you have mastered (or are at least comfortable with) the basic tools. While some basic tools are difficult to understand, practice and implement effectively, these are even more difficult and fought with potential land-mines. You must be confident in your abilities and your relationship before these tools make sense and can be implemented.

Advanced Tool One: Relationship Maintenance

When I mention relationship maintenance in this section I am speaking about a very specific method of repairing the relationship going forward. Chances are between you and your loved one with BPD, there are resentments, misunderstandings, grudges and all types of bad blood. Over the years, the failed expectations, emotional blow-ups, judgmental actions and outright animosity can build up on both sides of the fence. All of that being said, this tool seeks to deal with a very specific type of emotional injury: the unintended, yet real, injuries your actions as a Non-BPD have caused in the person with BPD.

That's why I held this tool off into the advanced section. This tool is impossible to use authentically if you're holding on to all of that bad stuff or if you feel you've been wronged so deeply by your loved one with BPD.

It's also impossible to use this tool if your loved one with BPD has zero trust for you. By employing the basic tools in this book, you can start to build up a modicum of trust. Once you've listened to and truly heard the meaning in the behavior and your BP senses that and becomes more comfortable approaching you with her feelings, this tool can be attempted.

Essentially, the essence of this tool is about taking responsibility for your past and future behavior. Do not use this tool if you don't believe the words I will instruct you to write or say. If you don't completely believe the content of the relationship repair message, wait until you do before attempting.

Here's how the relationship repair works:

1. You can only control and can only be responsible for your own words and actions.
2. For years, perhaps decades, you have been judgmental, advice-giving, insensitive and unable to make sense of your loved one with BPD.
3. Because of #2, you have UNINTENTIONALLY said and done things that have deeply hurt your loved one with BPD.
4. Relationship repair gives you to opportunity to acknowledge this fact and to resolve to change it.

Interestingly, most of my coaching clients are romantic partners, rather than parents of people with BPD. I have a few parents, but mostly adult men interacting with their wives or girlfriends. Often, they have no idea the impact of their "natural" words and actions of a woman with BPD.

A person with BPD will assume other people's (particularly attachment figure's) intentions and motivations are malevolent toward her. Why? The reason seems to revolve around three things:

1. The history of pain and suffering that this figure has caused in her life – i.e. trauma/invalidation;
2. The reading of neutral states as angry and aggressive and
3. The hair-trigger emotional tolerance that, through evolution (and possibly epigenetics), causes false positives to be safer than false negatives.

What you don't realize is that because these things, she has been thinking that you hurt her emotionally **on purpose**, and you've been wondering how you could have emotionally hurt her **at all**.

The way to address this disconnect is to approach the person with BPD and admit that you've hurt her. I instruct my consulting clients to essentially say (or write in an email) the following:

"I've been thinking about the other night [some emotional conflict situation that happened recently]. I just realized that when I said [what was said], it must have hurt you deeply. That was certainly not my intention; yet, by considering how that must have sounded to you, I realized it probably hurt a great deal. For that, I apologize and I will try to be more aware of the impact my words and actions have on you."

If no emotional conflict has occurred recently (although I find this unlikely), you can make a more general statement like:

"I've recently noticed how my emotions have affected my mood recently. Since I've become more aware of this, I can see how some of the things I said to you over the years probably hurt you emotionally. That was not my intention. I was ignorant of how my words could affect you emotionally. I will strive to be more mindful of the emotional pain my words may trigger."

What this does is it acknowledges that you have an awareness of how she feels. You are willing to take responsibility for even unintended pain you have caused her. You are willing to change the way you will approach her in the future to avoid causing emotional pain.

This tool can be very powerful. Don't use it until you can clearly see how your words and actions have hurt your loved one with BPD. Don't use it until you can authentically communicate the concept without sounding wooden or stilted.

If you still deep-down believe that the person with BPD is the cause of all the relationship problems, this tool will blow up in your face. People with BPD have exquisitely tuned bullshit detectors. In fact, their bullshit detectors are so finely tuned that they will detect bullshit where none exists. They see judgment in neutrality. You must believe the above statement all the way down to your very essence before you say it out loud.

Once you get to that point, and you're able to communicate the message above, the relationship will invariably improve. She will trust you more because you will be much closer to "getting" her. Yet, you MUST follow through on your promise to be more mindful of the impact your words and actions will have on your loved one with BPD.

Advanced Tool Two: Developing Emotional Agility

I believe that practicing the skills provided in the previous tools section puts you on a road toward (what I call) emotional agility. As you begin to develop it, it starts to become conditioned. It becomes "second nature".

Unlike the concept of emotional intelligence, emotional agility is something that can be learned and perfected. It takes practice and (sometimes) coaching.

Agility is the ability to change the body's position efficiently, and requires the integration of isolated movement skills using a combination of balance, coordination, speed, reflexes, strength, endurance, and stamina.

Emotional Agility is the ability to adjust a mind's position efficiently, depending on the conditions of other's minds around you. It is similar to mentalization (next advanced tool), yet the emphasis is on feelings, rather than general cognition.

It is the integration of isolated emotional skills including: emotional intelligence, emotional strength, emotional flexibility, emotional balance and emotional stamina.

Many years ago, Daniel Goldman wrote the book *Emotional Intelligence* which helped define and introduce the concept of Emotional (Intelligence) Quotient or EQ. Goldman recognized that a person's ability to successfully navigate emotional issues has a large impact on the person's life.

I came up with the concept of Emotional Agility (EA), because of a very important distinction in my mind between the concepts of intelligence and agility. Intelligence is an innate quality that fluctuates little throughout one's life. You are unlikely to become significantly more intelligent as you grow older. You can become more experienced, wiser and more aware of emotional influences on your life and other's lives, but since the very idea of intelligence is mostly in-born; your EQ is essentially stagnant.

Agility as a concept is completely separate and I have found more accurately reflects a person's ability to train one's mind, to practice and integrate a distinct set of emotional skills and to be effective and efficient in one's emotional life.

You can teach yourself EA or have someone teach you. However, even with an experienced teacher of EA, you have to practice, retrain your mind and reinforce the success. If you practice the emotional tools in this book, again and again, you'll naturally develop EA.

Emotional agility is like a playing an instrument: EQ represents your natural musical talents; EA represents your hard work. Once you have mastered EA, you can play anything you wish, including writing your own music.

But you have to put in the work and the practice. One of my list members posted an article on the support list about patience. The article talked about how firefighters practice putting on their equipment in slow motion, rehearsing each snap, zipper and strap. Only after rehearsing in slow motion over and over can they accomplish getting dressed and ready in under two minutes.

Have patience and don't try to rush to the end. Time takes time.

Advanced Tool Three: Mentalizing

The biggest development in the past 15 years for the treatment of BPD is mentalization-based therapy (MBT). The skills associated with MBT are useful to loved ones of people with BPD. Mentalization (or mentalizing) is a skill that can get the relationship to be about BOTH of you rather than solely about the person with BPD and their feelings.

Mentalizing is a complex and vast subject. Many people, when referring to mentalizing, will call it "mentalization." Mentalizing is an action in which people engage. It is not a static process.

I am not going to attempt to explain metalizing fully, either in theory or technique. There are other texts that do that in great detail. I will provide you with my limited understanding of mentalizing and how it has benefited me in my interactions with my loved ones with BPD.

As I indicated in chapter 3 (what causes BPD?), attachment plays a huge role in the formation of BPD, according to the pioneers of mentalizing in a therapeutic context. Rather than go through the attachment theory again (and I probably didn't do a good job of it the first time), I'd like to provide some comments about the nature of attachment.

Attachment and You

Even as adults, sometimes people need their mommy. People with BPD, being so emotional, need other people a lot. The people that are being needed are "attachment people." The first attachment that a person makes in their life is usually to their mother.

Some in the psychiatric community call BPD an "attachment disorder", meaning the initial attachment with the mother is disordered in some way and it models future attachments which also become disordered. The birth of the self and how one looks at oneself develops during the period of first attachment.

If this attachment is accomplished in a non-disordered way, the child develops a stable self-image, one in which they can locate their feelings and one that is not filled with shame. However, if this process is disordered in some way, the child will develop an unstable sense of self. This can lead to attachment issues later in life.

With BPD, the attachment system is hypersensitive and can be triggered too often and with little provocation. This can lead to the symptoms of BPD like fear of abandonment, a pattern of attaching and then leaving and a tendency to fall "in love" quickly. In other words, intimacy may be assumed before it is actually established.

Internally this unstable self can contribute to shame and self-hatred. In turn the self-hatred can be "flip-flopped" with what seems like narcissism. In reality, at least with BPD, the person will usually deep-down dislike themselves because their "self" is unstable and ever changing. They just don't know who they are.

When a person is unable to find themselves internally, they may seek to define themselves through others, moving from one attachment figure to another, searching for a "home" in which they can find their true self. As a loved one of someone in this situation, it can be very difficult and confusing for you.

The thing that you must keep in mind is that, because you are an important attachment figure in their minds, the stakes will be higher with you as opposed to the stakes with other people in their lives. This is the reason that some have postulated that there are "high functioning" people with BPD. I contend that it all depends on the importance of the attachment in the person's life.

The more important the attachment, the more that is at stake. Keeping this in mind can help you develop empathy, gentleness and compassion for them.

What is Mentalizing?

Mentalization is the connection of mind-to-mind in a particular exchange. It is about in-the-moment interaction, not about the past or future.

It is about communicating and understanding your and the other person's explicit and implicit expressions and motivations, feelings, goals, etc. It is about accurately expressing yourself and listening to the other person in a search for meaning. It is about internalizing the other's viewpoint and having the other internalize your viewpoint.

A really good example of mentalizing is an inside joke – both you and the other person completely understand the meaning of the joke and have internalized the meaning.

Jerry Holmes, a researcher who works with Anthony Bateman (a co-creator of mentalization therapy), calls mentalization the process of "seeing yourself from the outside and others from the inside."

Why mentalize?

We mentalize for several reasons. The main one is that mentalization is a "meeting of the minds" in which a personal connection is made. Mentalization encourages the integration of thoughts, desires, feelings, motivations, intentions, goals and all other internal mental elements and the communication and understanding of the same in others.

When we mentalize, we are out of "lizard brain" thinking and into the prefrontal cortex. That requires the reflection upon meaning and discourages emotional dysregulation, concrete thinking, bullshitting, dismissive attitudes, blaming and IAAHF.

One thing with mentalization is that you have to be authentic and be yourself. If you try to fake your way through it, the other person is bound to know, especially a person with BPD who can detect emotional fakeness a mile away.

Mentalization serves to:

- Improve trust - others feel that you "get them."
- Morph reflexive emotions into reflective emotions.
- Improve communication between two people – the meaning is exchanged.
- Build empathy and compassion – you can see the world through the other's eyes.
- Help work on a relationship – people take responsibility for feelings, words, and mental processes.
- Decrease misunderstanding and resentment – understanding another person's intent.
- Change viewpoints and assumptions – when the alternative meaning applies to situations, beliefs and assumptions can change.

How do you mentalize?

It is important to remember that mentalization is about NOW. It is not about any other moment than now.

Therefore, if you are dragging old issues or future worries into the conversation (or if the other person is) then you are experiencing a "failure to mentalize."

You mentalize by continually monitoring the progress and state of a conversation. You mentalize by asking questions about the current conversation, the feelings and intention of the other person and monitoring your own feelings and understanding of the current conversation.

It is a natural skill and is built into the human mind; however, it is also a difficult skill, because we are often not mindful of the current moment when having a conversation. We are often distracted by our own thoughts and feelings, assumptions and automatic thoughts, history and attachment to the other person.

If your mind meanders into these things, you are experiencing a failure to mentalize. Mentalization is done from a "stance," which is summarized as follows:

- Compassionate for yourself and the other person
- Focus on the other person's mind
- Humble about your viewpoint and not bullying
- Curious and interested, an authentic desire to see the other person's point of view
- Validating for additional information about inner mental states (before offering alternative perspectives)
- Normalizing and generalizing – "everyone makes sense (to themselves) at all times"

Mentalization is the true essence of love, compassion and understanding, because it allows you to internalize the accurate "image" of the other person's mind (and they can yours as well).

Mentalization is essentially done through asking questions, but not leading questions. One cannot ASSUME the other person's thoughts and feelings are what you think they are. You have to start with a blank slate each time.

I once met a woman with BPD in a support group for Non-BPD's. She was sitting in to understand what we were learning about her. After she let us know that she actually had the disorder and was "auditing" our group, she told us that she wished that her loved ones would "erase the board" each time before they spoke with her. What she meant was for her loved ones to cast aside the assumptions, prejudices and conditioned responses and interact with her afresh.

When you mentalize, you do just that. Every conversation is new and different. While there is some context for each conversation, the content should be fresh, like jazz musicians riffing.

You can "read" momentary feelings (such as recognizing micro-expressions) but the MEANING of those feelings is not always clear. If you don't know, you have to ask. If you assume the meaning of the feelings, you may fall into "Othello's Error" as Ekman calls it. From the site Mr. Media Training:

214

In Shakespeare's Othello, Othello is tricked into believing that his wife, Desdemona, cheated on him with his Lieutenant. When he confronts Desdemona, she weeps—a sign, Othello concludes, of her guilt. In a rage, Othello murders her, only to learn shortly thereafter that she hadn't committed adultery after all.

Othello made the mistake of assuming that he understood the source of Desdemona's anguish. He assumed that his wife's sobs when confronted were a sign of her guilt; he didn't understand that her grief was rooted not in guilt, but in her knowledge that there was no way to convince her husband of her innocence.

That tragic mistake—what psychologist Paul Ekman dubbed "Othello's Error"— teaches us that just because someone exhibits an emotion doesn't mean we understand the root cause. "Emotional signals don't tell us what brought them forth," Ekman writes in Emotions Revealed.

You cannot assume the meaning of the thoughts and emotions that are expressed in a conversation with a loved one with BPD. Instead, you have to be curious and ask.

You ask by being "dumb" and not assuming. For example:

- "I'm not sure I understand. Can you help me out and explain how you feel?"
- "Why do you think he said that?"
- "What happened?"
- "How did you feel about that?"
- "That'd make me feel sad. Do you feel sad about it too?"
- "What do you think was up with that?"
- "Could you tell me more about that?"
- "Really? That wasn't my intention. Perhaps we could talk about that more?"
- "I wonder if..." statements

The purpose is to probe the other person's mind and to get as close to a full understanding of the other person's internal mental processes as possible.

It is impossible without a true interest in the other person. It is impossible if you judge the other person, or if you get in your own way, entangled in your own mental processes.

Don't judge the other person's mental processes and feelings. It is important to focus on intention. You want to know what the other person intended to say and what the intention is behind their actions. You also want to communicate your intention. However, remember that intention does not rule out consequence.

In each conversation, you want to understand what the meaning is. What does that thought mean to them? You want to discover the treasure hidden below the surface of the ocean.

You want to be a detective, not a judge.

All people make sense to themselves in a given moment. If you can understand how your loved one with BPD makes sense, rather than judging them about how they make no sense, you've taken a big step toward relating deeply with your loved one. Mentalizing can help you get there.

This is especially true for parents of adult children with BPD. Since the "frame" of the situation is such that the parent is "wiser" and able to make more sense of the world, the parent will often not attempt to find the meaning (to the child) in the child's behavior. If the parent can find the "sense" their child is making – i.e. how does this behavior make sense to the child in this situation? – the relationship will start to make sense and, in my experience, will improve.

A failure to mentalize

Often, when speaking with someone who is a close "attachment person," misunderstandings, assumptions and ineffective modes of thinking creep into the situation. MBT identifies several "modes" of thinking that inhibit mentalization.

These modes are:

Psychic Equivalence – when the world is equivalent to the person's mind. This is the "feelings = facts" mode. "I think/feel it. I must be true."

Pretend – mental states are not anchored in reality. Pretending "as if" something is true, when external evidence shows the contrary. This is "bullshitting" mode.

216

Teleological – mental states can only be expressed in action. "If you loved me, you'd buy me a car." Only tangible actions count, not words or thoughts.

In addition, there are other ways of thinking that inhibit mentalization such as:

Concrete thinking – "But he said he hated me!" Taking something as gospel and ignoring the underlying mental states and their malleability.

Pseudo-mentalizing – seemingly understanding of mental states, but used in a self-serving fashion. This state of mind is dangerous to both parties. If the Non-BPD doesn't recognize the pseudo-mentalizing state, he/she will assume motives that are actually hidden.

When a break in mentalization occurs, you must intervene immediately. You cannot let the break go unnoticed or simply "let it go." You have to be attentive to the level of mentalization in the conversation and stop the flow of the conversation right away.

There are three basic ways of dealing with the break in mentalization, each used for a different intensity of the break. They are:

- Stop, Listen, Look (for minor cuts, bumps or abrasions).
- Stop, Rewind, Explore (for breaks, burns and internal injuries).
- Stop and Stand (for life-and-death struggles and near-fatal injuries)

Huh? What's up with those? You will notice that "Stop" begins each of these methods. MBT suggests actually holding up your hand, palm forward in a traffic cop sort of way and saying, "Stop..." (or some variant).

This "mentalizing hand" is the "shock to the system" that indicates a hold on further progress to a conversation. It is an indication that you can't continue the conversation without some sort of clarification of what just happened.

Stop, Listen, Look

This puts the conversation in "pause mode." It is to remedy a small break in mentalization. It is a reaction to the reaction of the other person.

If the person is triggered into an emotion by something that you said, you must stop, listen and look.

Some of the ways to do this are:

- "Wait. I'm confused. What I said seemed to have upset you. That wasn't what I intended. Can you clarify how you feel?"
- "Stop for a minute. You said I was being mean. I didn't intend for that to be mean, but I guess I was. What do you feel that's about?"
- "Hold on. You appear to be angry at that. Is that right?"
- "Hang on. I think what I said upset you. Can you help me out here and explain why?"

I know all of this seems rather clunky; however, the purpose of this is twofold: 1) to get the other person thinking about their thinking (a re-engagement of mentalizing) and 2) to communicate that you are really engaged in the conversation and interested in how the other person is feeling.

Stop, Rewind, Explore

This process is a bit arduous. It requires you to step back through the last few moments of the conversation and explore each, "frame by frame."

- "Let's go back and explore what happened just then. It seemed to me we were relating well and then something happened. What do you feel happened?"
- "Something happened just now. Let's try and rewind a bit to see where the conversation went astray, alright?"
- "Hang on a second. I feel like my intention and the way you felt about what I said are not in synch. Let's go back and see what happened."
- "Wait. There appears to have been a misunderstanding a moment or so ago. What do you feel about what I said?"

Then, you have to go forward, step-by-step, statement-by-statement and explore each one and see how those made the other person feel.

- "So, I said, 'maybe he was just tired' and you felt I was being dismissive of your feelings? Is that right?"

218

- "You said that you didn't want to talk about it and I continued. You felt badgered, correct?"
- "When I started talking about our daughter, you felt I wasn't being attentive to your feelings. Do I have that right?"

Stop and Stand

This process is for the big problems. It is the way that you apply your own personal boundaries to a situation.

When the other person is way down the path of emotional dysregulation or off the mentalizing track entirely, stop and stand can be the only option. It is basically your way of either ending the conversation or trying to re-frame it completely.

The mistake many people make is that they use boundaries (stop and stand) every time. This approach is not healthy for the relationship.

How to use stop and stand:

- "As far as I can tell, we are going around in circles about this. I don't see any point and continuing to talk about it."
- "I feel we have reached an impasse. You have your view and I have mine. I don't think going back and forth will do either of us any good."
- "I can't really discuss this anymore right now. Maybe we could discuss it again in the morning."
- "Let's talk about this later."

Remember: like any application of boundaries, this one is likely to cause an immediate strong reaction, but the "stand" part is that you have to stand your ground.

Advanced Tool Four: Becoming a Champ

Dealing with someone with BPD can be trying. If you practice the skills presented in this book, things are bound to get easier.

I have come up with an acronym for the "end-state" of using the skills. It is a CHAMP:

CHAMP

Compassion, Curiosity
Humility, Hope and Honesty
Acceptance, Authenticity, Affect Awareness*
Mentalization
Practice, Patience, Persistence

* Affect awareness means that you actively monitor the feelings of the other person and address those feelings as they arise.

Chapter 10: Wrapping it up

You may be thinking, "this is a lot of work!" Yes, in fact, it is a lot of work.

I decided that rather than dump my relationship with my wife with BPD, I'd undergo some changes to "fix" the relationship. Additionally, my emotionally sensitive daughter needed support and an effective approach as well.

I am happy to report that my marriage is (most times) strong and my daughter is thriving at college and in her social life.

BPD is a difficult disorder for the sufferer and for those immediately around them. It feels as though things will never get better.

My suggestion to you is to try the things I have laid out in this book. I know it's not "fair" that you have to do all the changing. Yet, when you change, the person with BPD is bound to change as well.

When you get more effective in the relationship, things will change, usually for the better. I have several members of my list that are women married to men with BPD. It is a difficult situation, because men are more likely to rage and become violent with their loved ones. I never recommend staying with someone if he/she has a history of physical abuse.

The interesting thing about these particular Non-BPD wives is that almost all of them have reported that the rages ceased when they began to practice these skills. That alone might be enough for you to decide to practice these skills.

I know that much of the things I have outlined in this book are counter-intuitive. Some feel as if you are "giving in" to the person's behavior. I don't feel as though there is a competition in a relationship in which one person wins and the other loses. Throw away the scoreboard.

I believe that all people deserve respect and understanding and that sometimes that is hard to provide. My guidance is that you practice the skills in this book until you have a complete mastery over them.

Once you have a complete mastery, they become second nature and you don't have to think about them – they become a part of you and your approach to the world. In my mind, that is where the true healing can flourish.

Best of luck.

Bon

Notes

Frequently Asked Questions

This section is a collection of frequently asked questions by Non-BP's. It has been culled from my Internet group and some other sources. I placed this section at the end of the book, because I thought that the answers would make much more sense after you had read the previous sections.

What is BPD?

The description of BPD that I put forth in this book is different than how others have described the disorder. I would describe BPD as a severe mental illness that is characterized by emotional dysregulation, impulsivity, shame and preoccupation with attachment relationships.

Clearly, people with BPD behave in a manner that is painful to you or you wouldn't be reading this book. I also suggest that BPD is not a "personality" disorder. Instead, it is a mood and impulse disorder. Many in the therapeutic community have suggested renaming and reclassifying BPD. One new name that has been suggested is Emotional Regulation Disorder (ERD), which many BP's and Nons prefer as a more accurate and descriptive term for this complex condition.

What causes BPD?

No one knows exactly. Some researchers believe it is completely biological, some that it is completely environmental. Some believe that it is a form of Post-Traumatic Stress Disorder. Others believe it is akin to a rapid cycling form of Bipolar Disorder. Turn to Chapter 3 in this book for more information.

What other disorders and conditions are often confused with BPD?

Several other disorders and conditioned are often confused with BPD. The main ones are:

- Post-Traumatic Stress Disorder (PTSD)
- Narcissistic Personality Disorder (NPD)

- Intermittent Explosive Disorder (IED) – also known as Episodic Dyscontrol Disorder or Behavioral Dyscontrol Disorder
- Dissociative Identity Disorder (DID) – formerly known as Multiple Personality Disorder
- Bipolar Disorder I & II
- Other Personality Disorders
- Other Emotional Disorders

Will the tools presented in this book work to help my loved one even if she doesn't have BPD?

They might. The tools are designed to work on modulating the emotional system of a person with an emotional disorder. Some of the above disorders are chiefly emotional and the tools are likely to work when dealing with someone with such a disorder. I have seen the tools work effectively with sufferers of PTSD and "Other Emotional Disorders."

PTSD shares many of the behavioral aspects of BPD, so these tools can be effective with a person with PTSD. Some people have both BPD and PTSD from childhood trauma.

My suggestion is that you try them and see.

However, if your loved one has Narcissistic Personality Disorder, I'm not sure these tools will be effective. I have seen the tools fail with someone with NPD, because NPD is not an emotional disorder. Sometimes when people have a hammer, every problem looks like a nail. In the case of these tools, they are widely varying in their application and applicable mostly to the problems described in this book.

Still, many people exhibit these types of problems and your loved one does not have to have BPD to benefit from the tool's application.

Why is this person raging at me?

In the support groups, rage is one of the most talked about aspects of BPD. Why? Because it is one of the most difficult for the Non-BPD to endure. Many people ask themselves, why is this person so angry (with me)? It seems to make no sense. A person with BPD will fly into a rage about seemingly nothing. The smallest thing that is out of place or not done the way that this person expects causes sometimes hours of anger and raging, yelling and screaming and sometimes physical violence. Again, many Nons ask: "what's up with that?"

Anger and rage are usually secondary emotions to other primary ones. Sensitivity to judgment plays a major role in the triggering of rage. The symptoms and feelings associated with BPD interact and, at times, feed each other. In the case of rage, I believe that it is fed by two other symptoms: shame and sensitivity to judgment (which is also fed by shame).

When someone with BPD feels shameful and when you (as a "Non") criticize or judge her behavior as "bad" or "negative," the trigger for rage is pulled within the person with BPD. Why? Because your judgment reflects her shameful feelings and resonates deeply into her core beliefs about herself. She panics that you are "finding out" that she is a bad person. She has to (at all costs) defend her "goodness."

What I have found with my own wife is that this is the point at which she will rage and introduce the "what about you?" argument. The "what about you?" argument is a way to rage at the Non and release anxiety about the Non finding out about her shameful "badness." Some people in the support community like to call this "projection" or "denial." I personally don't believe it is actually projection or denial (although there are times in which projection is clear). It is a form of misdirection to try to take the focus off her inner shame and refocus the discussion on you and your faults.

Nobody is perfect, not even you. When a person with BPD rages against you, you often feel very imperfect – especially if she uses the "what about you?" attack. When someone with BPD uses the "what about you?" technique she is usually deflecting blame and judgment on you. (Why? See below for an explanation of the symptom "Sensitivity to Judgment").

Ultimately however, you experience the rage as hurtful to your very self. You find that the rage "forces" you to defend yourself against her. That is what the "what about you?" attack/rage does best. That is its intention; it puts you on the defensive and shifts focus away from her and her behavior. As I said, it is form of redirection away from the person with BPD's shame.

One interesting thing about raging is that once the anger and raging is done, it is usually over. Sometimes the person with BPD will be exhausted after the rage and will just collapse and go to sleep. The same is the case with tired children. Sometimes a tired child will have a temper tantrum (which is a form of rage) and then, once the emotions are released, she will either go to sleep or sit placidly in your arms. The inner agitation has been released and she is done. It is the natural catharsis of the emotion.

Why is this person so selfish?

People with BPD can often come off as selfish, self-involved or not empathetic to other people's pain or problems. I find that Nons often complain about how completely selfish their loved one with BPD is. The entire genesis of this book was centered around the question: "What about me?" when in a relationship with someone with BPD.

While people with BPD seem very selfish and self-involved, it is difficult for anyone under the influence of strong (especially negative) emotions to see anything or anyone besides herself.

Yet, this characteristic of a person with BPD can lead to resentment and anger within the loved one. Often loved ones feel that the BP only thinks about herself and does not consider other people's feelings. This feature of BPD is often true. BPD involves strong negative feelings and those tend to overwhelm the BP, leaving little room for considering others. Additionally, the shame and sensitivity to judgment causes the BP to actively monitor the environment for disapproval. This can be outlandish and paranoid. My wife often attributes other people's actions as direct reflections of her feelings and that other people actively "hate" her. This personalization of the environment is an extension of the BP's own self-hate. Although it may seem on the outside that the BP loves herself greatly – in reality the opposite is true. She spends much time trying to detect whether other people can see her shame and hate her as well.

Why does this person fear judgment so much?

A person with BPD fears judgment almost to the point of being allergic to it. She is extremely sensitive to judgment from other people, even if that judgment is merely perceived. Because of the shame (the belief that she is a bad person and deserves to be deemed as such) and the rejection sensitivity, a person with BPD avoids situations in which her actions can be judged by others. When I say "judged" here and "judgment," what I am referring to is not "using one's better judgment" in a situation, but rather it is the sense that a person's actions or the person herself can be judged as "right or wrong" in a given context.

Interestingly, even with a strong fear of judgment of herself and her own behavior and self, she also tends to judge other's behavior and character harshly. How many times has your loved one with BPD told you that you were doing something "wrong" or that you are a "mean" or "bad" person?

Fear of judgment and emotional reactions to judgment (real or perceived) is a major issue for a person with BPD. Judgment of her actions causes emotional pain and to avoid judgment, she might lie or avoid social situations in which she feels she will be judged. If she is consistently concerned with doing something "the right way" or she feels that you think she "does everything wrong," it is likely that she suffers from a fear of judgment.

Additionally, there is a stigma associated with being "crazy" when a person has BPD. A person with BPD might feel "not normal" inside and might have felt that way most of her life. However, if the outside world labels her as "crazy" or "not normal" or "mentally ill," it becomes an external validation for what she might already feel. The fact that others "know" about her can make her feel exposed. It is a form of judgment and fear of it that reduces the likelihood that the person will "admit" she has   a   problem.

Why is this person trying to control me?

The reason that a BP will try to control you is that she feels so out-of-control of herself emotionally. That, in combination with the fact that she pins her hopes on others to solve her problems, causes her to try to control other's behavior. Sometimes she will think, "If only he did this, I would feel better." So she tries to make you do whatever she thinks at the time will salve her deep wounds.

When you do whatever it is that she wants and she still feels bad, she will select another thing. Not being self-aware can cause her to try to control the people closest to them. This idea of BP's not being self-aware requires some expansion. In *Sometimes I Act Crazy*, Dr. Jerold Kreisman notes that a BP can talk about herself for an hour and not really explain at all what she is really like. She might attribute her own qualities, particularly negative qualities, to others around her, rather than to herself.

If you use the "inserting your feelings" tool, you can cut off controlling attempts.

Why won't this person respect my personal boundaries?

I've already written a lot about boundaries in this book, and I hope that now you understand that this question really makes no sense. If she is violating "boundaries," she can only violate her own. You have to respect your own boundaries, and she has to respect hers. If it appears that she has no boundaries of her own, that is because emotional dysregulation takes place at a lower level of thinking than does the establishment of boundaries and values. When someone is emotionally dysregulated she will do anything to feel better and that includes violating boundaries and rules that she has established for herself. These "boundary violations" are typically attempts to self-soothe, which is a skill that people with BPD specifically lack.

Remember that your personal boundaries are about your behavior (sometimes in response to her behavior), not about controlling her behavior. You must respect your own personal boundaries, even if it appears that she can't respect her own.

Why can't this person hold a job?

Some people with BPD can't seem to hold a job - she will quit often and get fired repeatedly from even the most menial jobs. The reasons for this are varied. Sometimes it is because the BP can't get to work on time because of sleep-related issues. Other times it is because a menial job will reinforce her shame and she has to rebound by thinking that she is better than this "crappy job." The final reason that she may have difficulty holding a job is that if the job has long periods of inactivity, she may ruminate in those time periods. Ruminating leads to paranoia (which is born of shame) and paranoia leads to interpersonal conflict with co-workers, customers or supervisors.

Why can't this person keep friends?

In my experience the reason a person with BPD can't keep friends can be traced back to two features of the disorder: black-and-white thinking and impulsivity. When the BP detects that a friend has judged her in some way, she will likely "split the friend black," meaning she will suddenly assign the friend to the category of being evil. Rather than waiting for that opinion of the friend to subside, the BP may impulsively "burn their bridges" with the friend, communicating with the friend in a nasty and unforgivable fashion, causing the friend to abandon her.

Sometimes her friends will tire of the constant emotional crises and drop her. Since the BP is in constant need of reassurance, her friends can become exhausted by having to continually feed the BP's self-image.

Why can't this person stand to be alone?

I believe that BP's have trouble being alone for several reasons. Many in the therapeutic community say that this feature of BPD is due to the BP's unstable sense of self – that she needs others to help define herself. That is a part of it, but I think that the shame and tendency to ruminate also play a big role. Times of inactivity and solitude will kick off ruminating and that ruminating will lead to panic on the part of the BP. This panic is born from the feeling that everyone else can clearly see her shame and thinks that she is a "bad person."

Why does this person lie to me?

Lying is much discussed on my Internet board. On my blog (www.anythingtostopthepain.com) I receive more searches on "lying", "liar", "chronic liar", "lies" or some other form of "lying", "lies" or "liar" than virtually any other subject. Lying is a big issue when you are in a relationship with someone with BPD. You feel that your BP lies to you, even in the face of evidence to the contrary. Sometimes these lies are about trivial things and you can't figure out why a person would lie about that particular subject. It just doesn't make any sense.

People who feel lied to find the experience unnerving and "humiliating." The lying becomes wearying for the person in the relationship and it "poisons" the integrity and trustworthiness of the liar.

I believe there are several basic motivations to lie when you have BPD. There are also two types of lies: by admission (by telling) and by omission (by not telling). Both types are a problem with someone with BPD. The motivations for telling a lie (or omitting truth) by someone with BPD are as follows:

1. When it is more painful to admit or tell the truth.
2. When she wants the other person to think "better" of her than she thinks of herself.
3. To avoid the judgment of the other person or judgment of herself.
4. When she can't see the "truth" because of emotional reasoning brought on by the refractory period of the emotion felt. In other words, when feelings = facts.

The first three of these factors play a role in the lies of someone with BPD and they are often inter-related. If the person to whom the lie is told is likely to judge the person with BPD as "bad" or "deficient," the expectation of disapproval triggers first rejection sensitivity and then shame, because the person with BPD actually feels deep inside that, if she admits the truth, the other person will "find out" that she is a "bad person" and reject her fully. The last motivation is discussed in the "emotional reasoning" section below.

I bring up these motivations not to "let liars off the hook" but to point out something: a person with BPD does not live in the same "reality" as you do. Your truth is informed by what you see, hear, experience and what you believe about those inputs. A person with BPD is most often informed by her feelings about the experiences.

As stated earlier, these feelings can be misaligned with the facts and as Ekman notes a person overcome with strong emotions "cannot incorporate information that does not fit, maintain or justify the emotion." In effect the original lies can be motivated by the inability to see information that doesn't support the feelings. When someone is emotionally dysregulated, she just can't see the truth if it doesn't match what she is feeling.

In effect, she is not really "lying", but merely pointing out "facts" (or generating as we will see later) that support her overwhelming emotion about the situation. The subsequent lies, which are used to "cover up" or support the emotional reasoning, are typically done for one of the first three motivations, particularly the idea that you would think of her as less of a person (and deservedly so) if it was revealed that she lied in the first place.

I think there can be some argument about whether deep-down a person with BPD really believes the original lie (or any of those generated by motivation number four) when she exits the prolonged refractory period. My suspicion is that deep down a person with BPD is more concerned with the pain and shame the revelation of the lie will cause her than with repairing, rather than repeating, the lie.

While it is useful to know the motivations behind the lies, it still doesn't make the lies any less hurtful. Being lied to is a painful and hateful experience for the "Non." It destroys trust and personal integrity and leads to suspicion and paranoia. When someone specifically lies to you or is secretive, you end up feeling angry, saddened and disconnected from your loved one with BPD. It is a confusing, embarrassing and painful experience.

Why does this person try to manipulate me?

Manipulation is another hot topic of discussion when talking about people with BPD. Nons DO feel manipulated by their loved ones with BPD. Being manipulated is a difficult and irksome experience. It can make you doubt yourself and your ability to make sound decisions and it can build resentment toward the person with BPD. It invalidates your intentions in a given situation because you feel "forced" to make a particular choice.

That situation is bound to create angry, resentful feelings in you. I will repeat the quote from an anonymous source (a woman with BPD) about manipulation, because it helps to summarize my own attitudes toward manipulation and BPD:

I don't think that, in most cases anyway, that the "manipulative" behavior is deliberately so, despite appearances - thus it cannot be truly manipulative, by definition. These behaviors DO have a function and an objective, as do all behaviors (including brushing one's teeth), but we do not describe ALL Non-disordered people's attempts to find or maintain love or get attention or avoid pain manipulation - only when it truly is just that.

I think a new word is called for.

More accurately, the behaviors in question are more like "tools." Lacking a circular saw, I may try a hatchet to cut my board so I can cover my window and keep out the chill. It is not as effective, and is potentially damaging and will make a pretty ratty and half-assed covering, but it is the only tool I have to do what I need to do.

Granted, those with loved ones need to find ways to protect themselves, but applying such language ideas as "manipulation" does not give the "other" proper tools, either.

The overall effect is two people standing around with hatchets trying to make a straight cut down the length of an oak plank. Ain't gonna work.

- From an unidentifiable poster on an archived version of "Crazy Boards"

The point of providing this quote again is to demonstrate that a person with BPD will try to use tools (albeit deficient ones) to attempt to obtain her objectives. That being said, much of the decisions that someone with BPD makes are based in emotional reasoning and subject to strong emotions. Remember emotions are immediate, not long-term "designs" or "plans." A BP is often awash with these strong, negative emotions and will do anything to make herself feel better, including "manipulating" you.

The self-help book *Stop Walking on Eggshells* by Randi Kreger and Dr. Paul Mason talks about manipulation in the section "Manipulation or Desperation." Their book also uses the concept of "Nons" to denote those without the disorder but in a relationship with someone who has BPD. (As a brief side-note, I feel that much of *Stop Walking on Eggshells* is very effective in describing BPD and a Non's attitudes toward her. However, I disagree with the conclusions and the "prescription" of the authors of that book.)

It's no secret that Non-BPD's often feel manipulated and lied to by their borderline loved ones. In other words, they feel controlled or taken advantage of through means such as threats, no-win situations, the "silent-treatment", rages and other methods they view as unfair. We believe that, in most cases, the BP's behavior is not intentionally manipulative. Rather, this kind of behavior can be seen as desperate attempts to cope with painful feelings or to get their needs met - without the aim of harming others. [43]

[43] Kreger, Randi and Mason, Paul, *Stop Walking on Eggshells*, page 42

You feel manipulated by your loved one, but manipulation is not necessarily the best word to describe the person with BPD's attempt to "get their needs met."

Manipulation is a two-way street. The basic formula of manipulative behavior is "if you do (or don't) do this, I will do (or not do) that."

It can come in a form of a threat (I'll yell at you) or a reward (I'll have sex with you). Since it is a two way street, you can choose NOT to do (or to do) the opposite of the request or do something else entirely. Often, you feel bad or sad if you don't give into the manipulative request. In this way you are behaving as if you are the one with the BPD, because you are making decisions based on this negative emotion. I'm not saying that you are responsible for the attempted manipulation, but you must be responsible for your response to it.

Why does my spouse threaten divorce once a month?

Divorce threats arise from a fear of intimacy and a fear of abandonment. It may seem strange to include both fear of intimacy and fear of abandonment in the same section; however, with BPD, these two issues are closely related. Each fear is the flipside of the other and in a world of black-and-white, all-or-nothing thinking one can become the other rather quickly.

Strong, close relationships usually make people (all people) feel deep emotions. Closeness engenders strong emotions. Unfortunately, for people with BPD, these feelings can be overwhelming. The powerful feelings that come with being close can be, at first, invigorating and then exhausting. It is difficult for anyone, particularly someone with BPD, to maintain that level of intensity. Whether it is a "loss of control", or something else, the feelings overwhelm the person with BPD, and she has to push away for fear of being lost, adrift on a tidal wave of feelings.

On the flipside of intimacy is abandonment. In the case of people with BPD, abandonment is always a specter that haunts every relationship. Once the relationship is established, the fear of being left and abandoned can motivate many of the actions of the person with BPD. Clinginess, stalking and pleading can be a result of this fear. Constant phone calls, emails, even spying can result.

The problem of intimacy and abandonment is that in both cases the person with BPD feels that she is caught in a wave of emotions. Both experiences lead to a loss of control, but more importantly, these experience lead to a loss of the sense of self. The person with BPD doesn't feel "grounded" and in that way she feels empty or "selfless" in each experience.

Sometimes a person with BPD will decide to "run away" from a relationship (with associated "bridge burning") rather than experience this "lack of self" feeling that both intimacy and abandonment fears solicits. In other words, the person might "leave you before you leave me" (in the case of abandonment) or seek to show that "I don't need you" (in the case of intimacy). In this way the person with BPD can control the ending of the relationship without having to wait for the ending and obsess/ruminate about when it will inevitably end.

Why is this person so sensitive to rejection?

Rejection Sensitivity is the tendency to "anxiously expect, readily perceive and overreact to social rejection."[44] Someone with BPD will almost certainly have this feature.

Have you ever had your loved one ask you: "Are you mad at me?" Or has your loved one asked you: "Do you like me?" over and over again? Or have they said, "You could do so much better than me. Why are you even with me?"

These questions and others like them are indications that your loved one is suffering from rejection sensitivity. Someone with rejection sensitivity will also avoid tasks, meetings or other social interactions if there is any sense of rejection implied. She is unlikely to initiate social interaction or close personal contact. Often when forced to be in social situations, someone with BPD will constantly scan other people's reactions for disapproval or rejection. She might rely on others from whom the signals of possible rejection are less strong. In other words, she might ask you to do things for her (like make phone calls or attend meetings at school), rather than risk social rejection. This adaptation to rejection sensitivity is avoidance.

[44] Downey & Feldman, 1996, quoted from Baldwin, Mark, *Interpersonal Cognition*, 2005, page 83

When actual rejection occurs or is perceived by someone with this feature, especially when the rejection originates with someone who the BP feels is important to her, rage and even violence can occur. The person with BPD who perceives that she has been rejected by a significant person (one from which she is less likely to expect rejection), she "can become hostile not in general but specifically in reaction to potential rejection from a significant or important person."[45]

This feature is closely related to shame and to the fear of judgment. In both cases a person with BPD will judge herself harshly because of the shame (I am a bad person) and will reject themselves (I don't deserve acceptance). Additionally (and perhaps ironically), she may lash out, rage at or abuse people who do offer her acceptance, because she feels that she deserves the rejection. This is based on her deep-seated feelings of shame. In this way, the feelings around acceptance versus rejection are a "no win" situation for you – if you reject the person with BPD, she gets angry, but if you accept her, she may judge you as "stupid for accepting someone as bad as me."

She also anticipates negative emotions from future assumed rejections. Meaning, a person with BPD will think/say "I'm going to feel really bad when that person says 'no' to me." She may also have a diminished capacity to say "no" in social situations, even when she wants to. She does not want to accept the further rejection that might come from saying "no." Sometimes she might flip-flop between avoidance and accepting social situations that she feels are unpalatable. Both compunctions are generated by rejection sensitivity.

Why doesn't this person trust me?

A person with BPD has a marked lack of trust of the world and of other people around her. She often feels vulnerable and powerless. If her emotions can be engaged and dysregulated so easily and so often and her emotional reactions are so painful, she has to guard herself against that pain. In some cases, this leads to a lack of trust and a lack of intimacy. A person with BPD will not naturally trust you - even though you are a close loved one - because she fears the emotional pain that comes with trust. She might feel that this vulnerability is a form of emotional abuse, due to the severity of emotional pain that comes with it. In her mind the risk of

[45] Miscal, 1996, quoted from Hamel, John & Nichols, Tonia, *Family Interventions in Domestic Violence*, page 126

emotional pain outweighs any level of trust. If she is vulnerable, she is open to abuse again and therefore trust leads to vulnerability and to abuse.

I was abused and need shelter. But whatever shelter I run to, they will eventually abuse me. So I must be constantly on guard, to prevent being violated. If I let down my guard, I will be abused again. There is only one thing that leads to abuse: trust. [46]

She might believe that you don't understand her because the way in which you react to her emotional states (in her mind, not necessarily in the world) causes her pain. If you understood her properly, you wouldn't cause her pain, she believes. I am not saying that you actually are the cause of her pain. What I am saying is that she perceives that you are the cause of some of her pain (and others the cause of other pain) and that creates an inability for her to trust you. If the world is a malevolent place for her, it is not to be trusted.

Why does this person blame me for everything?

You might notice that when dealing with someone with BPD, everything that she feels and everything that goes wrong seems to be your fault. You probably feel blamed for many, many things including things over which you have no control.

Being blamed for everything is tiring to say the least. Coupled with the BP's inability to take responsibility (and blame) for her own actions, this aspect of BPD is maddening. It is impossible for one person to shoulder all the blame for everything in a relationship. One of my old therapists told me, "If you are responsible for everything, you are responsible for nothing." I truly believe that it is impossible for anyone to take all the responsibility and blame in a relationship.

Why does a person with BPD seem so fixated on blame-finding? (Which I like to call "blame-storming" in a nod to "brain-storming"). Why does she go to great lengths to assign blame to anyone else (including God, the world, everyone, etc.) other than herself? The reason seems to be similar to that of the inability to take responsibility for her actions. She does not want to be seen as the "cause" of problems or of pain. This would again make her "all-bad" and in being "all-bad" she deserves nothing less than

---

[46] from the "20 Rules" written by an anonymous member of the ATSTP list and cited in Chapter 4 of this book.

death. It is easier to find someone else (or something else, like karma or life itself) that is a more acceptable cause of her pain and problems. Some books call this "projection," but I don't think it is projection per se. It is more the fear of rejection, ridicule and emotional pain if she is at fault. It confirms her shame and that she can do nothing right. Through black-and-white thinking, if she is a bit at fault, she is doomed.

Sometimes I will hear my wife say that she "hates everyone" or that she feels "everyone is out to get her." Clearly, these statements can be seen as paranoid or misanthropic, but ultimately she is expressing her belief that forces outside herself are to be blamed for how she feels.

Why does this person idolize me one day and call me "the devil" the next?

Black-and-white thinking is the tendency for a person to believe that events or other people are either "all-good" or "all-bad" in any given situation. People with BPD will often vacillate between these two polar ways of thinking, sometimes about the same event or person. This way of thinking is also known as "splitting." In the support community, loved ones of BP's will say that they have been "split-white" (meaning, they are thought to be all good) or "split-black" (thought to be all bad). A person with BPD who thinks in this fashion will have an inability to see "shades of grey" in a situation or relationship. This approach can be extremely frustrating and confusing to the loved ones, because the BP might one day idolize you and then the next day think of you as evil or malevolent. You never know exactly where you stand with the person with BPD.

Black-and-white thinking can lead to "bridge-burning" behavior in which the person with BPD will cut all ties with another person (friend, parent, child or partner) during a period in which the other person is "split-black." She might say and do things that will destroy the relationship for seemingly no reason. I have seen people with BPD cut all ties with life-long friends over a simple disagreement. Usually, this "simple" disagreement will center upon abandonment fears or fear of judgment. If the person with BPD feels judged or if rejection or abandonment is seemingly imminent, she is likely to "leave you before you leave me" effectively running away from the "evil" person and damaging any additional hopes of a continued relationship. Sometimes a person with BPD will be regretful of the destruction, because the other person has returned to being all-good.

A BP is not immune from turning this black-and-white thinking upon herself, one day thinking that she is "all-good" (even god-like) and the next self-flagellating for being evil, broken, sinful and bad. Since shame is involved the "splitting black" of herself is total: she didn't just DO something bad, she IS bad. This pattern can lead to suicidal ideation because, if she is a "bad person", there is no reason to live. She can never be redeemed.

Some words that are hallmarks of black-and-white thinking are "always" and "never", "good" and "bad" (or evil),"everything" and "nothing" and other polar opposite words. Black-and-white thinking is also known as "all-or-nothing" thinking.

One way to combat black-and-white thinking is to come up with past situations in which the object of the thinking acted differently or in which the BP thought differently of the person. The "dialectical" part of DBT specifically speaks to black-and-white thinking. Dialectical philosophy takes two polar opposites (called the thesis and antithesis) and synthesizes them into a resolution – called the synthesis. DBT uses acceptance and change as opposites and tries to synthesize the two so that the BP begins to consider shades of grey in a situation and in herself. DBT operates under the premise that there are several "dialectical dilemmas" at work in the mind of a BP. These are opposites modes of thinking and behavior, and the BP will swing wildly between them. One purpose of DBT is to gain a balance between the polar opposites. The dialectical dilemmas are:

- Unrelenting Crisis (biological) - Inhibited Experiencing (social): the "balance" achieved through "Wise Mind" (for Unrelenting Crisis) and "emotional experiencing" (for Inhibited...)
- Active Passivity (biological) - Apparent Competence (social): the "balance" achieved through "Problem Solving" (for Active Passivity) and "Accurate Expression" (for Apparent...)
- Emotional Vulnerability (biological) - Self Invalidation (social): the "balance" achieved through "Emotional Modulation" (for Emotional...) and "Self Validation" (for Self...)

The notes here are based on my interpretation of the dilemmas and are not attributed to Linehan or any other DBT expert directly. I made this interpretation from a diagram of the dilemmas that I have posted in my Internet group.

Why can't this person listen to reason (or see the truth)?

It has been said in popular culture "if it feels good, do it." In the case of BPD, the saying should be more like "if I feel it, it must be true." Emotional reasoning is the inclination to believe that feelings actually equal (or cause) facts and events to happen. The feelings of someone with BPD are so immediate and overpowering; it is difficult for someone experiencing these feelings and emotions to believe that these feelings are self-generated. It is important to remember the function of emotions to understand why emotional reasoning takes place. As stated, the basic emotions function to detect threats to one's survival (or either body or mind). Fear is useful to protect a person from attack. Anger is useful to cut a threat off and attack back quickly and decisively. However, in the case of BPD, a person will react to threats that are not completely "true." Although she may feel that a situation is threatening, it is possible that she is detecting a threat that doesn't actually exist.

My wife had a sure-fire defense: 'You're cornering me.' But while I thought I was 'cornering' her into admitting the truth, she felt I was manipulating her into feeling something about herself other than what she felt. ATSTP member A. (male, divorced)

In the case of A's wife above, she detected a threat from him – that of "cornering" her – and would react with fear and anger. He didn't notice that she felt the threat because his intentions were not threatening. His intentions were merely to have his wife admit the "truth."

The problem with "the truth" when emotions are involved is that emotions lead to emotional reasoning and when someone is subject to emotional reasoning the only "truth" is how she feels. She will seek to mold the "facts" of a particular situation to match her feelings. This emotional reasoning is natural for BP's. As Ekman states in Emotions Revealed:

For a while we are in a refractory state, during which time our thinking cannot incorporate information that does not fit, maintain or justify the emotion that we are feeling. [47]

---

[47] Ekman, Paul, *Emotions Revealed*, Page 39

This is an important piece of information, which is why I re-quoted it here. He states "our thinking cannot incorporate information that does not fit, maintain or justify the emotion that we are feeling." During a period of emotional dysregulation, the person with BPD will be unable to "see the facts" if those facts do not support the conclusion of what she is feeling. Therefore, the person with BPD is likely to interpret or generate alternative "facts" that support what she is feeling. She cannot be "reasoned with" during this state because reasoning requires an objective view of the evidence presented. The strong (usually negative) feelings will drown out all reasoning or examination of evidence.

This aspect of BPD is one of the more frustrating ones for loved ones. Loved ones (especially partners) will often ask, "When will this person admit to the truth?" I have already covered lying previously, so I will not expound on the nature of truth. Instead I will only say that emotional reasoning is born from strong emotional reactions, whether or not these emotions are based in reality — whether or not the threat is real or imagined.

Why can't this person take responsibility for their own actions?

Very often in my online group, I hear that partners and parents of people with BPD decry the fact that this person can't seem to take responsibility for her words and actions. It is as if the person with BPD has no concept of personal responsibility and no idea that her behaviors can affect the feelings of others. She seems to be so caught up in her own feelings and emotions that other people's feelings and emotions are not in the equation. Even after the emotional dysregulation dissipates and the person with BPD returns to "baseline," she rarely admits her responsibility for her own (sometimes extremely destructive) behavior.

Years ago, before I started to understand and recognize the dynamics of BPD, I used to call my wife's periods of dysregulation "irresponsibility binges." She would do impulsive and sometimes extremely hurtful things and refuse to admit personal responsibility or to apologize for her actions. I found this aspect of BPD to be one of the most resentment-generating. Sometimes I would brood for periods of time, angry and resentful over my wife's not admitting that she was irresponsible or "wrong." I posted a quote (edited here) on my blog many months ago that reads like this:

When will my wife be willing to take responsibility for her actions? When will she try to fix the harm she has done to me and the kids? When will she finally admit that she is WRONG? - Paraphrased quotation from ATSTP group members

It is very difficult for a person with BPD to accept responsibility for her own actions. The problem lies within several other symptoms of BPD. The combination of black-and-white thinking and of deep shame causes the person with BPD to believe that if she does something wrong, SHE is wrong completely.

There is no middle ground between doing something wrong (and being guilty about it and admitting it) to being completely wrong and deserving death. Knowing this, however, does not make this situation any less infuriating for the loved ones. Living with someone who cannot accept responsibility for her actions is just that - infuriating. Once the black-and-white thinking can be addressed (through therapy) and the shame can be uncovered and assuaged (again through therapy), this feature is likely to dissipate.

Why does this person turn past events over-and-over in their mind?

Ruminating is the name I have given to the propensity of a BP to have "worry thoughts" about events and to turn them over-and-over in her mind. These events are usually in the past, although sometimes they can be about the possibility of future events linked with past events. Ruminating is an extended form of worry and anxiety in which the sufferer will examine events with an eye to find malignant intentions or judgments of others. Ruminating can lead to paranoia regarding the intentions of others.

When emotionally dysregulated, a person with BPD is experiencing strong emotions in the moment, but the meaning of those emotions is almost always linked to something in the past that she is angry about or something in the future that she fears. This is an important aspect of "ruminating." It is a thought pattern that turns things over-and-over in her mind, looking for danger or embarrassment in situations. It is very "not in the moment."

Often, the ruminating will extend over long periods of time, from hours to days, and will cause the person with BPD to look for hostile meanings within interactions with others. During this "search for meaning" the person with BPD may ask others about what is meant by certain actions or words while clearly implying that the BP believes that the other person is judging her or angry at her. Ruminating is a form of personalization and fear of judgment. The person with BPD will likely feel that situations which are not "about her" are, in fact, not only "about her" but are exclusively about how she feels about the situation.

Ruminating can lead to emotional reasoning – the situation in which a person's feelings equal actual facts. If she feels that there is a malicious intent or a negative judgment in a given situation, there MUST be one in reality (feelings created facts). Ruminating is a method of finding this negative and/or judgmental meaning. Ruminating most often occurs when a person with BPD either has time on her hands or is bored. It also can occur as the person with BPD tries and fails to fall asleep.

Ruminating can be combated with distraction with something the BP enjoys and engages her mind. Physical activities are a good salve for ruminating. Mindfulness, which is a component of DBT, also helps stop ruminating because the point of mindfulness is to be "in the moment" and not consider past or future events.

Why can't this person get up in the morning?

One of the physical aspects of BPD is problems with sleep. People with BPD are likely to have trouble going to sleep and trouble getting up in the morning. One of the reasons is the "ruminating" aspect of BPD I just discussed. Another seems to be that her brain chemistry is configured in such a way to utilize serotonin ineffectively. Many people with BPD will require sleep medications and sometimes will take these medications in large doses. This inability to sleep and awake punctually can also contribute to getting fired from jobs. If a BP can't get up on time and make it on time to a job, she might get fired.

How do I get this person to go to therapy?

Unfortunately, you can't force someone to go to therapy if she doesn't want to go (except through a court order). What I suggest is that you use the tools in this book for a while. After you do that for some time, the BP might begin to gather some self-awareness or to share her inner thoughts and feelings with you. It is likely that these thoughts and feelings will be filled with shame, self-hatred and worry. At that point, you say something like, "Boy, it must feel awful to feel that way about yourself. What do you think you can do to feel better?" or "That's so painful to feel that way. Maybe therapy can help?"

My wife has resisted going to DBT because it identifies her as a BP and she "doesn't want to be that person." She also resists because DBT seems like a therapy of last resort to her and, if she fails at it, she will have to be committed. I occasionally do reinforce to her that there are people who are trained to help her feel better and encourage her to look into it. She is in therapy, but not in DBT. My daughter does see a DBT therapist. She decided to go because she was so angry all the time, she felt terrible. She wanted to learn how to feel better. At some point, her emotional pain reached an intolerable level.

I have tried to model these skills in my life and, by doing so, shown my wife that I can more adequately cope with emotional situations, both personal and interpersonal. This modeling encourages my wife to consider DBT (or another emotional training program) to help her feel better. My suggestion is that you practice the tools in this book, master them and use your mastery over emotional situations as a beacon for your BP's healing.

Why does this person do such crazy things? (like cutting, drugs, etc.)

People with BPD are in a great deal of emotional pain. Since emotions are immediate and primal, emotional pain is also immediate and primal. As I have said, emotions represent a land-bridge between the body and the mind. Emotional pain manifests itself in both mental and physical ways. If you have ever been depressed or "fraught with grief" over the loss of something or someone important to you, you will know what I am saying in this regard.

Depression and grief can be a trying experience for anyone. You feel pain in every area of your body and mind. Sometimes you will just want to retreat to your bedroom and go to sleep for hours, just to get some relief from the physical and mental anguish you feel. The sleep represents a distraction of both the mind and the body from the experience of complete pain. You might also use alcohol to relieve the pain by "turning off your mind." Many people "drink themselves into a stupor" and, in doing so, extinguish the pain for a short period.

Pain-killers, whether over-the-counter or prescription, can also remove pain by working on the pain at its source (in the brain where pain is actually felt). Once, when I was asked by one of my daughters about how the Tylenol knew to go to her foot (which was in pain), rather than to her head (because she'd taken it for headaches before), I explained that it acts in the brain where she feels the pain, not where the pain actually "is." In the case of emotional pain, the pain seems to be both in the body and in the mind, but the pain-feeling area of the brain is where these drugs act. See below about substance abuse.

People with BPD are likely to feel emotional pain many times a day every day. Since these emotions are basic (like fear, sadness and anger) the reactions to them are both physical and mental. These emotional pain-states are powerful and have the ability to overpower rational thinking. When you are in pain, regardless of the source, the main reaction of the body and mind is to get out of or to relieve the pain as soon as possible and by whatever means necessary.

Earlier I used the example of someone who is literally on fire. This person will try to douse the flames in any way, without thinking about the people around her and what harm may come to others if the flames spread. This situation is analogous to a person in deep emotional pain. The person will do anything to stop the pain, which is why my Internet blog and Internet list are called "anything to stop the pain" (ATSTP). This "anything" includes self-destructive and relationship-damaging behaviors.

Self-injury

Self-injury can come in many forms and includes cutting oneself with razors or knives, burning oneself with cigarettes or matches, pulling out clumps of hair and picking at oneself (especially the nails and/or cheek) until blood is produced. Self-injury is one of the most difficult behaviors for the loved one to understand. In the case of BPD, self-injury is done for the purpose of pain relief, not to "get attention" or to manipulate the loved one. Most self-injury is done in private and done without the knowledge of the loved one.

Occasionally, the self-injury cannot be covered-up (i.e. the blood and/or scars are apparent or the hair is missing in large area of the head) and others notice the activities. The actions themselves are fraught with shame and may lead to even more shame for the person.

In the hospital, ER doctors take a dim view of those who injure themselves and a person who engages in self-injury often avoid hospitals to avoid the inevitable judgment and lack of compassion these doctors (and nurses) will exhibit toward her. What is important for a loved one to understand is that self-injury has a purpose and that purpose is usually pain relief, not self-punishment or attention-getting. The person who engages in this behavior may feel and describe a deep "itch" inside her body that she has to rid herself of immediately.

It reminds me of the experience that I have had with Restless Leg Syndrome (RLS). I have had this condition since I was very young, and I can best describe it as a pain, itch or burning sensation in one of my legs after a period of inactivity. When I am experiencing this sensation, getting rid of it is paramount in my mind and, if I thought it would be effective, I can understand how a sufferer might resort to extreme measures, such as self-injury, to rid oneself of this unpleasant and unnerving feeling. By generalizing that sensation to the rest of the body, I gain some insight into what the desire to self- injure must feel like.

While self-injury can provide relief from pain (through the release of endorphins, or natural, pain-killing substances within the brain), it can have risks and negative consequences. These include embarrassment, scars, infection and, in some cases, death.

Substance Abuse

As stated above, many people use alcohol and/or drugs to dampen the effects of emotional pain. With BPD, it is likely that alcohol and/or drugs will be used for this purpose. Drugs and alcohol CAN function to reduce pain. However, this pain reduction is temporary. What I have noticed from the ATSTP group is that people with severe BPD are likely to use large quantities of alcohol and/or drugs to deaden their pain. Some estimates of substance abuse by people with BPD are as high as 75%.

Many people with BPD use and abuse alcohol and drugs. Often, they will ingest large quantities (more than someone without BPD could handle) and not overdose or even pass out. They may take both prescription drugs with anti-anxiety medication, such as Xanax, Ativan and Klonopin (and others); painkillers, such as Oxycotin, Vicodin or Codeine (and others); or they may take illicit drugs, such as Marijuana, Cocaine, Heroin, or Methamphetamine (and others). The purpose, again, is to remove emotional pain.

Unfortunately, these substances, especially in the quantities consumed, can have several negative effects and consequences, including overdose, driving violations and an increase in impulsivity or dyscontrol.[48] These periods of impulsivity and dyscontrol and the behaviors that result (such as "risk-taking behavior" below) may cause more shame and self-punishment when the BP sobers up.

Risk-taking Behavior

People with BPD also engage in risk-taking behaviors of various forms. These behaviors include risky sexual behaviors, reckless driving and thrill-seeking behaviors. Many of these activities could be considered life-threatening either in the short term (by having a car accident) or in the long term (by contracting HIV or another fatal sexually transmitted disease). The people with BPD will, at the time of the risk-taking behavior, most likely not consider the consequences to life and limb – either physical or legal. Again, the purpose is to halt and/or deaden the emotional pain. In other words: "it seemed like a good idea at the time." Sexual activities can provide pleasure, dangerous driving can provide a thrill and other risky behaviors, like hanging out of windows or jumping off cliffs into lakes, can provide a rush of adrenaline that temporarily removes the emotional pain.

The point is for you, the loved one, to understand that the motivation of these behaviors, however short-sighted and ill-conceived you think they are, is to remove pain.

One member of the ATSTP group reported that her husband had totaled four cars in a period of eight years. These behaviors are impulsive and therefore not "thought through." They are another method to "put out the fire" within the person. Certainly, these behaviors can have significant consequences, physical, legal, financial and otherwise.

Eating Disorders

Another behavior that many people with BPD engage in (particularly females) is eating disorders. Whether it is starving oneself or binging-and-purging or overeating (especially secret overeating), the eating disorder is another tool someone with BPD can use to alleviate emotional pain.

[48] R. W. Cowdry and D. L. Gardner, 1998, from Abstract

Again, eating disorders can have negative consequences including starvation, ill-health, poor self-image and obesity.

Other Binge Behavior

Other binge behaviors (or indulgent/irresponsible behaviors) are binge shopping, obsessive plastic surgery and "running away" through binge travel. These behaviors provide temporary relief from emotional pain as well. And again, they can have negative consequences by damaging a relationship or financial consequences.

A final note on dangerous behaviors: it is important to prioritize when you are trying to help the BP halt or alter their behavior. You will want to start with the most dangerous first.

If your daughter with BPD is having unprotected sex and smoking marijuana, regardless of your feelings about drugs, the unprotected sex will have to come first. Also, you need to be practical about it. Giving her condoms and saying, "I can see how buying these or asking your boyfriend to wear one might be embarrassing to you" rather than insisting she no longer see the boy is probably more effective, again regardless of your feelings about premarital sex. Once the genie is out of the bottle, it is difficult to stuff it back in.

You can, however, help make it safer and you do so by being effective. Of course, you also have to be brave in this situation. It can be very difficult for a parent to talk to a child about sex.

Are this person's suicide threats real or just a "cry for help" or a call for attention?

Well, the short answer to this question is that a suicide attempt is probably all three: real, a cry for help and a call for attention. First, let me remind you that I am not a mental health professional and consulting with one if your BP loved one is suicidal is essential. All suicide attempts must be taken seriously and getting the authorities involved is most likely the prudent choice.

When a BP attempts suicide, they are in a great deal of pain and want to snuff it (real); they are in need of help with their pain (a cry for help); and they are trying to communicate their pain to other people (a call for attention). All motivations are valid and all probably play a part in the attempt.

In the brief before Congress about naming May "BPD Awareness Month" in the United States, it was indicated that: "BPD is a leading cause of suicide, with a suicide rate 400 times the rate of the general public." That floored me – 400 times the rate of the general public! With this in mind, the likelihood that your loved one with BPD will consider (or even attempt) suicide is large. Sometimes, since most suicide attempts are impulsive on the part of someone with BPD, these attempts are not planned out and are unlikely to succeed. "Only" (and I put that in quotes because it is still a large figure) about 8-10% of BP's succeed in killing themselves, while some estimates suggest more than 75% ATTEMPT suicide some time in their life. Even so, if someone is in enough pain to attempt suicide, their pain needs to be noticed and attended to. Dismissing a suicide attempt as a simple "call for attention" is dangerous and could be deadly.

Appendix: Integrating Skills for the Holidays

The holidays are a tough emotional time for everyone. There are expectations that the holidays be "jolly and happy" when, sometimes, the holidays are anything but. The get-together with relatives – many who don't understand the actions, feelings and behaviors of someone with BPD – can cause huge stress for those with BPD and for the loved ones. Expectations of a low conflict Christmas (or other holiday) are typical, but not often "delivered upon". Stress and the feeling of being "on-stage" or "good enough" for the family can cause emotional dysregulation and distress. Sometimes an invalidating family can compare the person with BPD with other, less emotional family members. You know, "why can't you be like your cousin?"

There are some emotional skills and other tools that can help us non-BPD people get through the holidays reasonably unscathed. These are an integration of the tools and advanced tools in this book.

In order to skillfully approach the holidays, I'd like to remind you of the following skills that can help you get through.

1. Frustration Tolerance. Sometimes we are overcome with frustration. We feel like we "can't stand it" or "can't take it anymore." When you feel that way, I would encourage you to ask yourself some questions that can help build frustration tolerance. Some questions are:
   - Can I really not stand it?
   - Am I really going to explode?
   - How does exploding/raging help me in my relationships?
   - What can I do to decrease the frustration?
2. Mentalizing with yourself in a search for meaning within other people's actions. Often people jump to conclusions or assume the intent and motivation of others. Sometimes these motivations are assumed to be malevolent, invalidating or uncaring. You can ask yourself the following questions to help understand the intent within yourself:
   - Do I really believe that he/she is being mean?
   - Is there another explanation as to his/her motivations?
   - What would he/she be feeling that could explain this action?

3. Mentalizing with others to understand others' internal mental states. Be curious. Ask questions. Don't "load" these questions. That is, ask "can you clarify what you meant, I'm not sure I understand your intention?" vs. "Why are you being so mean to me?"

4. Be validating toward yourself and others. Remember that emotions are a major influence on people's behavior. Listen to others and validate the emotions. Validation does not equal agreement with behavior. It shows that you have heard the other person's emotions and that it is ok to feel however one feels. Normalization can also be helpful here.

5. Don't label people, label events. In other words, rather than saying "he's an asshole", say "he did something that bothered me." This can be used on your own actions as well. Rather than telling yourself you're a "failure," you can say "I didn't do that as I would have liked."

6. Be mindful of the moment. Monitor interactions actively and in a way that is non-judgmental. Don't get caught up in past reactions or fear of future reactions.

7. Cheerlead yourself and others. This is not "positive mental attitude" statements. This is encouraging others to be brave and effective. The essence of this skill is "you can do/face hard/difficult things."

8. Consider the consequences of mind-altering substances. Too much alcohol and/or drugs can create impulsive situations and ones that you may regret later. Think before you drink.

Resources

- Bon's Blog: www.anythingtostopthepain.com
- The "Anything to Stop the Pain" Email Support List: http://www.anythingtostopthepain.com/atstp-group/
- Bon's coaching: http://www.anythingtostopthepain.com/coaching/
- A recommended reading list for Non-BPD's: http://www.anythingtostopthepain.com/reading-list-bpd-nonbpd/
- Bon on Twitter: https://twitter.com/bondobbs
- BehaviorTech: The main DBT technology "transfer" site http://behavioraltech.com/
- Borderline Research: Scientific Research on BPD http://borderlineresearch.org/
- DBT Self-Help: Excellent resource on DBT http://dbtselfhelp.com/

Lightning Source UK Ltd.
Milton Keynes UK
UKHW04f1854251018

331212UK00001B/105/P